Seven Steps to College Success

Seven Steps to College Success

A Pathway for Students with Disabilities

Third Edition

Elizabeth C. Hamblet

ROWMAN & LITTLEFIELD
Lanham • Boulder • New York • London

Published by Rowman & Littlefield
An imprint of The Rowman & Littlefield Publishing Group, Inc.
4501 Forbes Boulevard, Suite 200, Lanham, Maryland 20706
www.rowman.com

86-90 Paul Street, London EC2A 4NE

British Library Cataloguing in Publication Information Available

Library of Congress Cataloging-in-Publication Data

Names: Hamblet, Elizabeth C., author.
Title: Seven steps to college success : a pathway for students with
   disabilities / Elizabeth C. Hamblet.
Description: Third edition. | Lanham, Maryland : Rowman & Littlefield,
   [2023] | Includes bibliographical references and index.
Identifiers: LCCN 2022039837 (print) | LCCN 2022039838 (ebook) |
   ISBN 9781475864441 (cloth) | ISBN 9781538188415 (paperback) |
   ISBN 9781475864458 (ebook)
Subjects: LCSH: Learning disabled youth—Education (Higher)—United States.
   | College students with disabilities—Services for—United States. |
   Learning disabilities. | Universities and colleges.
Classification: LCC LC4818.38 .H36 2023 (print) | LCC LC4818.38 (ebook) |
   DDC 371.9/0474—dc23/eng/20220824
LC record available at https://lccn.loc.gov/2022039837
LC ebook record available at https://lccn.loc.gov/2022039838

∞™ The paper used in this publication meets the minimum requirements of
American National Standard for Information Sciences—Permanence of Paper
for Printed Library Materials, ANSI/NISO Z39.48-1992.

Contents

Preface   vii

Acknowledgments   xi

Introduction   1

Step 1	Learning How the Laws Apply to College Students with Disabilities	5
Step 2	Knowing a Student's Responsibilities and Rights	27
Step 3	Developing the Student's Nonacademic Skills	51
Step 4	Developing the Student's Academic Skills	75
Step 5	Identifying Colleges That Are a Good Fit	97
Step 6	Applying for College Admission	127
Step 7	Requesting Accommodations	141

Final Thoughts for Parents   175

Appendix A	A Picture of How the Laws Work at the National Level	177
Appendix B	Professionals Working with CLD Students	187
Appendix C	Additional Resources	193

Bibliography	197
Index	203
About the Author	213

Preface

Thank you for reading this book. By doing so, you are helping me on a quest I began in 2008 to help fill the information gap concerning the changes students with disabilities encounter when they enroll at college.

At the time I started writing on this topic and giving presentations, I had spent ten years working in college disability services offices, where some of my duties involved reviewing requests for disability accommodations. Over that time, I realized that my training as a special education teacher in the mid-1990s was missing something crucial. It hadn't prepared me to help my students make the transition from high school to college. I only learned what knowledge I lacked when I started working at a college myself. I regretted that I hadn't known enough to provide my high school students with the proper preparation for their next environment.

During that period, as I reviewed requests, I realized that I probably wasn't alone. Students sometimes asked for accommodations we didn't provide. It seemed likely their own special education teams hadn't known about the changes at college, either. I worried about how students would feel when they learned we didn't provide some of the supports they needed. That's why I decided to try sharing information with professionals and families.

Sorting Fact from Fiction

The challenge I continue to face on this journey is this—how do I get people to seek out the information I have to offer when they're hearing a variety of advice from their district, or from friends, colleagues, online posts and groups, etc.? In other words—how do I get them to question whether what they're hearing is correct? I offer lots of free information online and share it on social media, present webinars, and wrote this book and two previous editions to try to make sure students, parents, and professionals have access to accurate information. But unless people have a reason to think critically about what they hear, it's hard to get them to seek verification that the information is correct.

You yourself may have arrived at this book after first hearing a lot of different stories about the college environment and wondered what was accurate. Maybe you've only heard from one source. Perhaps this is your first step in learning about the changes in the college environment. Either way, I'm so glad you've found your way here. However you got here, I hope you'll share what you learn. Doing so can only help to make sure students have the preparation they need.

Be aware that what you learn here may contradict what you hear from others. I know it's hard to know what to believe when dealing with conflicting information. It's important to me that you feel you can rely upon the information this book provides. I have provided citations and resources to assure you that what you read here is based in the law and the experiences of professionals in the field. I hope that will give you a sense of security.

"Just when parents think they mastered the IEP process . . . "

If you're a parent or guardian, this message I received from a parent may speak to or for you. You've spent years advocating for your student and learning about how things work in the K–12 system. Now you've realized there's a different system at the college level.

I hear your concerns, and I empathize. The unfamiliar can cause anxiety, and the college environment does indeed hold some changes that may be worrying to you. You love your student, and you just want to make sure they have what they need.

I can't promise you that everything you read here will soothe your worries. It may depend upon the kinds of supports your student is currently receiving and how wide the gap is between those and what they are likely to find available at college. But I hope that learning about how things work, about which accommodations are commonly available and which aren't, will give you a sense of empowerment. You'll come away with a much clearer picture of what the next environment looks like, allowing you, your student, and the rest of the folks you work with to prepare your student for it, if attending college is your student's goal.

Please keep in mind that I am presenting information in this book in a matter-of-fact way to make sure you learn what you need to know. When I talk about the things that colleges don't have to (and therefore commonly don't) do, the discussion may make the college environment seem like a cold place. I don't want you to get the impression that the college system isn't inviting, though. The directors interviewed for this book are passionate people invested in serving students—that's why I chose them to provide the information shared here. I can't promise you everyone working in the college disability system is as welcoming as they are, but one thing students can do to empower themselves is to make sure they find a college where the people they'll interact with around their accommodations make them feel like they truly care about them. That may help ease your worries, too.

You Don't Know What You Don't Know

If you are a professional reading this, I assume you're seeking information to empower you to do what you can to prepare the students you work with for a successful transition. Thank you for taking the time to do this.

Given what I have learned in talking to some of your colleagues in my professional development presentations, some of you may be working in schools that operate based on misunderstandings about the college disability services system. (For instance, maybe your district moves all students on IEPs to a 504 plan because someone in the district believes 504 plans are valid at college. That's not true.) Or you may be writing assessment reports on students and making recommendations for accommodations and supports that may not accurately reflect what students can expect at college.

This isn't anybody's fault; it's just a result of the information gap. Like me, you may have received no training about what the college environment holds for your students. I hope you'll take what you learn here and share it with as many professionals as possible. Again—the more people who have information about how things work at the college level, the better the outcomes will be for students.

Many Paths After High School

I want to mention that the ideas in this book focus primarily on preparing students to attend a traditional four-year college. The reason for that is that it's the setting with which I am familiar (I am now working at my third such institution in more than 20 years in the field) and because it places so many demands on students, especially if they live at school. If students prepare for that environment, they'll likely have the skills they need to navigate life after high school, no matter what they choose to do.

This focus is not meant to diminish the value of other paths students can take. The only important goal for each student is the one they set for themselves. This is not an idea to which I merely give lip service, and it is a message I think applies to all students, not just those with disabilities.

I also recognize that the research covered here and the strategies suggested reflect the dominant American culture's definition of postsecondary success. Valenzuela and Martin (2005) reminded us that "individuals from different cultures may have different visions of successful transition outcomes."[1] The focus of this book is not meant to diminish those other visions in any way.[2]

Instead, I want to make sure that students with disabilities who *do* aspire to attend a four-year school know that this is an option. Based on conversations I've had and things I've read, I know that isn't always the message they're getting. I want to make sure they are aware of all the possibilities open to them.

Approaches Should Be Individualized

This book contains numerous suggestions for how parents can prepare students for college, and much of what is recommended will be helpful to them, no matter what they decide to do after high school. The ways I suggest that families work on the preparation should be seen as my own ideas, shaped by my own experiences in the field and my own personal culture. I recognize that families may have different ways of helping their student transition to adulthood. The ideas presented in this book are not meant to detract from those in any way. As you read, please don't take the suggestions about what parents *can* do as anything but suggestions. You may decide some can be helpful and use them exactly as described, modify them as you see fit, or not use them at all. They're here to offer you options.

With that, let's begin . . .

Notes

1. Rudolph L. Valenzuela and James E. Martin, "Self-Directed IEP: Bridging Values of Diverse Cultures and Secondary Education," *Career Development for Exceptional Individuals* 28, no. 1 (2005): 4–14. https://doi.org/10.1177/08857288050280010301

2. See appendix B for resources on working with students from culturally diverse backgrounds.

~

Acknowledgments

I am so grateful to everyone who helped me with this new edition.

I'd like to thank Tom Koerner at Rowman & Littlefield and my agent, Grace Freedson, for seeing the potential in this book, and the Rowman & Littlefield team for making it a reality.

If you find this book to be fluid and well-organized, you can join me in thanking Ross J. Q. Owens, my editor, for his guidance and feedback.

Jamie Axelod has been an incredibly helpful mentor and teacher. His advice has been invaluable, and his generosity with his time and knowledge has been an enormous gift.

I want to thank Meg Grigal, Laura Kazan, Jill Jansen, Leena Landmark, Elena Silva, and Pete Wright for educating me and making sure I didn't misinform readers.

And I want to thank all of the folks who shared their knowledge and expertise to make sure students with disabilities have the preparation they need for a bright future, whatever path they decide to take. They were chosen because of their knowledge and their passion for helping students. They are:

Deborah S. Braswell
Jane Thierfeld Brown
Margaret Camp
Joan K. Casey
Rick Clark

Elizabeth Cooper
Leann DiAndreth-Elkins
Laura DiGalbo
Eric Endlich
Catherine Getchell

Paul Harwell

Ann Knettler

Mike Langford

Sherri Maxman

Gabrielle Miller

Gregory Moyer

Doris Pierce

Jeremiah Quinlan

Stacey Reycraft

Jane Sarouhan

Jason Sarouhan

Keyana Scales

Spencer Scruggs

Korey Singleton

Sacha Thieme

Eric Trekell

Annie Tulkin

Scott van Loo

Jennifer Walker

Imy Wax

Jorja Weybrandt

Belinda Wilkerson

Marvin Williams

Lorraine Wolf

Finally, and as always, I want to thank my husband, who is—quite simply—the best.

Introduction

As students with disabilities move from high school to college, they move out of the coverage of the Individuals with Disabilities Education Act (IDEA) or Section 504 Subpart D (depending upon the kind of plan they've had) to an environment where Section 504 Subpart E prevails.[1] This book is designed to help build a foundation of knowledge, where the information in one step leads logically into the information in the next one.

This change in prevailing laws means there are changes to the way the system works, and in the part students play in this system. Step 1 details the differences and explains how they play out at the college level.

Within this new system, students who want to receive accommodations must meet certain responsibilities. They also have certain rights. Step 2 will explain these so readers can understand how things work.

As a result of the changes in the environment, students will need certain self-management skills in order to navigate the system. Step 3 explains what they are and offers ways to help develop them.

And since students will be in an environment where the demands are increased and structure is decreased, they'll need academic skills they can apply independently. Step 4 discusses these and provides ideas for ways schools can incorporate them into instruction, as well as strategies that students can use once at college.

Compared to those pertaining to high school, the laws that prevail at the college level place fewer and different demands on colleges in terms of the supports they are obligated to provide. Although some colleges will simply comply with the letter of the law, others will do more. As students compile their lists of prospective colleges, they can use this information to help guide their choices. This is discussed in step 5.

Furnished with a list of schools that provide the support they need and are a good fit overall, students should be ready to apply to colleges of their choice. In order to do so effectively, they'll need to know what the law says about how colleges can and can't treat them in the admissions process. This is explained in step 6.

Once they are at college, students may wish to use accommodations. Again, because the laws in place have different mandates, what is available may be different from what they received in the past. Also, having had accommodations previously doesn't guarantee that students will receive them at college, too, but the opposite is true, too. A lack of history of receiving accommodations doesn't rule out the possibility that a student might be found eligible for them at college. Step 7 explains how students register for accommodations, the paperwork they may need, what accommodations are and aren't commonly available, and what students can do if they aren't approved for the accommodations they request.

Notes on Language Choices

Opinions vary across and within communities on appropriate terminology. Given the wide range of opinions about the appropriate way to refer to individuals and groups, not everyone will find their preferred terminology used here. Apologies go out to those who are disappointed with the choices made. Since the goal of this book is to be inclusive, numerous references were checked in an attempt to make sure the language used was as sensitive and respectful as possible. These include:

ADHD—this will be used to refer to all of the different types of Attention Deficit Disorder.

Blind/VI—this will be used to refer to students who are blind, have low vision, or have vision loss.

Deaf/HOH—this will be used to refer to students who are deaf, hard of hearing, and/or have hearing loss.

LD—this will be used to refer to learning disabilities.

Neurotypical—this will be used to refer to students who don't have a disability.

When reading discussions of the research in appendix A, you may find some of the terminology used questionable and even offensive (e.g., emotional disturbance). Just for the clarity of the discussion (and for those who might want to read the studies themselves), the discussion uses those original labels but also points out that they were used by the researchers. The terminology used in the field has evolved since some of those studies were conducted.

This book uses the word "disability" because this is the word used in the laws. Use of the word is not meant to offend those who see students as having *differences, or being neurodivergent or neurodiverse.*

When discussing the role of caretakers throughout this book, the term "parent" is used. It is not meant to exclude those family members or guardians who might not be a student's parent, but who care for them. "Parent" is used throughout the book and meant to be inclusive of anyone assuming a caregiver role.

Postsecondary planning should involve the student, their parents, high school staff and faculty members, and any outside professionals who work with the student. For that reason, when the term "team" is used in this book, it is meant to represent all of these stakeholders.

Some of the parents reading this book may have homeschooled their children. These parents take on a variety of roles. For the purposes of the discussions in the book, they should see themselves in all of the applicable roles, including teacher and case manager.

Terminology from the College Disability Services System

There are some terms commonly used in the postsecondary disability field that are used extensively in this book. Again, terminology varies across colleges and universities, so the terms used here may not match what is used at a student's college.

DS—is the abbreviation for the disability services office, which is the one that typically provides accommodations. For the purposes of the book, any office, department, or individual who works with students on accommodations will be referred to as DS.

Coordinator—may be the name of a student's contact person at DS. This may be the director themselves, or another staff member. For the purposes of this book, this term will be used to represent the person who coordinates a student's accommodations and serves as their primary point of contact for this. The coordinator may, at some schools, be the sole employee of the office and also have the title of director.

OCR—Office for Civil Rights—is the government agency (part of the United States Department of Education) that students can appeal to if they believe their college or an individual at their college has discriminated against them on the basis of their disability.

SOP—Summary of Performance is a document that high schools have to create for graduating seniors who have had an individualized education program (IEP).

How to Use This Book

This book's overall goal is to educate readers about the college disability services system and to help students prepare for success at college. It is for informational purposes only. Nothing in this book is legal or medical advice or should be considered as such. Those who require legal or medical advice should seek it from a qualified professional.

Note

1. The Americans with Disabilities Act covers both settings, but the majority of the guidance for colleges comes from Section 504.

Learning How the Laws Apply to College Students with Disabilities

What You'll Learn in This Step

- The differences in the laws covering K–12 and those covering college and their purposes
- What the laws tell colleges they do and don't have to do for students with disabilities
- What it means to be "qualified" for protection
- How the laws define what constitutes a disability

As the saying goes, "knowledge is power." But new information can bring new questions. When a student is identified with a learning disability, they and their family members may have a variety of reactions. For some families, that identification can bring a sense of relief, as it can explain some of the struggles the student has experienced. For others, it may validate what they already thought. After they've absorbed the information, their thoughts might eventually turn to what students will do after high school; one question they may have is whether college is a possibility.

The short answer is yes. College is indeed a possibility for students with disabilities who are interested in going. While specific statistics about students with disabilities attending college aren't collected as frequently as we might hope or expect, the most recent data from the National Center for Education Statistics showed almost 20 percent of college students reported having a disability in the 2015–2016 academic year.[1] As you can see, students with disabilities *are* attending college!

For students who *want* to go, the focus of the planning for their high school years should be on developing the skills they'll need for college success. In order to be effective, planning must be informed by an understanding of the environment at the college level. This involves not just learning about the academic demands but also about how the system for providing accommodations works, and what it does and doesn't provide.

Which Laws Cover Students at College and Who Is Covered by Them?

You may have heard all kinds of conflicting things about which laws apply at college and what does and doesn't happen for students with disabilities there. There's understandable confusion. It's important not only to know which laws are in place but also to know what they're intended to do, because that helps to explain the shifts students will see in the services and accommodations (and how students get access to them) when students start at college.

Laws in Place and What It Means for High School Plans

If you're a K–12 teacher or other related professional working with students with disabilities, your training may not have included the laws that cover college students. If you're a parent, you may be seeing things online or hearing things from acquaintances that aren't accurate.

Here's what you need to know:

- The Americans with Disabilities Act Amendments Act (ADAAA) of 2008 (P.L. 110-325)[2] applies across the life span.

- The Individuals with Disabilities Education Act,[3] which provides eligible students with Individualized Education Plans (IEPs), applies only to K–12 schools, not colleges.

- Section 504 of the Rehabilitation Act of 1973[4] has Subpart D, which applies to K–12 schools (and under which eligible students get 504 plans), and Subpart E, which applies to postsecondary (after high school) institutions.

Why does it matter which laws prevail? It's because the fact that IDEA doesn't apply to colleges means that IEPs no longer have application as legally binding plans once students graduate from high school. A clearer way to put it is that those plans "expire." If you look at IDEA, you won't see that stated explicitly, but that is the effect.

This doesn't mean that colleges don't have to provide accommodations—they definitely do, and there are a lot of them. But colleges don't have to provide the same accommodations students had in their IEP simply because they were written into that plan. They get to decide what accommodations they will provide based on what they see as a student's needs. And there are some accommodations that they do not have to provide, even if a student's high school thought it was appropriate to do so. When it comes to *services*, there are also some that colleges don't have to provide; all of this will be discussed later in this step.

Even if you knew that IEPs aren't valid after high school, you might have heard that 504 plans are. This is an understandable misconception, since Section 504 applies to colleges, too. But again, Subpart D of Section 504 applies to K–12 schools, and Subpart E applies to colleges. These two subparts have decidedly different *mandates* (requirements for what they have to do). As with IDEA and IEPs, the shift between subparts as students move from high school to college means that Section 504 plans from high school are no longer applicable at college as legally binding plans.[5] Again—the law doesn't explicitly state this but, as with IEPs, 504 plans essentially "expire" once students graduate from high school.

You may have heard of someone who has received a 504 plan at college. What can cause some confusion is that some colleges may use the term "504 plan" in the letters or electronic notifications they write listing a student's approved accommodations. But these are not new 504 plans. (Subpart E doesn't require these, even though Subpart D does.) And they definitely aren't "extensions" of students' high school 504 plans.

The ADAAA applies both to K–12 schools and to postsecondary schools, but it doesn't provide for the creation of an individual plan for students at any level. Moreover, there are parts of it that specifically apply to colleges but not to K–12 schools. Although the ADAAA's mandates are not as extensive as those in Section 504, students are covered under both laws once they transition to college.

Purposes of the Laws

If colleges are also subject to disability-related laws, why aren't they required to provide the same services that students had in high school? The answer may lie in what each relevant law was written to accomplish.

The goals of IDEA include providing students with disabilities a free, appropriate public education (FAPE), improving their educational results, and ensuring that those students can meet state educational standards. The goals of Section 504 and the ADAAA are to prevent disability-based discrimination and to address such discrimination if/when it occurs.

The difference between services at the secondary versus postsecondary level is often summarized as an emphasis on helping students to achieve *success* under IDEA versus providing them with *access* under Section 504 and the ADAAA. What does this mean?

Colleges provide eligible students with accommodations that help them *access* college programs. For example, a student with a reading disability may get *access* to their required readings when their college provides their materials in a format that allows them to use text-to-speech software to read that text aloud. But if the student doesn't understand the reading and never seeks help from the professor or the campus tutoring center and fails an exam because of their lack of comprehension, the college isn't required to do anything more for them, such as allow them a do-over of that exam. In this example, the college did what was necessary to provide that student with a means for accessing the readings. But it wasn't responsible for making sure the student actually understood those readings.

Section 504 explains this idea. It says that "aids, benefits, and services, to be equally effective, are not required to produce the identical result or level of achievement for handicapped and nonhandicapped persons, but must afford handicapped persons equal opportunity to obtain the same result, to gain the same benefit, or to reach the same level of achievement" (34 C.F.R. § 104.4(b)(2)). In the example just discussed, the student was given access to the readings in a way that addressed their reading disorder. That was the extent of the college's responsibility. It was the responsibility of the student to seek help when they didn't understand them.

Another common explanation of how the laws apply at the college level is to say that schools have to provide accommodations that "level the playing field" for students with disabilities. They don't have to do more than that, though the way some colleges decide to accommodate students may be seen—positively—as going beyond the minimum the law requires.

As an example, a student whose GPA fell below the required level to keep their scholarship might request additional accommodations in an effort to raise it. If DS reviewed the student's disability-related needs and found they hadn't changed since the student was originally approved for accommodations, their college would have no obligation to provide additional accommodations *simply* because the student needed to raise their GPA. The college could *choose* to add accommodations if they thought it was appropriate, but, assuming there was no change in the student's eligibility or needs, they wouldn't have to do it for that reason alone. Accommodations are meant to make it *possible* for students to be successful, not to *make sure* they will be.

Why are the mandates for colleges not as extensive and the services not as supportive as those in the K–12 system? This isn't explained in the laws. It may be because K–12 education is mandatory, while attending college isn't.

Who Gets Access to Accommodations at College?

Now that you know that IEPs and 504 plans aren't valid after high school, you may be wondering what that means for students. Do only certain kinds of disabilities get accommodated at college, such as physical ones that affect a student's ability to get around campus? You may have heard that only students with such physical or obvious disabilities (such as students who are blind) are given accommodations at college. Research shows that a number of students don't think they're eligible for disability accommodations when in fact they may qualify.[6]

The laws in place at college provide protections for students who meet two criteria: 1) they must be "qualified" and 2) they must have a disability. Since one of the places where "qualified" applies is in the admissions process, it makes sense to start with this requirement.

Students Must Be "Qualified" in Order to Be Protected

As students move from high school to college, they may encounter limits that weren't a problem in the past. For instance, they may have been allowed to take an AP class in high school even if they didn't have the qualifying grade to get in. At college, something like that is less likely to happen, though it's always a possibility.

It starts with the admissions process. If you're wondering whether colleges have to make changes to their admissions requirements for students with disabilities, they don't. Any student—regardless of disability status—has to be qualified for admission. Section 504 says that in order to be viewed as "qualified," students must meet "the academic and technical standards requisite to admission or to participation in the recipient's education program or activity" (34 C.F.R. § 104.3(l)(3)).

For instance, if a student has a disability but doesn't have the GPA, scores, or something else required for admission at the colleges they apply to, those colleges don't have to admit the student. In other words, if the student isn't qualified for admission, the colleges don't have to accommodate them by bending their requirements.

Once students are admitted to college, they may have to meet other standards in order to be considered qualified. Some specific majors may have requirements for students to enter their programs. Although colleges can't just exclude students with disabilities from certain majors because they perceive that they won't be successful in them, they can set up requirements that all students must meet in order to be qualified for participation. These typically require students to have achieved a certain minimum grade in some *prerequisite* courses (classes students have to take before they're allowed to take certain other classes) to demonstrate that they have the skills and knowledge needed for further study in that field.

For example, if a student wants to major in engineering, and the engineering program at the university they attend requires students to get a C or higher in certain math or science classes in order to be admitted, the university doesn't have to let the student into that program if their grades don't meet this requirement. In this case, the program wouldn't be singling out students with disabilities. The limitation would apply to any student hoping to pursue that major, not just those who have a disability.

Students who register with their college's DS and are found eligible will receive accommodations. What may surprise some readers, though, is that having been found eligible by their high school doesn't guarantee that students will also be found so at their college. This is where the second part of the definition comes in: they must have a disability.

Disability

The ADAAA explains that a person with a disability is defined as one who has "a physical or mental impairment that substantially limits one or more major life activities" (42 U.S.C. § 12102(1)(A)). At § 12102(2)(A) and (B), it provides examples of those activities, which include not only walking and speaking but also learning, reading, and concentrating, as well as certain digestive and immune system functions, among others. (The definition in Section 504 is similar, but the ADAAA was written and updated more recently, so it will be used for this discussion.)

It goes on to explain that an impairment that is "episodic or in remission is a disability if it would substantially limit a major life activity when active" (§ 12102(4)(D)). For example, if a student has a depressive disorder that doesn't affect them every day but does have severe periods where they can't function, they would qualify as a person with a disability.

The ADAAA also covers students who use "mitigating measures" such as medication, prosthetics, implantable hearing devices, assistive technology, etc. At § 12102(4)(E)(i), it says that the determination of whether someone has a disability should be made without factoring in such measures. For example, if a student with ADHD took medication to help them concentrate, their college shouldn't conclude that because the medication helped them concentrate, they didn't have a disability.

You might assume that if students have previously been accommodated by their high school, their college will be required to provide them with accommodations. It may be surprising, but this isn't the case. This is because colleges get to interpret the "substantially limits" part of the definition. This can be where some students may have an issue.

When a student registers for accommodations (this happens after they enroll[7]), they will likely have to provide documentation that shows they are a person with a disability. Although the college is unlikely to reject the validity of the student's documentation, it may still conclude that the student is ineligible for the accommodations they've requested, even if they've received them previously. Although the ADAAA says its definition of disability should be "construed in favor of broad coverage" (§ 12102(4)(A)), it doesn't require colleges to accommodate students simply because they've previously been found eligible.

The ADAAA's definition does address history, but not in a way you might expect. It says a person meets the definition if they've been *discriminated against* because they previously either had a disability or were *perceived to have one* (§ 12102(3)(A)). Even so, this still doesn't translate into a mandate that colleges provide accommodation solely on the basis of that history if they aren't currently disabled.

The ADAAA also excludes from its definition any impairment that lasts six months or less (§ 12102(3)(B)). So, if a student was accommodated in high school with a scribe for tests and notetaking because they broke their arm, but the injury healed and didn't create a lifelong, substantial limitation in their use of that arm, that student wouldn't be eligible for accommodations at college (or afterward) on the basis of that history.

To reiterate, a student who has an impairment that substantially limits one of their major life activities will likely be found eligible for protection under the laws in place at college. (Many won't run into a problem.) So now that you know who Section 504 and the ADAAA cover, your next question may be—what do these laws require colleges to do for students with disabilities?

What the Laws Do and Don't Require

Though this may be surprising, the laws in place don't provide a lengthy list of specific accommodations that colleges must provide—but don't be alarmed. If you think about it, this makes sense. As technology advances and laws and academic programs evolve, and as students with more and more complex needs enroll at college, it would be difficult to keep such a list updated.

Instead, the laws provide parameters for how colleges have to treat students across different parts of the college experience. They also carve out some exceptions. Section 504 provides most of the guidance for colleges. While you don't need to know the details of the laws, seeing what they do and don't say can provide helpful context for understanding the differences in accommodations and services.

Colleges are educational institutions first and foremost, so they provide a number of academic accommodations. And many colleges are more than just places for learning. Those with housing also serve as living environments. Additional college offerings may include student services, activities, and more. It may be reassuring to you to know that the laws in place cover all of these.

Academic Accommodations

Section 504 provides most of the guidance for colleges. Subpart E includes some general rules, stating that:

(a) "No qualified handicapped student shall, on the basis of handicap, be excluded from participation in, be denied the benefits of, or otherwise be subjected to discrimination" in any part of a college's programs.
(b) Colleges have to provide "an equal opportunity for the participation of qualified handicapped persons."
(c) Colleges can't exclude qualified handicapped students "from any course, course of study, or other part of its education program or activity."
(d) Colleges have to operate their programs "in the most integrated setting appropriate."

The first three points have already been discussed. The last one isn't an issue that comes up very much, as colleges don't have special education classes. (Remember that IDEA, which mandates that K–12 schools provide students with specialized instruction, doesn't apply to colleges.) But it does mean that other parts of college programs (such as school-sponsored social activities) should be inclusive of students with disabilities.

The ADAAA adds some further clarifications. Among them, two points are especially important because they concern exceptions regarding accommodations. Colleges aren't obligated to provide accommodations that would:

- create an undue burden on their part;
- directly threaten the health or safety of others.

The law specifies that colleges don't have to approve accommodations that would "result in an undue burden" (42 U.S.C. § 12182(b)(2)(A)(iii)). The kind of burden is typically financial or administrative. But the law doesn't provide further clarification for determining when a requested accommodation would be too expensive or hard to administer. As a result, colleges may take guidance from Office for Civil Rights (OCR) decisions in cases where a student has filed a complaint and a college claims that it would create a burden.

The bar is high to support a college's claim of an undue financial burden. For example, if a deaf student complained to OCR that their college said it didn't have to provide sign language interpreting because it costs too much, OCR would consider the entire budget of the college, not just the DS office's budget, and would likely find in favor of the student.

In the case of an administrative burden, the college might not have as much trouble reaching the "undue" standard. For example, consider a request that a student who takes stimulant medication for ADHD might make. The student might request only day classes on the grounds that their medication would keep them awake very late if they took it in the late afternoon for an evening class. Clearly, it would create an undue administrative burden if the college had to reschedule all of the classes that student needed or wanted to take. (Imagine what would happen if colleges had to do this for all students who needed it.) Instead, the college would likely accommodate the student by letting them register for classes earlier than the rest of their class.[8]

Additionally, the college would be under no obligation to provide accommodations that would directly put others in danger (§ 12182(b)(3)). In many academically focused college programs, this prospect seems so rare as to be almost irrelevant. (For instance, it's hard to imagine something a student would be asked to do in a literature program that seems likely to create a danger to someone else's safety.) However, in vocational training programs where students work with dangerous equipment or chemicals near someone else, or where they are training for jobs in the healthcare field, some accommodations might not be allowable for this reason.

These general rules apply to all parts of a college's operations—classes, housing, etc. Not surprisingly, though, much of the additional guidance around how colleges have to treat students is focused on academics.

Academic Adjustments

Remember that the goal of the laws in place is to make sure students with disabilities have access to college programs and that they don't experience discrimination on the basis of their disability. Section 504 provides the bulk of the guidance for what colleges must or must not do. Essentially, the way colleges meet the mandate is by providing accommodations. There are four basic things the law requires. Colleges:

- may need to alter their requirements;
- can't deny certain accommodations;
- have to make sure tests measure a student's knowledge, not their disability; and
- have to provide auxiliary aids.

Each of these requirements gets some clarification in the law, and all but one includes exemptions.[9]

Colleges may need to alter their requirements (§ 104.44(a)).

- *What the law says:* Colleges have to "make such modifications to [their] academic requirements as are necessary to ensure that such requirements do not discriminate or have the effect of discriminating, on the basis of handicap, against a qualified handicapped applicant or student." The law lists possible "modifications," including course substitutions, additional time to complete a degree, and "adaptation of the manner in which specific courses are conducted."

- *Exceptions mentioned?* Yes. It also says that if colleges can show that their academic requirements "are essential to the instruction being pursued by such student" or are related to any licensing requirements, they will "not be regarded as discriminatory."

- *What it means:* Many colleges have what they may call "core" or "general education" requirements that mandate that students take a certain number of courses in different areas of study, such as two science classes, two social studies classes, etc., no matter what their major is. Colleges can choose to provide substitutions for these, but they don't have to do so if they determine that these courses are essential to their degree program. The same is true with required courses for majors; colleges don't have to offer substitutions for these (see step 7).

  The ADAAA echoes this. It says that colleges don't have to make "modifications in policies, practices, or procedures" that would "fundamentally alter" any part of their programs (42 U.S.C. § 12182(b)(2)(A)(ii)). Some DS websites alert students to this fact, noting that even if some accommodations might make sense for a particular disability, they may not be granted if they would create such a fundamental alteration.

This is a good time to address the way colleges use specific terms to categorize requests even though the laws don't. Section 504 Subpart E, as noted, uses "modifications" when discussing academic adjustments colleges have to make. The ADAAA uses "accommodations" to describe adjustments, but it also uses "modification" when stating that colleges have to change their "policies, practices and procedures" when necessary to accommodate individuals with disabilities.

Many colleges, though, use "accommodation" and "modification" to differentiate certain kinds of student requests from others. While these distinctions aren't made in the laws, many colleges view the terms differently. They use "accommodations" to describe adjustments that don't change what students will learn or how they'll meet standards in their classes and programs as compared with their neurotypical peers, while they use "modifications" to describe adjustments that do change the standards.

An example of a modification might be a student's request to be exempted from speaking in a public speaking class. (Some majors may require students to take a course like this, and some colleges may require all students to do so.) A student with an anxiety disorder or language-based disorder might ask to write a paper instead of giving a speech, but this would likely be considered a *modification*—that is, a fundamental alteration to the class objective of having students learn to speak clearly and comfortably. The student might receive an *accommodation* instead, perhaps by being given permission to deliver the speech just to the professor or to a smaller group. But if the professor can make the case that even doing this would fundamentally alter the course's objectives—in other words, that it would constitute a modification and not an accommodation—a review of this objection might agree.[10]

Colleges can't deny certain accommodations if doing so would be discriminatory (§ 104.44(b)).

- *What the law says:* Colleges can't "impose upon handicapped students other rules, such as the prohibition of tape recorders in classrooms or of dog guides in campus buildings, that have the effect of limiting the participation of handicapped students in the recipient's education program or activity."

- *Exceptions mentioned?* No.

- *What it means:* Students may need certain accommodations that may conflict with other kinds of school rules or result in challenges from faculty. In some cases, the accommodation has to be allowed. For instance, a professor may object to allowing students to record their lectures (as a notetaking accommodation). However, even in states where it's illegal to record a conversation without the consent of both parties, Section 504 prevails, meaning that the professor can't prevent students from recording their classes if this has been approved as an accommodation.[11] Similarly, although colleges are allowed to ban pets or emotional support animals from academic buildings, they must allow service dogs to accompany their students into those spaces.

This part of the guidance is not interpreted to mean that colleges have to provide *any* accommodation a student requests. Again, there are exceptions.

Tests should be designed in a way that measures a student's knowledge, not their disability (§ 104.44(c)).

- *What the law says:* Colleges have to make sure that tests are designed in a way that "represents the student's achievement in the course, rather than reflecting the student's impaired sensory, manual, or speaking skills."

- *Exceptions mentioned?* Yes. As already, noted, it goes on to say that colleges have to do this "except where such skills are the factors that the test purports to measure."

- *What it means:* The wording of this part of the law might make it seem like it's telling colleges to monitor how professors design their tests. While that could be true at some schools, this part of the law is usually viewed as meaning that colleges must provide accommodations so students with disabilities aren't prevented by those disabilities from showing what they know on exams. Again, you might find it surprising that Section 504 doesn't provide a list of test accommodations colleges *must* make.[12]

  But even if a student has been approved by DS for certain test accommodations, a professor may argue that some of them fundamentally alter what they are trying to assess with their tests. For example, DS may approve use of a calculator for exams for students with a math disability. At the college level, students may actually be *expected* to use a calculator in classes that involve math (e.g., statistics), so those students might not even need special permission to use one as an accommodation.

  But in certain classes or programs, use of a calculator might be seen as a fundamental alteration. If a student is studying to be an elementary school teacher, being able to complete math problems on a board or screen correctly without the benefit of a calculator might be considered "essential" to the program's requirements. In that case, the student's request to use a calculator would probably be denied.

Colleges have to provide auxiliary aids (§ 104.44(d)).

- *What the law says:* Colleges have to provide auxiliary aids, including "taped texts, interpreters or other effective methods of making orally delivered materials available to students with hearing impairments, readers in libraries for students with visual impairments, classroom equipment adapted for use by students with manual impairments, and other similar services and actions."

- *Exceptions mentioned?* Yes. This section says colleges don't have to provide "attendants, individually prescribed devices, readers for personal use or study, or other devices or services of a personal nature."

- *What it means:* Although colleges have to provide access to information and materials students need for their courses and other aspects of their programs, they don't have to furnish some other things. An example of a device "of a personal nature" commonly used to explain this rule is eyeglasses. You probably wouldn't expect colleges to provide those for students who needed them. But the exceptions the law does allow may be surprising.

  For example, if a student with disabilities is approved by DS to have any materials for their classes put into a format that can be read by speech-to-text software, colleges only have to provide that alternative format—they don't have to give the student access to such software for their personal computer. However, if a student is approved to use this software for exams, the college has to provide that software in test settings since those exams would be considered in-class activities (even for a student who is taking classes remotely).

  And since readers in libraries are also mentioned specifically, computers in the library should be equipped with text-to-speech software. Colleges may also load that software on some of the terminals in a computer lab. If students have to access physical books in the library because an electronic copy isn't available, the college has to provide a reader.

  Some colleges do provide students found eligible for text-to-speech with a copy of the software for their own computers. And some load these kinds of programs into their online system so that anyone with a student ID number can access it—they don't have to register with DS. But policies on providing software for use outside of test situations vary from college to college.

  When it comes to "attendants" or "services of a personal nature," this means that colleges don't have to provide a personal aide for a student who needs one. This applies to students with significant physical disabilities who require help in tasks of daily living such as showering and dressing, as well as to students with other kinds of disabilities, who might have had an aide in high school who redirected them, kept them on task, etc.

This doesn't mean that colleges won't allow students to have an aide as an accommodation—just that they don't have to locate someone or pay them to serve in that way. It is a student's responsibility to find any assistant they need and to pay for their time.[13] A family member may also serve as a student's aide. Regardless of who provides this service, the college may require a background check for any assistant who has access to campus buildings. The college may also require any aide to sign an agreement about what they may and may not do for a student.

The only "services of a personal nature" mentioned specifically in the law are "readers for personal use or study." While the law doesn't specifically state this, it's important to know that DS offices aren't required to provide specialized tutoring for students with disabilities. Indeed, many don't. Unlike in K–12, where students may have had access to learning disabilities specialists or teachers certified in special education, students at college are not "entitled" to meet with such a professional as an accommodation. However, some DS offices offer this for a fee, while others do so for free.[14]

Finally, students aren't entitled to specialized tutoring arrangements in the general campus tutoring center. For example, if the college's academic support center provides one tutor to a group of five students, a student with disabilities doesn't have a right to get tutored one-on-one or in a smaller group.[15]

While this list of requirements in the laws may seem brief and limited, the real-life effect of them is that colleges provide a number of academic accommodations.[16] And some colleges do provide certain accommodations even when the law does not require them.

Of course, academics are only one part of the college experience. Colleges have to provide accommodations throughout their other departments and offices.

Accommodations in Nonacademic Parts of College Programs and Services

Section 504 provides guidance on all facets of a student's experience, including housing, financial and employment assistance, counseling and placement services, social organizations, as well as other nonacademic services.

Housing (34 C.F.R. § 104.45)

Because they have to provide students with access to their offerings and avoid discriminating against them on the basis of their disability, colleges that provide housing must have housing that is accessible to students with disabilities. If a university's housing isn't usable by students with physical disabilities, it has to modify existing housing or build new housing to accommodate them.

But if a college doesn't provide housing to neurotypical students, it isn't required to do so for students with disabilities, either. Also, at colleges that don't have enough on-campus housing to meet the demand, students with disabilities aren't "entitled" to on-campus housing if their neurotypical peers don't have the same guarantee. If freshmen are the only ones guaranteed housing and their college doesn't have enough spaces, both neurotypical and disabled students who are sophomores, juniors, or seniors must find someplace to live off campus.

Colleges also may not use a student's disability as a basis for assigning them to housing that is different than that of their neurotypical peers, *unless* it is the only housing that can accommodate their disability. That may be the case at some schools.

Financial and Employment Assistance (§ 104.46)

A college can't provide less financial assistance to students with disabilities than it does to their neurotypical peers or preclude them from any scholarships the college provides. However, it may distribute funds from a private scholarship or fellowship, even if the rules of that scholarship or fellowship exclude students with disabilities from consideration.

Also, if companies recruit students at a college (by either listing job openings with their career services or attending a career services event), the hiring parameters for those jobs can't be discriminatory. And if an employer providing a good or service on campus employs students, it may not discriminate against students with disabilities seeking jobs. Colleges themselves are prohibited from discriminating against students with disabilities in hiring for their own job openings.[17]

Counseling and Placement Services (§ 104.47)

Assuming that students have met requirements to get into a program that prepares them for certain kinds of jobs, the college should not steer them away from certain kinds of jobs *just because they have a disability*. However, colleges *may* provide information about licensing and certification requirements in fields that are of particular interest to students.[18]

Sometimes, colleges offer personal counseling. Colleges may not provide different versions of these services for students with disabilities. The same rule applies to academic advising services. At the same time, colleges aren't required to provide *more* or *enhanced* counseling hours or academic advisement to students with disabilities than they do for their neurotypical peers.

Social Organizations (§ 104.47)

Social organizations on campus that receive funds and/or significant assistance from the university can't discriminate against students on the basis of their disability. This does not mean, however, that they *must* admit students simply *because* they have a disability. Organizations are still entitled to make rules for whom they admit, as long as those rules aren't discriminatory.

Other Nonacademic Services (§ 104.47)

Colleges are allowed to have separate physical education classes for students with disabilities as long as they allow *qualified* students to enroll in classes with their neurotypical peers. The same is true of athletic teams and clubs. Colleges have to allow qualified students access to these, and they can create separate opportunities for students who aren't.

High School Services Not Mentioned in the Laws

Now that you know the parameters for what colleges have to do (and don't), you may be wondering whether the laws require that colleges provide certain services that IDEA requires K–12 schools to. Even though Section 504 and the ADA don't specifically say colleges don't have to provide certain services, the effect of their absence in the laws might be seen as meaning that colleges don't have to provide them. And remember that IDEA doesn't apply to colleges.

You may find it helpful to know some of these specifics of what colleges don't have to do. Some of this may be surprising.

- *Locate students with disabilities and require them to register with DS*—Under the Child Find mandate of IDEA, K–12 schools have to seek out individual students with disabilities and refer them for services. As steps 2 and 7 will discuss, students who wish to receive accommodations have to register for them. Although colleges may alert students to the existence of DS and some of the accommodations they offer,[19] they are not required to actively seek them out individually and offer them accommodations.

- *Provide disability evaluations*—Part of IDEA's mandate includes evaluating students. Colleges don't have to do this for a student who thinks they might have a disability that wasn't previously identified. They don't have to test a student who acquires a disability while attending college (e.g., sustains a brain injury in an accident) and subsequently wants to register for accommodations. And if a student who had been evaluated before college has documentation that doesn't meet the college's requirements, their college doesn't have to provide them with testing that would provide what they need.[20]

- *Provide specialized instruction*—Colleges aren't obligated to provide specialized instruction to students with disabilities (such as Orton-Gillingham for students with reading disorders), something that IDEA requires K–12 public schools to do. If a college chooses to offer a special class just for students with disabilities, it may do so, but it can't *require* students with disabilities to take it simply because they have a disability. Moreover, the laws in place don't say anything about how such a class would have to be taught.

  Because colleges don't have to provide specialized instruction, they don't have to adapt the content taught in their classes, or the way it is taught, both of which IDEA requires. As already discussed, colleges are under no obligation to change what is taught in their classes if doing so would fundamentally alter the learning objectives. And while it would be helpful if all professors taught in ways that reach all learners, colleges don't have to—for instance—require them to use slides for their lectures or provide a summary at the end of class.[21] This also means that colleges don't have to offer an alternate list of books or topics for students who are struggling with what's on the *syllabus* (list of topics, exam dates, and assignments for each course).

  Some colleges have what are called *developmental* or *remedial* classes for students who didn't score above the designated cutoff on the placement test when they enrolled or who were given *conditional admission* (meaning they didn't meet admissions requirements and must do certain things to stay enrolled). However, these aren't classes just for students with disabilities; any student who doesn't meet the cutoff score may have to take them. These aren't considered special education classes, as special education doesn't exist at the college level. That's because IDEA doesn't apply there.[22]

- *Set annual goals for students, and monitor and report on their progress*— Colleges don't have to do any kind of planning for students with disabilities. As far as setting goals goes, students are on their own. Likewise, colleges don't have to check on a student's grades, or on their mental health, social adjustment, etc. A college may have a system where professors issue alerts when students aren't doing well. If so, they can set this up any way they like. For example, the alert may go to the student's advisor, rather than to the student. And the law doesn't require any notification to go to the parents.

Also, even if a college's policy states that an academic advisor is responsible for reaching out to a student if they receive notification that the student is doing poorly, the college is unlikely to require the advisor to make sure that student makes tutoring appointments, registers for accommodations, etc. Remember—it's literally impossible for an advisor (or anyone) to *make* a student do anything like this. And they don't have to try, or to take over that responsibility for the student. Colleges don't have to notify parents about their student's progress, either, even if students have signed a Family Educational Rights and Privacy Act (FERPA) release. That release doesn't create a new responsibility for colleges.

- *Check the effectiveness of their efforts to educate students*—Colleges aren't required to have someone check in with students to see how they're doing. If a student is struggling, it's their responsibility to seek help.

  On a related note, DS staff members aren't required to check in with students to see whether their accommodations are helpful. DS offices may decide to send an occasional email reaching out to students for this purpose, but as step 2 will discuss, students themselves have to let DS know if things aren't working for them. It is the responsibility of a student, not the DS office, to request additional accommodations if they need them.

- *Improve educational results for students*—Colleges don't have to make sure a student can meet any particular educational standard. For instance, a college doesn't have to keep adding accommodations in order to make sure a student can meet the cutoff for the minimum GPA required to stay enrolled. It also doesn't have to guarantee they get to take classes with certain professors they think would be best for them.

Summary

The college environment holds numerous shifts for students with disabilities that stem from the changes in the laws in place. While colleges do have to provide a number of accommodations, there are certain supports students received in high school that won't be available to them at college. It is vital to gain an awareness and understanding of the ramifications of these changes in the law so that you can make sure students are prepared for them. This knowledge provides a foundation for step 2, which outlines a student's newfound rights and responsibilities as they make the transition from high school to college.

FAQs

Do all colleges have to provide accommodations?

The answer to this is a qualified "yes." Because the laws in place are federal, they apply to all colleges that accept federal funds. Most of them do. Even colleges with huge endowments accept federal funds in various forms, such as students' Pell Grants, GI Bill funds, and research funds.

A college can only be exempted from complying with disability laws *if it meets three conditions*. Think of the conditions as three gates the college would have to get through:

> Gate 1—which is refusal of federal funds. If a college does this, it has to get through;
>
> Gate 2—which is that the school also has to be private. If so, it also has to get through;
>
> Gate 3—which is that it has to be a religious school, too.

Only then would that school be exempt. (Even if a college were exempt, it could always *choose* to provide accommodations.)

Families and professionals shouldn't make assumptions about whether or not certain types of schools have to provide accommodations. For instance, a college that accepts only students who are very academically accomplished still has to accommodate its students who have disabilities.[23]

Also, a school's budget doesn't have any bearing on whether it has to provide accommodations. As long as it takes federal funds, it's required to do so.

The U.S. Department of Education does not keep a list of the colleges that are exempt from relevant disability laws. There likely aren't many of them, because so many schools do take federal money. If a student is applying to colleges that are private and religious and is worried that one or more of the schools might be exempt, they can search online to see whether these schools have a disability services office or 504 compliance officer. However, it's very likely that these schools take federal funds and are therefore required to provide accommodations.

Do colleges have to provide course substitutions?

One of the accommodations students may ask for is a substitution for courses required as part of their school's general education requirements and/ or for required courses for their major. As noted, Section 504 specifically mentions course substitutions as a way colleges can accommodate students.[24]

When requesting a substitution, a student may be asked whether they took such a class in high school and—if so—what sorts of accommodations were offered to help them access the content. They may have to self-report their grades for such classes or provide a copy of their final high school transcript. If they received a waiver for a class in high school, DS may ask them to provide documentation of this. A college may even require that the student take the class in question with accommodations before it will consider providing a substitution.

If a college decides to grant a substitution, it can handle this in a variety of different ways. The college may waive the requirement entirely, but more typically, it will require the student to take another class as a substitution for the waived course (e.g., a course on French cinema taught in English rather than a course in French language). Or the college might allow the student to take the original required course and be graded on a pass/fail basis (instead of for a grade), and then allow the course to count toward fulfilling the relevant requirements.

A student whose substitution requests are not approved and who cannot pass a required class for their chosen major may have to choose another major (which means more time and more money for them to finish their degree). In extreme cases, if they can't complete the general education requirements, the student may have to transfer to another college to finish their degree. Students who are worried about this might want to focus their college search on schools that don't require students to take certain classes to graduate (see step 5).

All colleges' general and major-specific academic requirements should have been determined by a process involving members of different departments and offices that determined what was essential to their programs.[25] Even so, colleges still have to *consider* requests for substitutions when students make one, even when the courses in question have been determined to be essential.

When that happens, DS may forward the request to a committee or administrator (perhaps with a recommendation from DS as to whether they view it as supported by a student's documentation). The process for review will vary from college to college; the laws don't say anything about this process and what it should include. Even if DS recommends the accommodation, that may not have any bearing on the decision.

Colleges have a lot of discretion in deciding who is eligible for a substitution because the laws don't provide any details on this, either. They may decide that only students with severe disabilities in a related area may qualify for this (e.g., a student with severe dyscalculia may be allowed to take logic or computer science courses instead of their college's two math courses to fulfill the general education requirements). Or they may grant it for anyone registered with DS who asks for it. They have the freedom to decide who is or isn't eligible.

Notes

1. "How Many Students in Postsecondary Education Have a Disability?," National Center for Education Statistics, accessed March 1, 2022. https://nces.ed.gov/fastfacts/display.asp?id=60

2. Americans with Disabilities Act Amendments Act (ADAAA) of 2008, P.L. 110-325, 42 U.S.C. §§ 12101 et seq.

3. Individuals with Disabilities Education Improvement Act (IDEA) of 2004, P.L. 108-446, 20 U.S.C. §§ 1400 et seq.

4. Rehabilitation Act of 1973, P.L. 93-112, 29 U.S.C. §§ 701 et seq.

5. Some colleges accept a student's IEP, 504, or SOP as a form of *documentation* (paperwork showing the student's history of receiving disability accommodations) when they register with DS. See step 7 to learn more.

6. Emma V. Cole and Stephanie W. Cawthon, "Self-Disclosure Decisions of University Students with Learning Disabilities," *Journal of Postsecondary Education and Disability* 28, no. 2 (2015): 163–79. https://eric.ed.gov/?id=EJ1074663; Spencer Scruggs et al., "Impact of High School Transition and Accommodation Experience on Student Involvement in College," *Journal of Postsecondary Education and Disability* 34, no. 2 (2021): 179–90. https://files.eric.ed.gov/fulltext/EJ1319194.pdf; Michael Lyman et al., "What Keeps Students with Disabilities from Using Accommodations in Postsecondary Education? A Qualitative Review," *Journal of Postsecondary Education and Disability* 29, no. 2 (123–40). https://eric.ed.gov/?id=EJ1112978

7. See step 7 for further discussion.

8. This is known as "priority registration" and is discussed in step 7.

9. For specific, up-to-date information in any of these categories, please refer to the U.S. Code of Federal Regulations (C.F.R.), Title 34, Subpart B, Chapter 1, Part 104, Subpart E, Sections 104.41 through 104.47. https://www.ada.gov/pubs/adastatute08.htm

10. See appendix A to see the low rates at which students in a large longitudinal study received what colleges might view as modifications.

11. Colleges may require that students sign agreements outlining what they may and may not do with those recordings. For instance, students may have to agree not to post the recordings online.

12. See step 7 for a discussion of commonly granted test accommodations.

13. This may be done through students' regional office of vocational rehabilitation, if students are found eligible for those services.

14. See steps 5 and 7 for more on this.

15. See appendix C for resources from the U.S. Department of Education to learn more about this.

16. See step 7 for more discussion.

17. As is true with courses, though, students would have to be qualified for the jobs they're seeking, with reasonable accommodations or without them.

18. In some fields, students may not have access to the accommodations they had in the academic environment.

19. They may do this in their acceptance packets and/or orientation sessions, student resource tabling events, etc.

20. See step 7 for a discussion of documentation.

21. You may have heard of the concept of Universal Design for Learning. This is a framework that suggests ways of designing instruction that is accessible to all learners. Colleges may support professors in using this, but they aren't required to do so.

22. If you hear about a college that has a great special education department, this refers to a department that trains students to teach in that field; it isn't a department that serves students with disabilities or provides special classes for them.

23. Any student requesting accommodations will have to be found eligible for them. See step 7 to learn about this.

24. While students may ask for a course "waiver," this specific term would mean that students wouldn't have to take any course to make up for the required one they hope not to have to take. Colleges typically don't approve waivers, and will instead provide a substitution, if students are approved for this.

25. Neither law provides any guidelines for this.

Knowing a Student's Responsibilities and Rights

What You'll Learn in This Step

- The typical tasks of a college student
- The process for accessing disability accommodations
- The part students play in the accommodations system
- The student's right to not request or use accommodations
- Protections for students if they register for accommodations

When a student thinks about college, what they may envision is being in control of their own destiny—taking steps into adulthood. One thing that may especially excite them is the freedom they'll enjoy there, especially if they plan to live on campus.

Of course, with freedom comes responsibility, an idea that understandably may not be front of mind as they get excited about their college transition. In the context of the college environment, this means the student has to take responsibility for themselves and for doing a number of things they might not have had to do before, such as registering for housing. And if they want to receive accommodations, they have to register with the disability services office. This will be a new experience, and it will lead to additional ones related to the accommodations process.

The laws in place at college don't explicitly spell out what college students have to do or what their rights are.[1] Instead, their responsibilities and rights are shaped by the absence of certain mandates and the interplay of other laws (such as FERPA).

27

The Student Takes Charge

In K–12, a student's case manager drives the accommodations process. It is the case manager who calls annual meetings, collects information from faculty members, and reports on the student's progress.

At college, the student drives the system. They initiate the registration process themselves and—if they are found eligible for accommodations (most students will be)—they typically have some tasks to complete as part of the professor-notification process.

For some students, this may be the first time they've had any involvement in the accommodations process or with arrangements for their accommodations. Preparing them ahead of time may reduce the risk that they'll be anxious about registering for accommodations at college. It will also give them the information and understanding they'll need to complete the process.

Everyday Responsibilities

College students with and without disabilities are expected to meet certain standards of comportment and to complete processes related to housing, scheduling, etc. All students, including those with disabilities, are expected to complete paperwork and other responsibilities on their own, which may differ from their previous experiences.

Follow the Rules

When it comes to students with disabilities, high schools have to follow special rules pertaining to discipline and have to find appropriate placements for students based on their needs. But college students with disabilities are expected to adhere to their school's honor, behavioral, and/or other kinds of codes, just like their neurotypical peers do. If a student commits a violation, the college might consider whether their disability contributed to that violation and might even seek feedback from DS on this matter, but it will likely handle these situations in the same way it would for students who don't have a disability.[2] In other words, if a student breaks the school's rules, having a disability is unlikely to automatically exempt them from any consequences (or mean they'll experience different consequences).

Complete the Typical Tasks of a College Student

Students (regardless of whether they have a disability or not) are expected to fulfill the tasks associated with their education, such as completing enrollment forms, registering for courses, meeting with their advisor, etc., and to do so according to an established timeline. Neither academic advisors nor DS offices are required to help students with these processes, though—if students ask—they might receive some assistance at the start so they can complete them independently next time.

At college, students are usually expected to purchase any materials they need for their classes (e.g., textbooks, art supplies, lab coats). Colleges don't typically purchase anything for students with disabilities that their peers are expected to buy. For instance, if students in a medical program have to purchase their own stethoscopes, DS may help a student who is Deaf/HOH locate a specialized one that meets their needs, but they won't purchase it for that student.

In addition, students are typically expected to attend class (though some professors might not have a requirement for this). Although those who suffer brief, intensive episodes related to their disability (e.g., students with mental health or physical/medical disabilities) may be allowed some flexibility in class attendance, there will usually be a limit to how many classes they can miss. A student who needs to be hospitalized for several weeks, for instance, may be told that this would exceed the allowable number of absences.

Maintain a Certain GPA

At many colleges, students must maintain a certain minimum GPA in order to stay enrolled. Schools do not have to hold students with a disability to a lower standard for this, and they don't have to keep adding accommodations until a student can meet that requirement.

Just like their neurotypical peers, a student with a disability who doesn't maintain the minimum GPA after their first term may be placed on *probation* (meaning the college is giving them one more term to get their GPA up). As part of this probation, they may be required to do certain things in the next term, such as meet weekly with their advisor, attend tutoring sessions, etc. If their GPA still isn't high enough after the next term, the student typically will be dismissed from their college. Again, having a disability doesn't mean that a student will be treated differently than their neurotypical peers.

Meet Deadlines

College life is full of deadlines—for registering for classes, housing, etc. Students who have disabilities are expected to complete the same tasks as their neurotypical peers and within the same time frame. While extended time for an in-class exam is a common accommodation, colleges don't typically extend it to processes such as filing a form for graduation—it is generally applied to academic tasks only.[3]

What Are Add/Drop Deadlines,
and Why Do Students Need to Know about Them?

Before they arrive at college, students should know what an *add deadline* and a *drop deadline* are and why they need to pay attention to them. Sometimes these dates are the same; sometimes they're not.[1] Each term, this cutoff sets a final date for when students can *add* a class to their schedule after the semester has begun or *drop* a class for any reason. Depending upon how colleges charge for *tuition* (the cost of taking classes), students may get a refund for a class they drop before the deadline, but not if they miss that deadline. Dropping a class may also affect the amount of financial aid a student receives; students should ask the *bursar* or student accounts office about this.

If a student decides *after* the drop deadline or schedule adjustment period that they don't want to take a certain class anymore (e.g., because it's too hard, because they're taking too many classes, or for any other reason), they can do so, but this may count as what is called a *withdrawal*. Withdrawal policies vary; the class may appear on their transcript with a W next to it (to show they withdrew), or it might have a WP (Withdrew Passing) or WF (Withdrew Failing). Whether the class is calculated into their GPA will also vary from college to college.

At a lot of colleges, there is a deadline for withdrawals as well. Students who ask to withdraw after that time may have to get permission from the college. And colleges may not allow what would be referred to as a *retroactive* withdrawal (typically because they didn't earn a good grade), meaning that after a student has completed a class, they can have it removed from their transcript.

The rules regarding all these deadlines generally apply both to neurotypical students and to students with disabilities. Although colleges may choose to show some flexibility for students with disabilities who miss them, they don't have to.

The reason to be aware of these policies is because in high school, some students with disabilities are not "allowed" to fail courses. For instance, they may be allowed to retake a test in the hopes of receiving a better grade, something not typically approved at the college level. As a result, they may not recognize the need to drop a class before a very low grade compromises their GPA.

Note

1. The period between the start of the term and the latest of these deadlines may be called the *schedule adjustment period*.

Specialized Responsibilities for Students with Disabilities
In addition to the list of obligations they share with all college students, students with disabilities have some specialized responsibilities that relate to their need for accommodations and services. Unlike in K–12, if they want accommodations, they have to register for them, and they may have additional responsibilities once those accommodations are approved. For some students, this will require them to step up in ways that haven't had to in the past.

Register with DS If They Want Accommodations
  If a student needs accommodations, it is their responsibility to register and request them. As noted in step 1, colleges are not required to locate students who have a disability and guide them through the process. Students who want to use accommodations must find and complete the school's process for requesting them. This is true even if they disclosed their disability when they applied to college.[4]
  An anecdote in one study shows why students need to be told this directly. A college freshman who applied for accommodations *after* he was placed on academic probation said that because he mentioned his disability in his application for admission, he "thought that would be it."[5] He said that no one informed him that he needed to formally register.[6] Other studies have shown that students who get transition planning services are more likely to register with DS.[7] It is important to tell students explicitly that in order to receive accommodations, they must register with DS.
  At most schools, the process isn't time-consuming. Typically, students have to complete a brief form, upload documentation of their disability, and (at some schools) attend a short meeting where they may be asked some questions about their needs.[8] It's a relatively simple process—much simpler than the process for applying for financial aid, for example.
  Given that some students with disabilities struggle with organization and other executive functions, you might wonder what happens to a student who fails to complete the entire registration process. For instance, what happens if they turn in their documentation but not their registration form or if they turn in all of the paperwork but don't attend the mandatory meeting? In most cases, unless they complete all of the steps, they will not considered registered, and DS will not review their requests. Moreover, DS offices aren't required to follow up with students who don't complete their registration process, though some may do so voluntarily (but not necessarily more than once). It's the student's responsibility to initiate and make sure they complete their DS registration.

Although colleges aren't required to identify students with disabilities and suggest that they register with DS, they may inform incoming freshmen and transfer students about the existence of accommodations and explain how students can access them. Colleges may do this by putting information about DS in the student handbook, sending information describing services with the student's acceptance letter, posting disability-related information on their website, or holding information sessions during new student orientation or setting up a table at a student services fair. However, it remains the student's responsibility to contact the DS office to begin the process of applying for services if they want accommodations.

Once students complete their registration and are approved for accommodations, they won't have to go through the process again as long as they stay at their current school. If they transfer from College A to College B, they will have to go through College B's registration process, even if it is similar to College A's. College A's disability services office isn't required to send copies of the student's documentation to College B (they're unlikely to know the student is transferring), but the student can ask if they'll do that. The student can also ask College A's DS office to provide a letter confirming what accommodations they had there. But B does not have to grant the same accommodations that A did.

Notify Professors about Accommodations

Many of the DS directors interviewed for this book said their office uses an online system for managing accommodations (a popular one is called Accessible Information Management, or AIM). Once accommodations are approved, DS will prompt students to log in. From there, students may be asked to indicate:

- which professors they want notified of their accommodation
- which accommodations they want each professor to know about

It is their decision whether to share everything with everyone or be selective about what they share, and with whom they share it. At some colleges, the student will then be in charge of sending the electronic notification to professors. At others, this information may go into a queue, and the DS director or other staff member may send the notifications out in batches.

Some schools use a system that generates a letter listing all of the accommodations for which a student has been approved. Students may be responsible for emailing these to professors or for printing them and delivering them to professors by hand. They may even be required to have professors sign the letters, and students may then have to deliver the signed copies back to DS to confirm that professors have seen them. (This is for students' own protection—in case professors later say they weren't aware they were approved for accommodations.)

Many of the directors interviewed for this book indicated that—no matter how the accommodation notification is communicated to professors—they advise students to contact their professors in a more direct way at the start of the term in order to make sure everyone understands how things will work. (The directors said they don't typically check up on this, but they strongly recommended doing it.)

Complete Processes Related to Accommodation Requests and Do So in a Timely Way

Students are often expected to play a role in the administration of their accommodations. And when they do, they have to complete tasks in enough time to allow DS to do what it needs to do. DS is not responsible for reminding them about those tasks if they don't complete them and isn't obligated to take over for students or rush things in order to compensate for students who failed to meet the required deadlines.

For instance, a student who needs accommodations for exams may have to submit a form to DS ahead of the test date (e.g., two weeks in advance). This is done to provide DS with sufficient time to go through all the necessary steps involved in arranging their accommodations in time for the exam, such as finding a room for the testing, hiring a proctor, and getting the exam from the professor in time to have it delivered to the testing site. If the student doesn't submit the form by the DS deadline, they may not receive their accommodations for that particular exam.[9]

At some colleges, DS may be not even be involved in exam accommodation arrangements, leaving it up to students and professors to work out details, such as exam location and timing. If this is their college's procedure, a student may be able to get some assistance from DS, especially in their first semester, but DS will not generally take over the process for them. It is considered reasonable for a college student to take the lead in arranging their own accommodations.

As already noted, although college offices and departments can choose to make exceptions for students with disabilities who fail to meet deadlines for college processes, they are under no obligation to do so. And there are certain cases where a missed deadline creates a situation that they are unable to fix.

For instance, when it comes to deadlines, such as those for requesting housing accommodations or reserving space in the university testing center, colleges may *choose* to consider requests from students who don't meet the deadline. But they aren't required to, for example, remove another student who did meet the deadline from their dorm room or testing space in order to accommodate a student who didn't.

When it comes to submitting forms for upcoming exams, even those DS offices that want to be flexible may be unable to coordinate accommodations in time if students miss the deadline. For instance, if DS is already providing accommodations for several students in a large class, such as Introduction to Humanities, taught by the same professor, they may have the materials and instructions they need to be able to include a student who has missed the deadline. But if the student is taking a different class and DS isn't already set up to accommodate someone for that specific exam, if the student shows up the day before, it's unlikely that DS will have enough time to get the exam from the professor and find a room and proctor. In short, they are not required to move heaven and earth just to get the arrangements in place for a student who missed a deadline.

If a student is approved for e-books that DS has to order for them, they are responsible for informing DS of what they need in a timely manner so the office (or person) can order them in time. The same is true when DS offices convert physical texts to e-text; the student will have to get the books to DS according to certain timelines, so the converted texts will be ready when they need them. If a student were to file a complaint because they received their materials late and felt that it affected their ability to complete their work, an investigation would likely close without finding DS at fault if it discovered that the student took a long time to submit what they needed to DS.

Notify DS of Any Accommodation-Related Needs or Problems

DS offices may or may not check in with a student to ask how their accommodations are working; as noted in step 1, they're not required to do so. They also don't typically check in with others involved with a student's accommodations (such as professors or notetakers) to see if there are any problems. It is the student's responsibility to report any issues and to do so quickly so that DS can respond effectively.[10]

For instance, if a student gets copies of notes from a peer for a math class, and the notetaker drops that class, the student who receives the notetaking accommodation shouldn't expect the notetaker or the professor to contact DS. Because it's the student's accommodation, they'll need to let DS know. And if they wait until the end of the term to tell DS about a problem and file a complaint, any subsequent investigation is unlikely to require the college to provide the student with relief once the delay in the student's notification of DS is revealed.

Students are also responsible for letting DS know if they want a change to their accommodations for any reason and to do so in enough time to allow DS to consider their request. Sometimes DS will not grant a student's requested accommodation but might instead provide a different accommodation that the office deems appropriate. A student who fails to request a new/different accommodation until close to the end of the term (if at all) is unlikely to receive any relief if they later file a complaint that blames their disappointing academic performance on the absence of a needed accommodation.

Also—while this is unlikely to happen—one director interviewed for the book mentioned that on occasion, a professor will attempt to persuade a student to try doing without their accommodations. A student is under no obligation to do this, even if a professor suggests it. If this situation should arise, the student should notify their coordinator as soon as possible so that the coordinator can speak to the professor. They shouldn't assume the professor will tell DS that they've convinced the student to forego their accommodations.

A professor also might object to one or more of a student's DS-approved accommodations. At the time that students initially register and receive notification that they have been approved for their requested accommodations, their coordinator may tell them what they should do if they run into this situation. If they don't, students should ask.

The stated process may be for professors to contact DS when they are notified about a student's accommodations so that they can discuss anything they consider problematic, but students should not assume that professors will do that. And they should know DS doesn't typically check in with professors to see if things are going well with a student's accommodations. Instead, students need to contact their coordinator regarding the professor's objection as soon as the professor refuses the accommodation.

Once the student does this, the DS coordinator should take over. Students should not have to argue for or negotiate around their DS-approved accommodations with a professor.

If they encounter a situation like this, students should be aware that timelines apply to such notifications. If they wait until the semester is over to let DS know that a professor refused them an accommodation throughout the semester, they may not get the resolution they want.

Take Responsibility for Their Decision Not to Register or to Delay Registration

Even though this may not seem like an *action* students take, they assume responsibility for whatever happens if they don't register with DS initially, or at all. A student can choose to delay registration right up until just before their last exams in their last term before they graduate; nothing in the law says that they can't. But once they register, the college has no obligation to provide them with any relief for any bad outcomes they experienced *before* that point by doing something like allowing them to take a makeup exam, asking a professor to *expunge* (remove) a bad grade from their record, etc.

It's important to make sure students are aware of this, and that they know just how simple the DS registration process is. In one study, students who eventually registered for accommodations after one or two terms said they didn't do so earlier because they thought the process would be time-consuming. These students had lower GPAs and earned fewer credits than those who registered upon starting at college.[11]

Again, while these kinds of responsibilities may not be what students have in mind when they dream of college, they're part of the picture. But the news isn't all bad. While they will have to handle some responsibilities at college, students will also have rights that may correspond more closely with their image of independence.

Students' Rights

Learning what the college environment doesn't do for students with disabilities and what it requires from them may make it seem as though there's not much offered *to* students. However, students do have rights at college, although this may not always be immediately apparent. As already discussed, students don't have to register with DS. But should they choose to do so, they are granted some procedural rights within the accommodation process, as well as the right to privacy about their disability.

Procedural Rights
Students should dedicate some time to familiarizing themselves with the accommodations process, which will be fairly similar across colleges. The more they know about how the process works, the better position they'll be in to recognize their procedural rights.

Students retain certain rights when it comes to requesting accommodations, filing a complaint if those accommodations are denied or administered improperly, and even opting out of talking to the DS office or using accommodations entirely.

Requesting Accommodations
Students who request accommodations are understood to have the right to an individual review of their requests and, if they're found eligible, to

receive those accommodations for free. In order to ensure that the accommodations are effective, they should be provided in a timely fashion.

Though this isn't specifically mentioned in the laws, the general understanding is that colleges will review requests for accommodation on an individual basis, meaning based on each student's disability, its severity, the course in which the accommodation is being requested, etc. DS offices don't typically have a standard list of accommodations they grant to students with a particular kind of disability, such ADHD. That's because not all students with ADHD experience the same symptoms, and even when some do, those symptoms are likely to vary in their intensity.

A request for a significant accommodation (e.g., substitution for a required course), too, has to be reviewed even if the school has already undergone a deliberative process and determined it to be a fundamental alteration. Of course, this review doesn't have to find the accommodation appropriate.

Also, a professor's objection to an accommodation that DS approved shouldn't be allowed to stand without undergoing some kind of review process. Until such a determination has been reached, colleges may require professors to temporarily grant the student the accommodation in question. Each college can make its own policy, as this isn't specifically covered in the laws.

That right to an individual review also means colleges can't deny a student access to certain programs *simply* because they have a disability. If a college thinks a student isn't qualified for entrance to a particular program, it has to make an individual determination about this. Discussion should include consideration of the standards and any technical requirements for the program and whether the student can participate through the use of reasonable accommodations (e.g., a spellchecking device) or without accommodations at all.

Providing the equal opportunity discussed in step 1 would not typically include allowing students into programs unless they've taken the prerequisites or passed those prerequisites with a certain minimum grade. The same restrictions apply to neurotypical students and to students with disabilities.

It is crucial for students to know that a college can't charge a fee for them to register with DS. If they are found eligible, their college also can't charge for any basic accommodations they receive, such as taking tests with extended time, or getting notes from a peer. However, as discussed in step 1, colleges may charge for things they *aren't* required to provide. Students who hope to receive services not required by law (e.g., specialized tutoring) and who don't want to pay extra for them will likely need to focus their college search on colleges that provide these for free.[12]

Of course, whether they're free or not, accommodations may not be helpful if they aren't granted and implemented in a timely fashion. Laws covering accommodations for students with disabilities in the postsecondary setting don't specify how many days any part of a DS process should take. However, Section 504 does say that accommodations should be "as effective" as services provided to others (§ 104.4(b)(iv)), and it is generally understood that in order to be effective, accommodations must be provided quickly enough to allow students to make use of them for most of the term.

Although it is reasonable to allow a few days for a notetaker to be assigned or to receive copies of text in an alternative format, if the delay is too long, a school will be in danger of denying a student their legal access to college classes. But the law doesn't provide any guidelines to help students know how long it's reasonable for them to wait.[13]

Appealing the Decision If an Accommodation Is Denied

Although it won't happen often, a student may be found ineligible for the accommodations they requested.[14] That student has a right to appeal the decision and, if they wish, to file a complaint.

Every college should have a process for students to appeal such decisions, although the laws don't provide rules for how this process must operate. Processes vary—sometimes the first step in an appeal is informal (e.g., another meeting with someone in DS), and sometimes students may be asked to complete a form or write a statement that may get reviewed by the DS director or staff or administrators outside the office.

Although nothing in the prevailing laws mentions a complaint process, colleges are required to have one for their DS office. Hopefully, a student won't have any problems with their accommodations, have their privacy violated, or be treated in a discriminatory manner. However, if they do experience any of these problems, they should let their coordinator know right away so it can be addressed.

What happens next will vary from college to college. Sometimes the coordinator will reach out (if it's a professor issue), or they may direct the student to file a DS-specific complaint form or write an email explaining what happened. If the coordinator is unsuccessful in resolving the problem in an informal way, they may then direct the student to file a formal complaint.

Occasionally, a student's problem will involve the DS office itself. If that's the case, they don't have to talk to their coordinator first; they can simply follow the process for filing a formal complaint. The steps for filing a grievance can usually be found on the university's website, perhaps as a link from the DS page. There is no fee to go through a university's grievance process.

If the student prefers, they can file a complaint with the OCR. They do not have to go through their college's process first.[15] There is no cost for going through OCR, but it is likely to take longer than the school's grievance procedure, as each office reviews complaints from regions that cover a few states.

As another alternative course of action, students can file a lawsuit. (This doesn't happen very often at the college level.) Of all the options, this is the most time-consuming. Moreover, filing a lawsuit will typically incur a cost for the student's legal representation.

No matter which of these processes a student pursues, they should pay attention to any timelines or statutes of limitations on complaints. If they wait too long, a complaint might be dismissed on that basis.

It is important for students to know that if they file a complaint, any investigation will look not only at what the college did (or didn't do) and the timeline for any actions it took, but also at the student's action or inaction. A student who's failed to follow the proper procedures around receiving accommodations may not get the resolution they want. For instance, if a college requires students to give five days' notice if they want to use their accommodations for an exam, and the investigation reveals that a student did not request an accommodation until the day of the exam, it is unlikely to end with the resolution the student seeks.

Students should know, too, that when OCR reviews a student's complaint that they didn't receive a specific accommodation, investigations tend to focus on the *process* a college uses to make its decisions, rather than on the decisions it makes. Even if OCR finds a college's methodology faulty, they won't *necessarily* require the college to provide the contested accommodation.

All of this said—students should exercise their rights if they have a complaint. It's always possible they'll get the outcome they desire.

Opting Out of Accommodations

Even though doing so can be helpful, students who don't want to use accommodations are under no obligation to register with DS. That is their right.

They can also choose to delay their DS registration. But if they register at any point after classes have begun, they don't have the right to *retroactive accommodations* (i.e., a "do-over" of any exams or assignments they completed before they requested accommodations), even if they are convinced that those accommodations would've led to better grades or other desired outcomes.

Also, even if they've used accommodations at any point in a term, no one can *force* a student to use their accommodations for the remainder of that term, or in subsequent terms. For instance, if a student decides they don't need test accommodations anymore, it's their choice not to fill out the form they'd otherwise use to let DS know they have an upcoming test. Although DS might still send reminders about those forms, if a student doesn't complete them, DS won't contact professors about arranging the accommodated testing, find the student on campus, and walk them to an accommodated test setting.

And if the DS process requires them to reach out or respond to an email each term to confirm they want to continue to receive accommodations, students don't have to respond. It's up to them. They just have to be aware that if they later change their minds and want to use accommodations again, DS doesn't have to provide them with relief for any bad grades they received between their last contact with the office and their request to renew their accommodations.

Students can assert their rights by not registering with DS, but if they do, the laws provide them with a number of rights related to their accommodations. In addition to these procedural rights, college students have certain privacy rights, too.

Privacy Rights
A part of the college experience that may excite students is the chance it gives them to establish their identity with a new group of peers and teachers who don't know anything about them or their history. For some students, this may mean not letting anyone know that they have a disability. For others, it may be more nuanced; they may not mind if people know.

If a student wants to receive accommodations, at least a few people will have to be made aware of their disability. Even so, a student might prefer to limit what they disclose to others. For them, the laws in place provide privacy regarding their disability information.

The Family Educational Rights and Privacy Act, or FERPA,[16] provides students with privacy rights around their educational records, which includes their records at the DS office. And while Section 504 and the ADAAA don't explicitly state what a student's rights are concerning their disability-related information, in some ways, they help to shape those rights by not allowing colleges to ask certain questions about their disability or require students to register for accommodations.

It's important that students know what protections they'll receive at college as a person with a disability. They have a right to choose whether to identify themselves as a person with a disability and to protect the privacy of their disability information.

Choose Whether to Identify Themselves as a Person with a Disability

A student's right to privacy about their disability starts with the application process. Colleges can't ask students applying for admission whether they have a disability.

Once they enroll at college, students don't have to tell anyone about their disability, unless they want to request accommodations, in which case they'll have to go through the DS registration process. Students should know that even if they disclosed their disability when they applied to college, they are still under no obligation to register with DS once they enroll, as long as they don't want to have accommodations.

If this seems a little strange, think of it this way: a college couldn't require all students whose parents recently divorced to register with the counseling office. Students have a right not to disclose private details of their lives to anyone or to utilize the services available to them.

Protect Their Disability-Related Information

Some students may be reluctant to disclose their disability by registering with DS because they fear stigma or because they want to get a fresh start without having their disability established as part of their college identity. They should know that colleges treat information about a student's disability with great care. As already noted, even accommodation notifications typically don't state what a student's disability is.[17] Nor do DS offices send out a list of all the students who have registered with DS to all faculty and staff members at the start of the semester.

Again, the only people who need to know about a student's accommodations are those who will be directly involved in them. However, it is important to note that some DS offices employ student workers to perform a variety of tasks in the office (as may the counseling center and other offices on campus). Although it's likely that these student workers are expected to maintain the privacy of students using the DS office and other supports on campus, if the idea of peers knowing about that makes students uncomfortable, students with disabilities may wish to focus their college search on colleges where DS doesn't do this.

At some schools, when a student receives notes from a fellow student as an accommodation, those notes may be shared in a way that keeps the identity of the disabled student private. For instance, notetakers may upload their notes to an online folder but have no idea who they are for. However, this may not be the case everywhere; colleges aren't required to arrange this accommodation in that way. A student may decide they don't want to apply to colleges where they aren't comfortable with how the notetaking is handled.

Of course, students' professors will need to know about their accommodations. But they don't have a right to know all about a student's disability *simply* because they're involved in providing accommodations. That said, FERPA allows educational records to be released (without the student's permission) to school officials who demonstrate a "legitimate educational interest," and colleges can determine that professors generally meet this requirement.[18] That said, it is unlikely any professors will attempt to learn about a student's disability by accessing their records at DS. Students who have concerns about this should (as they conduct their college search) ask DS offices how they would handle a situation like this.

Professors themselves are expected to respect a student's privacy with regard to their use of accommodations. They should not single students out in front of their classmates or comment on their need for accommodation. For example, at some schools, professors are involved in the process of identifying notetakers for students in their class who have been approved for one. (They may do this by asking for volunteers to contact DS.) Professors should not disclose the name of the student who needs the notetaker or in any way reveal their identity. Any student who feels a professor has violated their privacy rights or is treating them in a discriminatory manner should report the incident to their coordinator as soon as possible.

Some students who decide not to register with DS may do so because they're concerned about how this information might be shared after they graduate from college. In fact, colleges don't put any kind of notation on transcripts or include any additional information to show that students used accommodations. As is the case with special education departments when students transition from high school to college, college DS offices aren't involved in sending any records to a student's graduate school. However, a student may request a letter from the office to document that they used accommodations (to help them support their requests), and DS will write one, but they will do so only when the student asks them.[19]

It is important as part of the transition planning process for students to be made aware of their rights at college. If they don't know what to expect, they might not request accommodations that can be useful to them.

Empower Students by Educating Them

A lot of the impediments that prevent students from disclosing their disabilities may be easily overcome. Many of them are based on fear, misunderstanding, a lack of information, or a combination of these factors. Speaking to students explicitly about how things work at the college level can address most of these issues. The most important thing transition planning can do is explicitly tell students and their families that accommodations are available at nearly every college in the country, as research shows that ignorance about this is one of the reasons some students don't register.

A lot of students decide not to register because of things they don't understand. It's important to know what information they lack so you can address it.

Creating a Transition Packet: How High Schools Can Prepare Students to Register with DS

Consider creating a one-page handout explaining how students can locate information about the process online, being sure to have it translated into the languages of the community so it will be accessible to parents who don't speak English as a first language, allowing them to help their student. Provide an example of what the process may look like, using directions and screenshots from the process at a local college. In addition to reviewing the handout, actually demonstrate in person how to do this, so that students have a chance to ask questions. Just showing a student who hasn't made a decision yet about where they're going (or who isn't planning immediate transition to college after high school) how to do this can be helpful.

It may be beneficial to provide each student with a "transition packet" that contains that handout plus two items they'll need to register with DS: 1) some notes on the accommodations they want to request and why they need them; and 2) if the school has tested the student, a copy of the most-recent evaluation. Even though a number of colleges won't require the IEP, 504 plan, or SOP, provide students with a copy (letting them know that it might not work as stand-alone documentation). It could be helpful as additional documentation, just to confirm what accommodations they've received in the past.[1]

Have a meeting to review the packet with the student and be clear on why you're providing it. Hand them a copy of the physical packet at the meeting, but also email them copies of the two items and suggest they keep that email. It will make it easier for them to download a copy of their documentation that they can then upload to the college's DS registration system. Encourage them not to hand or email anyone the list of accommodations but to use the list as a resource when they complete the registration form.

Such activities will help to make it clear to students that you're preparing them to register for accommodations. Even if they decide to work instead of attend college, they can use this knowledge and documentation to request workplace accommodations.

Note

1. See step 7 for a discussion of the documentation they might need.

Research shows that some students don't register for accommodations because they don't know enough about themselves to do so.[20] As step 3 will discuss, preparing students for the transition to college must include activities to enhance self-knowledge and awareness of their disability that will help them to make the most appropriate decision regarding requesting accommodations at college.

Research also shows that some students think that they don't need accommodations.[21] This may be true for some of them. For other students, this may not be the case, but they may not realize that because some of the supports they receive are provided in ways that aren't obvious (e.g., students aren't aware that their classmates aren't getting a copy of the teacher's notes) or have been built into the way classes are run (e.g., when teachers provide a set of guided notes to everyone in the class). Make sure students are aware of the kinds of supports they're getting that won't be provided at college without being requested[22] and encourage them to register with DS as a sort of "insurance policy." Tell them that even if they register for accommodations and get approved, they still have a right not to use the accommodations they are approved for, making sure they understand the potential consequences of registering after a first disappointing grade (or not at all).

Be aware that some students' experience with certain accommodations in high school is negative, and that it may explain why they are reluctant to request them in college. For instance, if they are granted extended test time for taking the ACT or SAT, they may have to stay in the testing room until the end of the time period. They can't leave when they're done, and they can't have a book to read, their phone, etc.; some may find this experience very unpleasant, and it may be the only time they're truly aware of receiving that accommodation. This may dissuade them from asking for the same accommodation at college. Make sure they understand that in college, once they've completed their test, they're usually permitted to leave.

Sometimes, students take co-taught high school classes where a paraprofessional or co-teacher checks in with certain students to make sure they're paying attention, prompts them to start an assignment, etc. Some students don't enjoy this kind of support; it may make them feel embarrassed or annoyed. In order to make sure this isn't why they're reluctant to register for accommodations, inform them that this kind of thing doesn't happen in college classes.

The research shows that some students don't register because they're worried about a peer's potential jealousy, and some students feel it's "cheating" if they use accommodations.[23] When talking to students about accommodations they use at the high school level, frame them as a tool that "levels the playing field," not an unfair advantage over their classmates. Make sure they know that the same is true for accommodations at the college level. This may help them feel less reluctant to request them. And because students may overestimate how much attention their use of accommodations may get from their peers, let them know that their peers may not give any thought to the accommodations other students receive. In many cases, they probably don't even notice. This may help to encourage them to request accommodations at college, too.

Since the research indicates some students don't register for accommodations because they want to keep certain information about their disability private, educate them about what their right to privacy looks like in the context of the college disability services environment. Tell students that FERPA is designed to protect a student's educational records from being disclosed inappropriately or without that student's permission; this includes information about the student's disability. DS directors across different kinds of colleges (public, private, large, small) stated in their interviews that the only people on campus who know that a student is receiving accommodations are those who need to be involved with their delivery. Even then, the accommodation notifications don't specify *what* a student's disability is. Make sure students know this.

A great way to provide students with real-life examples to support all of these points is to connect them with a local college's DS office. See if students can visit and ask staff members to discuss how their system works, and have them talk about the other supports available on campus.

Another way to educate students (and their families) is to host a transition night with a DS representative from a local college who could review that school's services and procedures. Enhance the program by inviting current college students to speak about their experiences—either some suggested by the DS representative or high school alumni who are home on break or go to college nearby. Students may be more receptive to the information if it comes from people working or studying at the college level.

Summary

The college setting offers an exciting entry into adulthood. Students must take on some very adult responsibilities—everyday ones as well as those specific to students with disabilities. In addition, they hold certain rights, procedural ones as well as rights of privacy. Team members can help by informing students of these new rights and responsibilities and by easing some of the concerns that may rise from this transition. Both this information and the support from a student's team can aid in preparation for the next step, which involves developing nonacademic skills.

FAQs

Do colleges have to accommodate for or provide help with college paperwork and tasks?

DS offices make accommodations, but they don't have to provide personal services. Assistance with typical student tasks and DS-related tasks might be viewed as examples of these. It is generally considered reasonable to expect college students to complete tasks related to their own education. And while there's no data on this, it's unlikely that many college DS offices or other offices help students do things like complete their housing forms. Of course, any student—with or without a disability—can always ask campus offices for help with forms. Although it's generally not considered an accommodation for DS to help with forms not related to the office's own processes, they can choose to do so. If DS does help students with their processes, this may be only for a limited time and then DS may expect students to complete them independently (or at least without help from DS).

Can students ask professors for accommodations directly?

Students who don't want to be associated with DS may try to speak directly to professors about accommodations. The laws in place at college don't say whether this is "allowed" or not. The way such requests might be viewed will vary from school to school and even from professor to professor.

It's important to point out that if a student secures accommodations directly from a professor without going through DS, then DS will be unlikely to support them if they are turned down by other professors for those same accommodations. (Professors are not required to provide any accommodations DS has not approved.) If DS is not involved in these informal accommodations ("informal" because they were not approved by DS), the office may refuse to have any involvement in any other negotiations students have with professors about them. This also applies to situations where students who do go through DS but aren't approved for everything they requested ask professors for those accommodations that DS didn't grant.

At some colleges, DS and professors alike may view a student's efforts to secure accommodations outside of the DS process as inappropriate attempts to circumvent the system. Before making additional requests, students may want to learn their college's philosophy and gauge the receptiveness of their professors.

In some situations, a professor may ask a student what additional adjustments might be helpful. If this happens, the student is certainly welcome to respond; they should just remember that the next professor with whom they speak will be under no obligation to provide the same accommodations.

Can parents or someone else facilitate or complete a student's DS registration?

Parents may be worried that their student won't register for accommodations and wonder whether they can start the process for them (or finish it if students started but didn't get all the way through). If they've been working with an advocate or other kind of professional while their student was in high school, parents may also wonder if they can assign the task to that person. The answer will depend upon the philosophy of the college's DS office, but typically, the answer will be no.

Some offices won't speak to family members or anyone outside the school at all without the student's permission. DS directors interviewed for the book said that if they don't have a signed release from the student, all they can share is general information about the process that students have to follow to get accommodations and suggest that they contact their student with the information. Some might offer to contact the student and let them know that a parent asked them to reach out about the availability of accommodations and offer to answer any questions students might have. However, colleges are not obligated to do this, and some may not, believing it intrusive to contact students who haven't expressed any interest in their offerings.

Without a release from the student, DS may not be willing to talk to parents or outside professionals at all beyond this. And since DS usually offers students the option to sign a release during the intake process, they're unlikely to have a release from students who haven't contacted them about accommodations.

But even if a student has signed a release with DS but not otherwise started or completed the registration process, DS offices may not allow parents or someone else to do that for them. The exception is that they typically will allow someone to send in a copy of a student's documentation if they don't have it with them at college.

A release simply gives DS permission to talk to parents or someone else designated by the student, but it doesn't *require* DS to allow them to take over this process for the student by completing the forms or being in the intake meeting without the student present.[24] Many of the DS directors interviewed for this book said they won't communicate with parents or other outside advocates without the student's being present (if it's a conversation) or copied (if it's an electronic or print communication).

It can be frustrating for parents when their student refuses to register for accommodations. However, even if DS allowed them or someone else to complete the process without the student's participation, it seems unlikely that students would utilize accommodations they had no part in requesting.

For parents, their best bet is to work with their student and with their high school and any other professionals that consult with them to make sure that their student leaves for college ready to ask for accommodations and prepared for whatever the procedures require. They can suggest that their student register as an "insurance policy," meaning accommodations will be in place (if they're approved) but they don't have to use them if they don't need them.

Do DS offices communicate with parents?

In short, the answer is no. Parents who have already had a student attend college may know that FERPA's protection means that even when parents are paying the tuition bill, no information about a student's performance (e.g., grades, class attendance) or any other part of their college experience will be shared with them. This includes information regarding their interactions with disability services. Some colleges have a release that covers the whole university; some have different releases for different departments, including DS.

If students have signed a release, DS may answer certain questions for parents, but some directors interviewed for the book indicated they don't share certain information, such as grades.[25] And some said that even if they have access to the grades, they won't share them with parents. They instead encourage family members to contact the student directly in order to get this information.

Also, FERPA releases allow DS offices to respond to questions, but they don't require them to answer every question that parents may ask. And they don't create an obligation for DS to seek information they don't have (e.g., grades) or to report on a student's progress.

FERPA releases typically have an expiration date (e.g., they may be good for a year). That means, even if a student provides DS permission to communicate with their parents one year, they can decide not to do so in subsequent years. Some DS directors interviewed for this book also said that when they present students with a release in their initial intake meeting, they let them know that they can withdraw permission at any time without waiting for the release to expire.

Notes

1. See appendix C for an OCR resource for students that provides some guidance.

2. A student with a disability is entitled to accommodation during any investigation or hearing phase of conduct proceedings (e.g., having copies in writing, large print, sign language interpreters, etc.).

3. Of course, colleges can *choose* to show leniency for any student; they just don't *have* to do so because that student has a disability.

4. Students don't have to mention their disability when they apply to college, though they may choose to do so. See step 6 for more on this.

5. Kirsten L. Lightner et al., "Reasons University Students with a Learning Disability Wait to Seek Disability Services," *Journal of Postsecondary Education* 25, no. 2 (2012): 152. https://eric.ed.gov/?id=EJ994283

6. Lightner et al., "Reasons University Students Wait,"159–77.

7. Lynn A. Newman and Joseph W. Madaus, "An Analysis of Factors Related to Receipt of Accommodations and Services by Postsecondary Students with Disabilities," *Remedial and Special Education* 36, no. 4 (2015): 208–19. https://doi.org /10.1177/0741932515572912

8. See step 7 for a thorough discussion of the process.

9. This applies only to any exam for which a form was submitted late; if they submit it before the next deadline, they should be able to receive their accommodations.

10. "Transition of Students with Disabilities to Postsecondary Education: A Guide for High School Educators," U.S. Department of Education, accessed February 22, 2022. https://www2.ed.gov/about/offices/list/ocr/transitionguide.html?exp=1#note12

11. Lightner et al., "Reasons University Students Wait," 159–77.

12. See step 5 to learn how to research which schools offer certain non-mandatory services for no cost.

13. As already noted, a delay caused by the student (e.g., when a student turns in a test accommodation form late) does not create a need for DS to rush their process. It may also not be possible to rush some accommodations, such as when DS needs a vendor to produce a Braille version of a text.

14. See step 7 to learn more.

15. "Transition of Students with Disabilities to Postsecondary Education: A Guide for High School Educators."

16. Family Educational Rights and Privacy Act of 1974, 20 U.S.C. 1221 et seq. (2008).

17. If a student is worried about this, they can ask the DS office at the colleges on their list to tell them what does or doesn't go into their accommodation notifications to professors. They can decide to avoid applying to any school whose DS office shares disability information in the NOA (notification of accommodations), though it's unlikely they'll find any DS offices that do this.

18. "The Family Educational Rights and Privacy Act: Guidance for Eligible Students," U.S. Department of Education, accessed February 1, 2022. https://studentprivacy.ed.gov/sites/default/files/resource_document/file/FERPAforeligiblestudents.pdf

19. The student may be able to use this letter to request workplace accommodations.

20. Emma V. Cole and Stephanie W. Cawthon, "Self-Disclosure Decisions of University Students with Learning Disabilities," *Journal of Postsecondary Education and Disability* 28, no. 2 (2015): 163–79. https://eric.ed.gov/?id=EJ1074663; Spencer Scruggs et al., "Impact of High School Transition and Accommodation Experience on Student Involvement in College," *Journal of Postsecondary Education and Disability* 34, no. 2 (2021): 179–90. https://files.eric.ed.gov/fulltext/EJ1319194.pdf

21. Cole and Cawthon, "Self-Disclosure Decisions," 163–79; Scruggs et al., "Impact of High School Transition," 179–90; Maureen Squires et al., "Emerging Adults: Perspectives of College Students with Disabilities," *Journal of Postsecondary Education and Disability* 31, no. 2 (2018): 121–34. https://files.eric.ed.gov/fulltext/EJ1192068.pdf; Valerie Thompson-Ebanks and Michelle Jarman, "Undergraduate Students with Nonapparent Disabilities: Identity Factors that Contribute to Disclosure Decisions," *International Journal of Disability, Development, and Education* 65, no. 3 (2018): 286–303. https://doi.org/10.1080/1034912X.2017.1380174

22. See step 7 to learn what accommodations are and aren't commonly available.

23. Cole and Cawthon, "Self-Disclosure Decisions," 163–79; Scruggs et al., "Impact of High School Transition," 179–90; Michael Lyman et al., "What Keeps Students with Disabilities from Using Accommodations in Postsecondary Education? A Qualitative Review," *Journal of Postsecondary Education and Disability* 29, no. 2 (2016): 123–40. https://eric.ed.gov/?id=EJ1112978

24. Sometimes, parents have power of attorney or guardianship over their student. State laws vary in what this allows them to do.

25. In some cases, DS may not have access to grades, anyway, and they're not required to request it in order to answer a parent's questions.

STEP THREE

~

Developing the Student's Nonacademic Skills

What You'll Learn in This Step

- How self-determination skills help students at the college level
- What schools and families can do to support the development of a student's skills
- How professionals and families can help students self-advocate
- Additional skills that are important in the college environment
- How schools and families can promote a student's independence

Students Have to Self-Manage at College

Many students look forward to the independence they'll experience at college, especially the freedom to make their own schedules, choose what classes they'll take, and decide how to spend their time outside of class. Again, many may not be thinking about the demands this atmosphere of freedom will place on them.

At college, students will be truly independent. No one will wake them for class or make sure they eat regularly and well. They will be responsible for choosing a class schedule that works for them. They'll have to meet deadlines for important processes like registration and housing. That's why it's so important to make sure they've achieved an appropriate level of independence before they make the transition to college.

Additionally, at many schools, no one will be checking up on their academic progress. Some schools do have alert systems where professors can send a notification to advisors or other staff members if a student is doing poorly, but those staffers may not be required to do anything in response to such a notification.[1] Professors themselves may not be aware when students are struggling and suggest they come for help, either. So if students are lost, they'll need to show up during their professor's *office hours* (set times that professors are available to students outside of class) or make an appointment at the tutoring or other support centers.

This independence applies not only to their academic status but also to their mental well-being. If they are feeling depressed or anxious, they'll need to make an appointment at the counseling center. No one else is likely to do it for them.

For many students, this level of self-management will be a relatively new experience. This is especially true for those who are accustomed to receiving regular assistance from adults in managing various aspects of their lives.

DS Directors' Tips for Success

DS directors interviewed for this book were asked to share what makes students with disabilities successful at college. Their answers were quite similar, and many apply to all students, whether they have a disability or not. They included keeping up with academic responsibilities, demonstrating persistence and resilience, engaging with all elements of the college experience, taking a sense of ownership, and using available help.

Keeping Up with Academic Responsibilities

It may seem obvious, but part of the key to college success is going to class. While some professors may take attendance, or some class grades may include a participation grade, in other classes, professors may not count it against students if they don't attend regularly. Students who don't attend regularly risk missing important discussions of class content, changes to the syllabus, etc. They also miss having a chance to engage with class content on which they'll be tested.

Doing work on a weekly basis is also important, as it can quickly pile up. Once students get behind, they can struggle to prioritize what to do first and risk missing deadlines. Anxiety can affect working memory, so worries about the amount of work students have to do when they're behind can actually affect their ability to do that work. And if they've not done readings for several weeks, they may literally not have enough time to do them before an exam.

Demonstrating Persistence and Resilience

College is meant to be challenging. Students who are accustomed to receiving high grades in high school may find this harder to achieve at college. They'll need to take the initiative to figure out how they can do better. They may need to increase their time spent studying, seek help, try new approaches to their work, etc. Most students will have to work harder than they used to in order to meet academic expectations. If they give up in frustration, they're not likely to succeed.

Engaging with All Elements of the College Experience

A sense of connectedness can be important to a student's well-being. Research shows that the more engaged students are, the more likely they are to persist at college.[2] This means that students are more likely to be successful (and to stay enrolled) if they make connections.

Students can seek like-minded peers in a variety of clubs and activities. At many colleges, freshman orientation activities include a "club fair" or other opportunity to see what intramural sports teams or other kinds of clubs they can join. If they're worried about such activities cutting into their study time, they can use a time-management calculator or weekly scheduling tool to see how much time they actually have each week.[3] It's likely they'll find there's enough time for everything they want to do. In fact, they may find that having something to look forward to motivates them to get work done, and that having these activities on their calendar provides helpful structure to their week.

Students should think beyond their peer group, too. They can seek relationships with professors they like, members of the library staff they find helpful, and any other faculty and staff members who make them feel welcome.

Taking a Sense of Ownership for Themselves and Their Actions

Students are on their own when it comes to managing their daily lives and their academic responsibilities. If they need help with something, it's their job to seek it out. They have to make decisions about how they use their time. If they study too little or wait until the last minute to start a big paper or project, they may not get their desired result. Students who are successful see the link between their actions and their outcomes. They understand it's not anyone else's job to make sure they're successful and they don't blame others when things don't go well that were their own responsibility.

Using the Help Available to Them

Colleges expect students to find the academic demands challenging. This is why many colleges provide free tutoring, and some may offer access to peer mentors or coaches, academic coaches, etc.[4] But no one will make students go for help. They have to seek it out.

Colleges also understand that students may struggle with adjustment and mental health; this is why many of them offer counseling services. But they can't make students utilize them. Students have to take the initiative to set up an appointment.

And, of course, colleges offer accommodations to students who are found eligible. It's a student's choice to use them or not. DS directors said their students who use theirs tend to be successful.

Comments from directors echo what the research says are keys to success at college. The actions they describe are outcomes of executive functioning, self-advocacy, and self-determination, three constellations of skills that overlap with each other.

Three Skill Areas to Develop in College-Bound Students

When students move to the college level, they enter an environment where they are responsible for themselves and their success. It's up to them to stay on top of things and to speak up when they need something; no one will be looking after them. This is why the literature on students with disabilities at college emphasizes the importance of three overlapping sets of skills—executive functioning, self-determination, and self-advocacy. It's helpful to know what skills students need so that planning can include strategies to develop them.

Executive Functioning

Most of the DS directors interviewed mentioned *executive functioning* (EF) as being crucial to college success. In fact, some of the other success strategies they mentioned are examples of how students *use* executive functioning. EF describes a set of skills that play a role in all kinds of success (academic, professional, life).

To understand the idea of EF, it may help to visualize the role of a company president's executive assistant (EA). The EA is responsible for keeping the president's calendar and for prioritizing what should be done and when. An EA reminds the president of upcoming appointments and tells them when they should start preparing or leave the office to get to one on time. An EA also reminds the president of upcoming deadlines and keeps others from disturbing the president so that they can focus on the work they need to do. A president may call an EA in to take down a bunch of notes for them so they don't have to remember everything. Having good executive functioning means taking care of all of these responsibilities.

Unlike company presidents, most college students don't have the luxury of hiring an EA; they have to be one for themselves. No one provides them with that kind of supervision or direction. And not only do they have to perform the tasks just described, they also have to manage themselves internally, making sure that frustration or other emotions don't get in the way of their functioning.

Dr. Thomas Brown, an ADHD expert, identified a six-component model of EF.[5] These ideas are also echoed in the comments from directors. Brown's model includes:

- *Activation*—Rather than addressing when students start *doing* work, activation involves *getting ready* to do work. It's not enough for students to know what they need to do each week. They have to figure out when they're going to do it and how long it will take so they can plan when to do other assignments.

  This is why one of the subcomponents of activation is the *prioritization* that directors referenced in their comments. Successful students complete assignments in an order that makes sure that what's due first is completed first. Activation also requires another subcomponent, *organization*. When students are ready to work, they need to have the right materials on hand. (This may mean purchasing a text at the bookstore or downloading readings or problem sets from the course management system.)

  Organization can be seen to have a broader application, too, especially for students living on campus. While they keep on top of work, students have to make sure they take care of themselves (e.g., eat well and get enough sleep—both of which require planning), get their laundry done, read and respond to emails, etc.

- *Focus*—Obviously, students need to focus on what's being discussed in their classes and on their assignments. College requires long periods of concentration. Students also have to go from studying/thinking about one subject to focusing on another so they can keep on top of work for all of their classes and keep on top of life responsibilities like laundry, completing college forms, etc. This requires something called *cognitive flexibility* (the ability to shift from one topic to another).

- *Effort*—In some classes, students don't have assignments to submit to show they've done the readings; they may just have two exams. Without *deliverables* (assignments students turn in to show professors they've completed them), it can be quite easy for students (with and without disabilities) to let those assignments slide. This overall process of keeping up with work in college requires students to make a continuous, sustained *effort*.

According to Brown, another aspect of effort involves regulating alertness. When students try to study for too long at a stretch, they may lose focus. They need to be aware of when this happens to them and take a break (and then return to their work). It may be helpful to them to drink a caffeinated beverage or chew gum while working and/or to work in numerous short study periods with brief breaks between. They may have times of the day when they are more alert, and they can try to use those optimal times for their most challenging work.

Another subcomponent of effort is *processing speed*. Brown says students may go too quickly and make errors when working on assignments, or they may take a long time, which can lead to fatigue. Although students can't make themselves process information more quickly or slowly, what they may need to do is leave time to correct inattentive errors (if they are fast processers) or start work well ahead of time (if they process slowly).

- *Working memory*—On a daily basis, students have to remember what they have to do (academic assignments plus everyday tasks, meetings, etc.) and then also keep information in mind while reading, writing, and problem-solving. Students may find it helpful to use to-do lists or voice memos to offload information from their working memory so they have more capacity to focus on the task they're currently working on.

- *Action*—Interestingly, this refers not only to what students *have* to do but what they *should not* do. College students' obligations are fairly obvious—go to class, complete assignments, etc. But what may not be as clear is their need to *monitor* and *self-regulate*, two subcomponents of action. As an example, if a student has a test on Monday, they'll need to think about what could happen if they go out Saturday night and wake up late on Sunday. Not only do they need to decide to stay in but they also need to assess the challenges in their environment and take action. For instance, they may need to avoid distractions by turning off their phone or studying in the library so friends won't disturb them. (This requires *inhibitory control*, meaning that they appropriately handle an impulse to do something they know they shouldn't. In this case, the student's decision to stay in and away from distractions would be an example of how they showed such control.[6])

- *Emotion*—Taking care of all of these parts of self-management may be tiring for some students. Even if the responsibilities of college life aren't a strain, students have an interior life that will be full of ups and downs. And while students shouldn't be suppressing their feelings, they will likely have to put concerns aside at times in order to focus on their work.

  This was reflected in comments from some directors about how students view their struggles and respond to disappointing grades. Students need to avoid or move beyond their frustration and seek help.

It's clear why executive functions are so important in college. Students are in charge of themselves and their obligations, and that includes getting their own needs met. That's why self-advocacy is also a big theme in the literature.

Self-Advocacy

If college students don't take care of themselves, who will? As already noted, college DS coordinators don't have the same responsibility for looking after students as high school special education case managers do, and professors aren't responsible for checking in with students to see if they're struggling. What this means is that those students have to seek out the assistance and support they need. This is likely why the DS directors included many of the components of self-advocacy in their list of keys to success.

What does it entail? In order to make sure that K–12 schools help students develop the skills they need, transition expert David Test and colleagues created a framework of four components that make up self-advocacy. Given the demands that the college environment can put on students, it's easy to see why these skills are so important, especially for students with disabilities. They include:

- *knowledge of self*—In order to effectively request accommodations, students need to know enough about their disability and how it affects them to request accommodations that will be a good fit.
- *knowledge of rights*—As discussed in step 2, professors don't have the right to withhold DS-approved accommodations without a review of their objections. If a professor tells a student they can't have an accommodation that DS approved, that student needs to communicate with their coordinator to *address violations* (a subcomponent of knowing their rights).
- *communication*—Again, since students will be responsible for requesting their accommodations from DS and talking to professors about how

those will be implemented in their class, they need to be able to communicate effectively about their needs.[7]

The self-advocacy model also includes a component for leadership. Given
that students have to work with DS and professors (and roommates and other
members of college staff), it makes sense that these skills are essential to success in the college environment.

Students will use self-advocacy skills to get what they need at college. It's
all part of how they'll take responsibility for themselves. Another part of self-
management involves goal-directed planning, which—for students—means
planning how they'll earn their college degree. This is why self-determination is also a theme in the transition literature.

Self-Determination
The college experience is, in essence, a marathon of decision-making. The
decision to attend college in the first place is an example of what's called
self-determination (making decisions for oneself), specifically about what to
do after high school. And the rest of the process—from application through
graduation—is full of situations that require students to make decisions, large
and small, that determine how their path through college progresses.

Researchers Wehmeyer and Schwartz identified four characteristics of
self-determination:

- *autonomy*—acting according to one's own interests/preferences and doing so free of undue influence or interference
- *psychological empowerment*—feeling that one has the skills needed to do
  things to help shape their outcomes
- *self-regulation*—making decisions about what to do based on a situation's demands and the individual's own skills and formulating a plan,
  revising it if needed
- *self-realization*—using knowledge of one's strengths and weaknesses to
  determine one's own actions[8]

These components may seem abstract. It can help to demonstrate how
they help students operate in the college environment.

Students who have a strong sense of *autonomy* make their own decision
about what to do after high school, be it work, college, or another kind of
experience, and do so because it's what they *want* to do, not because they
feel pressured to make a particular choice. Choosing a major is another opportunity for autonomy. This doesn't mean that autonomous students don't

seek advice from others but rather that the decision they make is informed by their own preferences and any advice they choose to heed, not one that they arrive at because someone has exerted undue influence over them.

In order to make these decisions autonomously, students need a sense of *psychological empowerment*, the confidence that they can take care of themselves, make good decisions, and complete the tasks of a college student on their own. Again, this doesn't mean they can't consult others before making a decision. But a psychologically empowered student does that as part of their own process. They use it as another tool for achieving the goals they've set for themselves and are working toward.

Once they have chosen a college and enrolled, students will need to use their *self-realization* and *self-regulation* to make choices about how they use their time—to sleep, to study, to research possible internships, etc. For instance, a student with ADHD who has good skills in both of these areas will reduce distractions in their study environment so they can make good use of their study time and earn good grades. A student who is a slow processor will decide not to join friends for a weekend away because they have an assignment deadline coming up and know that they'll need the whole weekend to complete it in time. Self-realization can be a factor in their choice of major—a student may decide not to pursue a particular field of study because they feel some of the requirements may be more work or challenge than they want to take on.

In other words, everything about college—from the decision to go (or not) to the choices students make about how they use their time at college to make sure they graduate—requires self-determination. So many small daily decisions will help to shape their experience and their progress.

Two other closely related elements of self-determination are the student's *internal locus of control* (a sense that they have the power to control what happens to them) and what Wehmeyer and Schwartz call "positive attributions of efficacy and outcome expectancy" (meaning that when good things happen, the student can see that they are the result of their own effort).[9] Directors echoed these elements when they stressed the importance of the student's taking ownership of their outcomes.

The same elements also overlap with the concept of academic *self-efficacy*, which is a student's belief in their own abilities. Barry Zimmerman said that self-efficacy can both affect a student's effort and persistence and be affected by that effort.[10] A student's belief in their ability to do well will likely affect how long and hard they try something, and their performance on a task can, in turn, affect their confidence for the next time they attempt a task.

Many of the same themes occur in various models and frameworks for student success. For example, experts in the field of transition have created and validated a framework of college and career readiness skills. Some of the components include:

- *academic engagement*—learning through engaging with content in core subject areas (e.g., math, language arts) and perseverance, which combines several of the keys already discussed, such as work habits, self-regulation, and the ability to cope with failure
- *mindsets*—having a sense of belonging and ownership of learning, having a growth mindset, and showing perseverance
- *learning processes*—using strategies for test-taking, notetaking, group work, organization, and time management
- *critical thinking*—interpreting, making inferences, analyzing, and explaining (college students have to use these skills frequently)
- *social skills*—communicating, showing empathy and social awareness, taking responsibility
- *transition knowledge*—understanding the differences students will find at the college level[11]

Clearly, students need a number of skills so that they can be independent at college, where they are responsible for themselves. So what can be done to make sure students have them?

Assessing a Student's Skills

Before making any kind of plan for developing a student's skills, it's a good idea to figure out what (if any) areas need bolstering. The National Secondary Transition Technical Assistance Center offers a list of assessments, including interest inventories to help students identify their postsecondary goals, suggestions for task analysis to be used in direct observation, and measures of intelligence and academic skills.[12] In order to know what skills to assess, you'll need to know students' goals for themselves; this will help inform the list of skills they'll need, and what assessments you'll need to measure them.[13]

When and How Planning Should Be Done

Once the team knows where a student's skill levels stand, this information should inform the planning process.

The IEP for ninth grade is an ideal place to start the process of developing college readiness.[14] Although some states start earlier, IDEA requires that transition services begin no later than age 16. Ideally, transition planning will begin sooner so that there is sufficient time to develop the skills that students need before they graduate.

Every year, plans should include:

- measurable, appropriate goals based on a student's stated postsecondary goals
- updates to goals if they change
- consideration of services that could help students to reach their goals
- a course of study that will help students achieve those goals[15]

If assessments identify areas for improvement, the plan should include explicit instruction for developing these skills.[16] Students who aren't being educated in the general education setting need these skills for postsecondary success, too; the instruction they receive in those other settings shouldn't neglect these skills.[17]

Opportunities to Build a Student's Skills

As students transition to and progress through high school, there are other natural opportunities to build communication, decision-making, critical thinking, and other important skills. Such opportunities can include identifying postsecondary goals, selecting high school courses, conducting a college search, as well as some others.

Identifying Postsecondary Goals

Any high school plans should be based on a student's own goals. When IEPs are written for ninth, tenth, and even eleventh grade, students may not be clear about what they want to do. Case managers can use interest inventories to help those students identify what gets them excited and what kind of career options exist (and what kind of education they'll require). For students who don't yet have any particular leanings, the idea of postsecondary education in general can serve as a goal to drive planning. Or they may change their postsecondary goals as they progress through school, meaning their IEP's goals and objectives may need to be changed.

Selecting High School Courses

As a student enters high school, there may be questions about what level of classes they should take. Inclusion in general education is a predictor of postsecondary education participation.[18] The IEP meeting in eighth grade where ninth grade class placement is discussed provides a great starting point for students to exercise their self-determination skills.

If student input is considered in class placement decisions in high school, the case manager can provide information about the level of class that the student's teachers have recommended and seek the student's input about how they view those recommendations. If students want (and are allowed) to choose a higher level of placement than is recommended, case managers can talk to them about appropriate accommodations and also discuss those that might not be available after high school. This way, students can make a conscious choice to challenge themselves academically while using accommodations they may not have access to at college. Given that this can make the transition more challenging, students may decide to stick with the recommended course levels with accommodations they know are likely to be available at college.

Case managers can also educate students and their families about typical college admissions requirements so that students choose the range of classes they take with that in mind.[19] For instance, in order to be eligible for admission at some colleges, students may need four years of high school math. If their high school only requires three years and they find math challenging, they should be aware that not taking a fourth year could limit their college options. Case managers can show students how to locate college admissions requirements online, so students can learn how to do this for the colleges that interest them.

If anyone on the team (the student, parents, or high school staff member) suggests the student receive a waiver of their high school's course requirements because of their disability (e.g., for foreign language), the case manager can explain that this could affect eligibility for admission at some colleges. In order to maintain the widest range of options, the student may prefer to take those classes with accommodations. This is an opportunity for empowerment.

Participation in IEP and Meetings

One obvious opportunity for students to develop numerous college-readiness skills is to actively participate in these meetings. Students can be invited to discuss what accommodations they are using and how effective they are.

To encourage the student's participation, the case manager can find different ways for them to be involved, perhaps by first asking them to provide feedback (e.g., by responding to questions from the case manager about their goals or the effectiveness of their accommodations). The case manager can then try to encourage the student to take on increased responsibilities in subsequent meetings.

Although some students will be comfortable playing a larger role in their meetings, others won't be for reasons that can include social anxiety, communication difficulties, or cultural and familial norms around interacting with/speaking to authority figures.[20] Like everything relating to IEPs, student involvement in the IEP meeting should be individualized.[21] Case managers can try to find a balance and encourage their students to find a way to participate while also respecting their anxiety and being mindful of the power dynamic between high school students and their teachers.

Of course, there's more than one way for a student to work on college readiness. They don't have to be running their own meetings; there are different levels of participation that all offer their own opportunities. Case managers can meet with students prior to their IEP meetings to solicit feedback on the goals and accommodations in their plans. They can then check with students verbally at the end of each section of the meeting to make sure they feel their goals and views have been represented. This is a way of keeping students comfortable while also involving them in the process.

Should a student show great reluctance to run their own IEP meetings, it doesn't have to be a cause for concern. After all, the format for these meetings doesn't share much in common with what they'll experience at college. Intake meetings are typically one-on-one, where the student talks only with their coordinator. No faculty members will be present. It's extremely unlikely that students will ever be seated in a meeting with their coordinator and professors while they're at college, so don't feel it's imperative that the student have this experience while in high school.

At college, the power dynamic will be somewhat different when students meet with their coordinator. Because colleges treat students as adults, the coordinator-student relationship has a different tenor than the typical relationship between a high school case manager and a student. Therefore, rather than focusing on perfecting the student's ability to run an IEP meeting, it may be more helpful to role-play meetings with DS staff or professors—experiences that will be more analogous to those that they will encounter in the college setting. Case managers can contact a DS staff member at a local college to see whether they could visit or do a Zoom talk where they model how these conversations might look, with a high school case manager playing the role of a student in the demonstration.

No matter how much of a role students play in meetings, case managers should make sure they have the necessary self-knowledge to provide input about their needs. A student should know what their strengths are as a learner and what qualifies them for disability accommodations and services. Although conversations should always lead with the positive, the case manager shouldn't shy away from speaking to the student in a sensitive but direct way about their disability.[22] The student will need this information to request accommodations after high school, whether they go to work or attend a postsecondary institution.

The College Search Process

The college search provides numerous opportunities for students to work on self-determination. Do they want to attend college or do something else after high school? If they decide to go, what kind of school do they want to attend, and where, and what might they want to study? This process will also require organization (of application materials), communication (college essays), and ownership of the process overall.

Other Opportunities for Skill Development

Although identifying postsecondary goals, selecting high school courses, and conducting a college search can all provide opportunities during the high school years for a student to develop and practice important college-readiness skills, there are other chances to build these skills, too, including:

- asking for clarification of material taught in class
- telling a teacher about their disability
- making an appointment to speak to a teacher about something (rather than trying to have this conversation between classes, when it's likely to get interrupted)
- discussing their need for a particular accommodation
- seeking assistance at the library in getting sources for a paper
- contacting the DS office at some of their target colleges with questions about services
- asking high school teachers for recommendation letters

Students who are homeschooled may already have a lot of chances to work on self-determination as they choose what to study. If you homeschool your student, the two of you can think about other opportunities to work on communication, as well as time management and organization of materials.

Working on Communication

What's central in all of these activities is communication. Whatever your role is in a student's transition, you can take advantage of opportunities to help them develop and practice this important skill.

Serve as a coach by asking the student what they plan to say in an upcoming meeting or appointment, by helping them take notes about what they will say if they're afraid they'll forget or go off-course, and even by rehearsing these conversations with students, if they are interested. In situations where communication will be written (e.g., a note, letter, or email), offer recommendations for rephrasing (if needed), being sure to explain the reasoning behind any changes you suggest.

Help the student think about communication by using questions:

- *Who will they be communicating with?*
- *What and why will they be communicating?* If they need information from someone, what do they need? If they need to share something, how much detail is helpful?
- *How will they communicate?* Is this a situation where a conversation (whether in person or by phone/Zoom) would be more efficient than email? Is there a risk that tone could be misinterpreted?
- *When and where will they be communicating?* If students want to speak to teachers, when are the teachers available? (Trying to talk to a teacher while they set up for class or prepare to leave may not be ideal—either for the teacher, who may be trying to get somewhere else, or for the student, who may not get the privacy they'd like for the conversation.)

Granted, not every interaction needs to be run through this kind of questioning. But for students who struggle with communication, it can be a way to prompt some critical thinking about the outcome they're hoping for and how best to achieve it.

Other Forms of Readiness

For students who plan to live at college, readiness includes additional dimensions not typically covered in the literature. In their interviews for this book, college admissions consultants who specialize in working with students with disabilities shared how they assess readiness for students with whom they work.

Many of their comments echoed those by the DS directors—they spoke about organization, time management, and self-advocacy. They also addressed some additional points. If you are a parent, you may find the questions the consultants said they pose to clients helpful in thinking about where your student may need some additional development:

- Do they get up by themselves and get ready to leave for school on time?
- Do they manage their own medication (including ordering refills and taking it without prompting)?

- Can they settle conflicts with siblings without an adult to mediate? (They'll likely have a roommate at least once in college.)
- Are they successfully balancing schoolwork and other activities (clubs, sports) along with responsibilities at home (chores)?
- Do they start, complete, and submit homework without assistance?
- Do they approach teachers/coaches/other adults when they have a question or issue, or do they rely on parents to do that?
- Can they manage a bank account?

Eric Endlich, founder of Top College Consultants, said he thinks that too often, families don't think enough about all of the skills students need to get through college. He made a distinction between what he calls being *college capable* (meaning having the academic preparedness needed) and being *college ready* (meaning using all of the skills discussed in this step).[23]

Elizabeth Cooper, educational consultant at the College Consulting Collaborative, echoed Endlich's comment. She said, "College readiness is so much more than getting good grades or high standardized testing scores. College readiness is an integrated, mindful, and deliberate process that develops over time."[24] These questions can serve as a guide for families to assess their student's skills and figure out what they need to work on before the transition.

How Parents Can Help Students Prepare for Transition

Although developing skills such as executive functioning, self-advocacy, and self-determination are ultimately the student's responsibility, it's natural for parents to wonder in what sort of ways they can support this important process without impeding it. With this in mind, it can be helpful for parents to evaluate the amount and kind of assistance they are currently providing, to evaluate other forms of adult support that their student is receiving, and to aid in the development of their student's life skills.

Evaluate the Amount and Kind of Help Parents Are Providing

Parents want to help their student be successful, and they do numerous things to help them toward that goal. Their student's journey may have involved struggles and failure experiences before their disability was identified and they received supports they needed. (And sometimes they didn't receive them.) Or perhaps their student's disability was identified earlier, and even with supports, they have had difficulties in school. In all of these cases, parents have advocated for their student. This is so important.

So even when parents know their student needs to be independent to be successful post–high school (whatever they decide to do), it can be challenging to know where to scale back their involvement. They may worry that if they don't do things like, for example, rushing to the school with something their student forgot at home, the student will have a failure experience, which will damage their self-esteem and sap their motivation.

It's natural for parents to want to protect their student from experiencing the consequences of not doing something that's hard for them as a result of their disability. It's a sign of their love for them. But as already discussed, students will have to be completely independent in so many ways at college, and there aren't different performance standards for them. If they don't have a chance to discuss what is getting in their way before their transition to college (e.g., procrastination, failure to use a reminder system, etc.), then they'll miss the opportunity to work on strategies to help themselves with that particular task or function.

These experiences can be seen as opportunities for them to work on so many of the keys to success—self-efficacy, resilience, self-knowledge, self-motivation, and activation. It's hard to do this, but it's how students can learn valuable lessons. In *The Gift of Failure: How the Best Parents Learn to Let Go So Their Children Can Succeed*, author Jessica Lahey says, "Help [your student] problem-solve and find lessons in the failure . . . [the] goal should be to help [them] regain a sense of control over the experience of failing. The real learning happens when kids begin to understand how to pick through the wreckage, find the pieces that still work for them, and devise a strategy for future success."[25]

In short, instead of jumping into action, parents can best help their students by allowing them to experience the expected consequences, reviewing what happened, and making a plan for the next time.

Remember, too, that rescuing them can take away the chance to learn something that can improve their sense of their own competence. In their book *What Do You Say? How to Talk with Kids to Build Motivation, Stress Tolerance, and a Happy Home*, Dr. William Stixrud and Ned Johnson say, "When we rescue kids, we keep them from being inoculated. We take away their sense that they're in control and deprive them of the opportunity to learn that they can handle things when they get hard."[26] And as this chapter has already discussed, they need that sense of psychological empowerment to be successful not just at college but in life.

The truth is that no matter how hard you try as a parent, you can't save your student from everything. And there may be peril in trying to do so. Lahey says, "Protecting kids from the frustration, anxiety, and sadness they experience from failure in the short term keeps our children from becoming resilient and from experiencing the growth mindset they deserve."[27] She says that when parents "avoid or dismiss these opportunities, in order to preserve children's sense of ease and short-term happiness . . . [they] deprive them of experiences they need to have in order to become capable, competent adults."[28] In other words, understanding that life can't be worry-free, the best plan is for you to help your student by allowing logical consequences to occur, and then talking to them about how well they handled it, and showing them that such situations are not the end of the world. This can help build their sense of psychological empowerment, too.

A recent study on helicopter parenting (HP) provides some interesting insights. Although HP is a term that is understandably offensive to many parents, the study may shed some light on the kinds of support that can help and on those that may have a negative effect.

For this study, students in the general college population were given questionnaires and rating scales. The construct of HP it used included numerous parenting behaviors reported by students *who were already at college.*[29]

Researchers grouped related behaviors into different factors or categories:

- *information seeking*, including helping students make decisions, asking about their grades, and knowing their daily schedule
- *academic/personal management*, including calling to wake students, reminding them about tasks and classes, helping with projects, and rewriting papers
- *direct intervention*, including intervening with the student's roommates, friends, and romantic partners
- *autonomy limiting*, including preventing the student from making mistakes and failing to support their decisions[30]

The study found that certain information-seeking behaviors, when not combined with behaviors from other factors (e.g., autonomy limiting) were actually viewed by students in a positive way as a form of parental care. Of all the behaviors, these were the only ones that correlated with GPA.[31]

That said, the study found that overall HP was associated with both greater depression and anxiety in students, and with a "more dependent and avoidant—but less rational—decision-making style."[32] The researchers hypothesized that if students weren't allowed to make their own decisions over the years because of the HP behaviors of their parents, some either avoided making important decisions or avoided them as much as possible. As the researchers observed, "Perhaps surprising to the parents who engage in them, behaviors like helping complete school projects and reminding students about exams . . . were seemingly counterproductive given that they were associated with lower perceived college academic achievement and a weaker attachment to college."[33]

Again, this study looked at the effect of HP behaviors on students who were already at college, meaning that these parents continued to try to support their students *after* they made the transition. The researchers noted that students might have relied on their parents for help with their academic and personal lives because they "might not have developed the skills to do so when more independence is needed (e.g., in college)."[34]

The researchers commented that the students themselves may have sought assistance from their parents. They hypothesized that "HP behaviors send subtle messages about individual self-efficacy—or lack thereof—that youth internalize."[35]

Because this study wasn't focused on students with disabilities (and there's no way to determine whether some of the students in the *cohort* [the group being studied] had a disability), parents of students with disabilities may decide that it isn't relevant to their family. Indeed, it's not necessarily meant to suggest that it is. It's discussed here simply to provide information for parents who wonder how they can effectively support their student and to consider what might be unhelpful in the long run.

By doing things on behalf of their student, well-meaning parents may interfere with that student's opportunities to develop a sense of ownership for themselves. Even if a student works with an academic coach or peer mentor, or an EF coach or learning disabilities specialist (whether they're available on campus or the family provides one), they're likely to have only a few meetings a week, at most. In these meetings, the specialist/coach/mentor may ask the student if they're keeping up, going to class, or whether they've started an assignment that's due soon. But no one can be with a student every moment of the day and literally *make* them do the readings, start the paper, get to class, etc. In the end, in order to be successful, they'll have to activate themselves.

Providing too much parental or professional support can run the risk of undermining a student's confidence in their abilities. Failing to give the student a chance to function independently can limit their self-efficacy. It can deprive them of an opportunity to learn what they can do without help. In addition, it may inadvertently relay a message that parents don't think their student can be successful without such help. This, too, can undermine their self-confidence.

Of course, this advice is not meant to suggest that parents should immediately pull supports away. They can start by talking to their student about all of the supports being provided to them by adults. Ask which ones they think they truly need. They may feel that not all are necessary.

If there are supports the student thinks are crucial, speak to them about how those won't be available at college and ask if they want to start working toward building the skills they'll need so they can have a smooth, perhaps more comfortable transition later. If so, work on strategies while still providing supports and then gradually pull them back. For instance, talk about what gets in the way of their remembering items they need for school and help them figure out the steps it will take to do this independently. As Lahey says, "The key is that competence must come out of a child's own efforts."[36]

A student may have an unrealistic sense of how much they rely on others. Scaling back supports can provide them with some feedback on that. If their grades start slipping, that can serve as a prompt to suggest they engage with teachers and with you about developing independent strategies. Establish the link between lower grades and factors such as missed homework, failure to seek help, and brief or ineffective study sessions.[37]

Of course, it's possible that some students won't be interested in preparing themselves for future independence, even though they plan to transition to college right after high school. At that point, parents can decide whether they feel it's a better choice to maintain those supports. They may conclude it's important to keep them in place. Or they may want to probe their student's thinking about how things will be different when they are on their own at college.

Again, there are on-campus supports available (see step 5 for more on these), and families can find off-campus ones, too. But accountability check-ins and wake-up calls can only do so much. Students have to motivate themselves to do the work. If a student doesn't feel self-driven at the end of high school, to the point that they can't accomplish certain basic tasks without a lot of adult support, prompting, and direction, parents may want to think about whether an immediate transition after high school to a traditional college environment (meaning one where students live away from home) is the appropriate next step for their student.

Evaluate Other Forms of Adult Support

Whether their student works with in-school or outside tutors or specialists, parents can talk to these professionals about *what* support is being provided, *how* that's happening, and *how often* it's being provided. If a student needs help mastering the content of a challenging class, tutoring can be appropriate. But it might be helpful not to provide it every day, as that can impede a student's development of important strategies for independence, such as making a note to ask the teacher a question when they don't understand something (or sending an email), seeking help right away through online video tutorials or resources, or asking a classmate for assistance.

If their student is working with a subject-matter tutor or other kind of specialist (e.g., learning disabilities specialist, ADHD coach, executive functioning coach), parents can ask that this person start sessions by *asking* the student what they need to work on, not by *telling* them what they'll work on together. This person can ask what should be first on their list, so that the student learns the important skill of prioritization. They can teach them strategies for organization and time management, rather than giving them a schedule to follow. The focus can be on making the student as independent as possible.

Parents can ask tutors and specialists about how much use their student is making of their sessions. If the student seems resistant to working with someone, it may be a bad match. If so, families should see if they can find someone else. (This may not be available for school-based supports.) But if a student just won't engage, their parents may decide it's better to remove the support for a time until the student feels motivated to utilize that support.

In addition to speaking about what they see as the keys to college success, the DS directors shared their view of what has gone wrong when they've seen students who weren't successful. Besides remarking that some students didn't do the things associated with success, they made comments that spoke to a lack of self-efficacy and self-advocacy.

They gave numerous examples, including students who failed to use their accommodations and other campus supports or failed to take action after they did poorly on their first test. A theme running through their comments was that these students lacked the ability to function independently. This, again, is a good reason for parents to consider scaling back supports while their student is still in high school.

Some of what parents often handle are school-related decisions and meetings. To help their student to develop the self-advocacy skills they'll need, parents can ask the student's opinion or input in meetings before offering their own. Although high school students often select their courses on their own, parents can coach them by asking questions that help them create a plan and make choices and by reminding them about college admissions requirements, if college is that student's goal. (Maybe they're not feeling ready yet.)

Help Students Develop Life Skills
Parents can also help their student to develop essential life skills before they leave home, so that the everyday aspects of their independent lives do not

add additional stress. If they do not already do this, families can help them develop a weekly routine to take care of their responsibilities, including:

- doing laundry regularly
- using some kind of planning system (importantly, one that *works* for students) to manage their commitments, such as rehearsals or club meetings
- organizing and staying on top of email a few times a week
- organizing their backpack and papers
- cleaning up their actual and virtual desktops weekly
- being responsible for waking up on time for school and other commitments
- taking care of any essential forms (e.g., enrollment forms for sports or other activities)
- making their own medical appointments and other arrangements (e.g., carpools)

By teaching these things, parents can provide their children with the experience and confidence they'll need to handle life at college and beyond.[38]

Summary

Once students, families, and professionals understand the amount of independence students are expected to demonstrate at college, it should become clear that those students must strengthen their executive functions and develop the self-determination and self-advocacy skills needed for college while they are still in the structured, supportive high school environment. There are a number of opportunities for building such skills. Parents can play a vital, albeit limited, role in this process. Of course, since college is an educational environment, students will need academic skills, too.

Notes

1. Even if a school alerts a student that they aren't doing well, the college may not require them to attend tutoring or meet with their professors, at least not until they are put on *probation*, meaning they have one more term to get their grades up before the college dismisses them.

2. Ketevan Mamiseishvili and Lynn C. Koch, "First-to-Second-Year Persistence of Students with Disabilities in Postsecondary Institutions in the United States," *Rehabilitation Counseling Bulletin* 54, no. 2 (2011): 93–105. https://doi.org /10.1177/0034355210382580

3. See step 4 for a discussion of these tools.

4. See step 5 for more on what supports may be available at different colleges.

5. Thomas E. Brown, "Executive Functions: Describing Six Aspects of a Complex Syndrome," *Attention* (February 2008): 12–17. https://chadd.org/wp-content/uploads/2018/06/ATTN_02_08_Executive_Functions_by_Thomas_Brown.pdf

6. Peter Baggetta and Patricia Alexander, "Conceptualization and Operationalization of Executive Function," *Mind, Brain, and Education* 10, no. 1 (2016): 10–33. https://doi.org/10.1111/mbe.12100

7. David Test et al., "A Conceptual Framework of Self-Advocacy for Students with Disabilities," *Remedial and Special Education* 26, no. 1 (2005): 43–54. https://doi.org/10.1177/07419325050260010601

8. Michael Wehmeyer and Michelle Schwartz, "Self-Determination and Positive Adult Outcomes: A Follow-Up Study of Youth with Mental Retardation or Learning Disabilities," *Exceptional Children* 63, no. 2 (1997): 245–55. https://doi.org/10.1177/001440299706300207

9. Wehmeyer and Schwartz, "Self-Determination and Positive Outcomes," 253.

10. Barry J. Zimmerman, "Self-Efficacy: An Essential Motive to Learn," *Contemporary Educational Psychology* 25, no. 1 (2000): 82–91. https://doi.org/10.1006/ceps.1999.1016

11. Mary E. Morningstar et al., "A College and Career Readiness Framework for Secondary Students with Disabilities," *Career Development and Transition for Exceptional Individuals* 40, no. 2 (2017): 79–91. https://doi.org/10.1177/2165143415589926

12. See a link to this resource in appendix C.

13. June E. Gothberg et al., "Successful Transition of Students With Disabilities to 21st-Century College and Careers: Using Triangulation and Gap Analysis to Address Nonacademic Skills," *TEACHING Exceptional Children* 47, no. 6 (2015): 344–51. https://doi.org/10.1177/0040059915587890; Dawn A. Rowe et al., "Updating the Secondary Transition Research Base," *Career Development for Exceptional Individuals* 44, no. 1 (2021): 28–46. https://doi.org/10.1177/2165143420958674

14. If you are a parent who does the planning for your homeschooled students, consider yourself your student's case manager in the rest of this discussion.

15. Valerie Mazzotti et al., "Linking Transition Assessment and Postsecondary Goals: Key Elements in the Secondary Transition Planning Process," *TEACHING Exceptional Children* 42, no. 2 (2009): 44–51. https://doi.org/10.1177/004005990904200205

16. See curriculum and other instructional strategies in appendix C.

17. Jessica Monahan, Allison Lombardi, and Joseph Madaus, "Promoting College and Career Readiness: Practical Strategies for the Classroom," *TEACHING Exceptional Children* 51, no. 1 (2018): 144–54. https://doi.org/10.1177/0040059918802579

18. Jay W. Rojewski, In H. Lee, and Noel Gregg, "Causal Effects of Inclusion on Postsecondary Education Outcomes of Individuals with High-Incidence Disabilities," *Journal of Disability Policy Studies* 25, no. 4 (2015): 210–19. https://doi.org/10.1177/1044207313505648

19. Learn more in step 6.

20. Tiana C. Povenmire-Kirk et al., "A Journey, Not a Destination: Developing Cultural Competence in Secondary Transition," *TEACHING Exceptional Children* 47, no. 6 (2015): 319–28. https://doi.org/10.1177/0040059915587679

21. See strategies for helping students run their own IEP meeting in the "Additional Resources" section in appendix C.

22. Using the term "learning difference" with a student who actually has a learning disability in order to frame their challenges in a positive light is well-intentioned. Just be sure to explain that this is how you look at it, but that they qualify as a person with a disability, which affords them certain rights. If you are a professional using "learning difference" in your reports or other work with a student because the student *doesn't* have a disability, let the student and their family know that it's your professional opinion that they don't have a disability, based on their testing, which the college may interpret the same way. Tell them to request accommodations anyway but be aware that their school might not find them eligible.

23. Eric Endlich (Independent Educational Consultant), in conversation with the author, December 21, 2021.

24. Elizabeth Cooper (Independent Educational Consultant), in conversation with the author, November 19, 2021.

25. Jessica Lahey, *The Gift of Failure: How the Best Parents Learn to Let Go So Their Children Can Succeed* (New York: HarperCollins, 2015), 70.

26. William Stixrud and Ned Johnson, *What Do You Say? How to Talk with Kids to Build Motivation, Stress Tolerance, and a Happy Home* (New York: Viking, 2021), 51.

27. Lahey, *The Gift of Failure*, 36.

28. Lahey, *The Gift of Failure*, 24.

29. The researchers didn't comment on whether these were new behaviors or ones parents had engaged in when students were still in high school.

30. Aaron M. Luebbe et al., "Dimensionality of Helicopter Parenting and Relations to Emotional, Decision-Making, and Academic Functioning in Emerging Adults," *Assessment* 25, no. 7 (2016): 841–57. https://journals.sagepub.com/doi/10.1177/1073191116665907

31. Luebbe et al., "Dimensionality of Helicopter Parenting."

32. Luebbe et al., "Dimensionality of Helicopter Parenting."

33. Luebbe et al., "Dimensionality of Helicopter Parenting."

34. Luebbe et al., "Dimensionality of Helicopter Parenting."

35. Luebbe et al., "Dimensionality of Helicopter Parenting."

36. Lahey, *The Gift of Failure*, 37.

37. These can be challenging conversations for parents to engage in with their student, who may be reluctant to talk about these subjects. Parents can ask the case manager to try to have these conversations with the student. If they work with an outside coach or specialist, that person may be the best one to approach the student.

38. Find additional resources in appendix C.

~

Developing the Student's Academic Skills

What You'll Learn in This Step

- How the academic environment at college differs from the high school environment
- Academic challenges students may encounter at college
- Strategies and tools high schools can teach students to get them ready
- Strategies and tools that students can employ on their own
- Supports students can seek out at college if they're struggling

The thrill of forthcoming independence at college can sometimes obscure a fundamental fact for students: First and foremost, college is an environment focused on academics. Students excited about attending college may be looking forward to it because it's a step into adulthood—a chance to live on their own. It's also a chance to decide what to focus their time and energy on by choosing a major—this is freedom they likely haven't experienced before. What many students may not be thinking about is the academic demands they'll encounter at college, which are likely to be different from what they experienced in high school.

Unfortunately, students may not be getting the preparation they need to meet those demands. A recent study that surveyed students registered with their college's disability services office found that only half of students said they were prepared or very prepared for college. Those who did reported that instruction in time management, notetaking, and writing had helped. Unsurprisingly, comments from the 30 percent who said they were unprepared or very unprepared expressed a need for instruction in study and literacy skills as well as in executive functioning.[1]

It's not just students with disabilities who feel unprepared. A large separate study of college students in the general population found that:

- only 20 percent thought they'd been very well prepared for college
- 50 percent said they had been somewhat well prepared
- 19 percent said they'd been somewhat poorly prepared
- 9 percent said they'd been very poorly prepared

(Two percent responded that they didn't know.) Asked what skills they wanted to develop further, 40 percent said time management, 39 percent said exam preparation, 29 percent said "general study skills," 15 percent said independent thinking, 13 percent said writing, 9 percent said subject knowledge, 8 percent said reading, and 9 percent said studying to understand/remember. Clearly, not enough students with or without disabilities are transitioning to college feeling confident about their preparation.[2]

How High Schools Can Help Students Prepare

Based on studies like these, it seems clear that high schools need to address these skill deficits. As part of the high school-to-college transition process, schools should look for opportunities to present *all* students—not just those with disabilities—and their families with information about what to expect at the college level. This kind of information can be especially important for students who will be the first in the family to attend college at all, or the first to attend college in this country, where the system may work very differently from what their parents experienced. Inviting high school graduates who have already started at college to speak about their experiences, and perhaps asking them to mention some of the things they wish they had known before they started college, can be an effective way to do this.

Preparing Students for Changes in the Academic Environment at College

It's never too early to learn organizational and academic strategies. In fact, it would be ideal if districts could integrate these strategies into the curriculum before high school—preferably in late elementary or middle school—so that students could get accustomed to using them. Researchers whose work focuses on how students learn posited that "one reason why they may underuse effective strategies is that many students are not formally trained (or even told) about how to use effective strategies, perhaps because societal attitudes and assumptions indicate that children and adults do not need to be taught them."[3]

Again, focusing on these skill areas would benefit *all* students. Although students with disabilities need this kind of instruction, many other students (including those who are academically advanced) can derive some value from being introduced to strategies that may be different from those that they have been using instinctively, although perhaps not as effectively.

There are a number of significant shifts in academic expectations that students will encounter in the college environment. Although most of the elements, such as exams, studying, reading assignments, writing assignments, and notetaking, are already familiar to high school students, they carry a lot more weight in a college setting. Schools can help students prepare by incorporating some needed skill development into their curriculum, counseling, and guidance programs. And they can teach strategies that students can employ once they get to college.

Exams

What's Challenging

In high school, exams are often just one tool of many that teachers use to assess a student's academic performance. At college, a student's entire course grade might be based on just two things: a midterm exam and a final exam, each of which may cover half the semester's topics. College exams may consist of essay prompts that ask students to take a position and support their view using information from the readings and lectures.

Some exams are based on *identifications*, or IDs. In these exams, the professor provides numerous quotes from the readings in a literature class, pictures or other works in art history classes, or snippets of music in a humanities class, and students might have to identify who created it, what period or movement it represents, why it is important, etc.

Although some question types, such as multiple-choice, short-answer, or fill-in-the-blank, will already be familiar to students, college exams are likely to have numerous items and be quite lengthy. Students aren't typically approved for modification of exams, such as having fewer answers to choose from on a multiple-choice test.[4]

Some professors may give *open notebook* exams to the whole class, where students can access their own notes. Or they may permit all students to bring a notecard of a particular size or a piece of paper with reference notes that students create for themselves. In these situations, students with and without disabilities are expected to create their own notecard or sheet; neither professors nor a DS staffer has to make one of these up for the student.[5]

How High Schools Can Help Students Prepare

Districts can coordinate across the high school curriculum to make sure that students are taking different kinds of exams within their courses, a policy that would benefit *all* college-bound students.

High schools can also explicitly teach test-taking strategies to all students, including how to eliminate options on multiple-choice exams or how to brainstorm before starting to write on essay exams.[6]

A meta-analysis looking at the study strategies students used found that many were ineffective.[7] Explicit instruction in effective study strategies would benefit all students. Even those who do well in high school without studying can benefit from learning some techniques before moving to college, where demands increase.[89] In fact, it would be ideal if this kind of instruction began in middle school, so students could have time to see what works for them and practice it before they get to college.

Looking specifically at students with disabilities—when teams discuss a student's IEP or 504 plan each year, if someone recommends modifying tests for students, the case manager should make sure the student knows that the chances of getting modified tests at college are very small. This will give the student a chance to decide whether they want to accept this significant accommodation at the high school level, knowing they may find the shift to college exams even more challenging if they become accustomed to working under modified demands.

And if instruction in test preparation strategies is not included in the general education setting, case managers should be sure they're included as part of a student's high school IEP, and special educators can provide direct instruction.

What Students Can Do Once They Get to College

At college, regularly visiting professors and TAs (teaching assistants) during their office hours can help students get clarification on class concepts they haven't grasped, and give them a sense of whether they have been focusing on the important ideas. It can also demonstrate to professors students' interest in the class and in their own performance. Keeping up with readings and assignments can help them avoid the necessity of cramming. Some students may find it helpful to form study groups, where classmates quiz each other, share notes, etc., to make sure they haven't neglected studying any important information. This can also be a great way to ensure that students remain engaged while reviewing information, as it's a more active way to study. (The social aspects of study groups can also be a benefit of this approach.) And of course, students can request and use any exam accommodations for which they've been approved.

"Studying"

What's Challenging

Whereas in high school, students typically use "studying" exclusively to refer to preparing for a test, "studying" in college often covers a range of tasks, such as keeping up with readings even when there are no questions to answer or homework to turn in, completing any weekly assignments that do have to be submitted, and reviewing material far in advance of upcoming tests. Engaging in these tasks effectively is a form of test preparation, in that it serves as a review of the materials, though students may not think of it this way.

Professors don't typically provide their classes with study guides that indicate what students should focus on.[10] If they do, these may be long lists of terms that students need to know. Rather than including definitions or explanations, professors may expect students to supply these themselves, gleaning them from readings or from their class notes.

Studying may prove particularly challenging for students with disabilities when it comes to:

- identifying appropriate times during the week to complete their work
- having a sense of how much time is "enough" time to spend studying, especially when there are no assignments to turn in
- falling behind when they don't have to complete and submit assignments

How High Schools Can Help Students Prepare

Across curriculum areas, teachers can tell students that studying at college is different; it likely will require more of their time, as the reduced amount of class time means that professors expect them to learn more outside of class. It can be helpful to:

- demonstrate and have them try a "time management calculator" to gain a better sense of how they spend their day.[11]
- engage students in an experiment by having them estimate how much time they spend each week on assignments, asking them to record those times, and then discussing how accurate they were in their estimations.

- ask students to estimate how much time they plan to spend studying for an upcoming test and to explain what strategies they plan to use. After the exam, ask them how their plan worked out, and what, if anything, they would change for the next test.
- help students develop the habit of setting weekly goals, committing these to paper or digital file (this can make tasks seem more real), and check in with them to see whether they accomplished what they set out to do. These can include both academic and personal goals.
- get students thinking about their ideal study conditions by encouraging them to complete a study strategy inventory.[12]

These activities can help raise awareness of the student's own time management and scheduling skills.

Of course, students may have no idea how many hours they should spend on academic work at college. This makes sense: How can they know until they get there and can see for themselves what's required of them?

Teachers and case managers can suggest that students start by following the common suggestion of scheduling two hours of study activities outside of class for each hour they spend in class. This would mean that for each course they take (where they'll typically be in class for three hours a week), they can start by planning six hours a week of reading, doing problem sets, etc. for that one class.[13] Of course, six hours of study time may not be necessary for some classes, and it may not be enough for others. But it's generally a good idea for students to plan *some* amount of study time for each class in the first week, just so they have a plan to follow. Then, depending on how things go the first week, they can adjust those times either up or down.

When it comes to studying, "down" time can be almost as important as "up" time. Students who make up their own schedules sometimes find themselves working too long without a break. The resulting fatigue can mean they work more slowly and less efficiently.

Teachers and case managers can suggest that students try the Pomodoro Technique, a strategy that some college students use to structure their time.[14] Using this strategy, students would devote a "Pomodoro session" for a particular class by:

- studying (i.e., reading, doing problem sets, writing part of an essay) for 25 minutes and then taking a five-minute break; they can use a timer to make sure they don't exceed that time
- studying for another 25-minute block and taking a five-minute break
- repeating the study/rest periods again

- repeating the study block, but following this fourth one with a more significant break (e.g., 30 minutes)

They can then repeat the whole process with another class.

Studying in 25-minute blocks may prove too brief for some students and too long for others. Educators can emphasize that students vary in their study stamina: some students may be able to study for longer periods, whereas others may not be able to be productive for 25 minutes at a clip or for 2 hours with only brief breaks—at least not initially. Students may want to experiment with time blocks of different lengths to determine what works best for them.

Special educators can also work with a student on techniques specific to their disability to help them bypass or compensate for an academic weakness. Although some students develop these techniques on their own, often without realizing they're doing it (especially students whose ADHD or learning disability isn't identified until later in their education), many students don't.

What Students Can Do Once They Get to College

Students can review the syllabus for each course prior to or during the first week of classes and place all exam and assignment due dates on a calendar so these dates don't sneak up on them. They can also (or alternatively) enter them in a spreadsheet and cross them off as they complete them.

Once they have their assignments in a list and/or plotted out on their calendar, they can compose a weekly study plan to structure their time and make sure that they keep up with work.[15] For instance, they might plan to complete their biology readings and assignments on Tuesdays, Thursdays, and Sundays from 2:00 to 4:00.

In devising a plan, students may want to consider their "best" or "prime":

- studying time, meaning when they are most energized and attentive (is this morning, afternoon, or late night?)
- location (do they get more done in their dorm room, or in a library *carrel*, or booth?)
- conditions (using earplugs? listening to music?)

A student can also consider additional preferences as part of this plan. For instance, do they prefer to tackle the work they like least first, or do they feel more motivated if they start with a subject they like or a brief assignment that can give them a feeling of accomplishment? What motivates them (or at least encourages them to get started)?

Students can try to stay on track with their study and assignment goals by keeping to-do lists, crossing items off as they complete them; by creating a Post-it note for each task, throwing each one away as they get the work done; or by using online goal-tracking tools or apps—whatever works for them. If they are comfortable with this, they can set specific work-completion goals (e.g., do this week's readings for political science) and ask a friend or family member to follow up with them at a prescribed time of the day or week to check on their progress.

Some students find study groups helpful for getting assignments done, too. They can be a way of creating a sense of responsibility for completing readings or other work. Sometimes students work on problems together, or they do them separately but help each other.

Such collaborative efforts can carry social benefits and may give students a sense of whether they've spent as much time preparing for class as they need to. If a student has been working on study strategies before college, they may discover that they have the best study strategies in the group. They may also benefit from teaching something to others. If being in a group is not a comfortable strategy, students can also try to find a single "study buddy" with whom they can review class material.

A modification of the study buddy idea is for students to find another student and agree to meet at a certain time and place to get work done. They can sit at opposite ends of a study table or in library carrels near each other. The idea is simply to create an outside motivator to get students to go somewhere and get the work done. In other words, students may be more likely to get to the library to do work because someone is expecting them, and they won't want to let them down. This kind of meeting plan can also be an adaptation of the idea of "body doubling"–working silently alongside someone who also has a task that needs completion, keeping each other on track. (Jokingly, this might be seen as a useful adaptation of the "misery loves company" idea.) If students can't find a fellow student who will do this, they might try asking a family member or friend to join them on FaceTime or Zoom.

Students who are struggling with class content should take advantage of the regular office hours that most professors or TAs maintain and/or by taking part in review sessions. They may also find it helpful to look online for videos that explain concepts or provide examples.

Reading Assignments

What's Challenging

Weekly reading loads for college classes can be large (as many as 200 pages per class), and generally will be more sophisticated than what students have previously encountered, and they may contain a lot of new vocabulary. Although professors may assign readings that are not covered or discussed in class, information from these may still be included on an exam. Reading assignments might include books that students need to purchase or articles to download from the course management system.

How High Schools Can Help Students Prepare

The more practice students have with different kinds of readings, the more comfortable they may be with handling these independently at college. Districts can make sure their curriculum includes a variety of kinds of texts—not just textbooks but also newspaper articles, opinion pieces, plays, and research studies. Again, this approach can benefit all students, and even students who don't plan to attend college will benefit from the literacy and critical thinking skills.

Schools can also teach strategic approaches to reading (e.g., SQ3R[16]) that promote engagement with the text and taking notes from it that students can use to prepare for exams.

In some classes, students may not have physical texts to read but instead have articles and studies in digital form (PDF). Research on this is still developing, but there's some evidence students read more effectively on paper.[17] Schools can try an experiment and have students try reading pieces of similar length and challenge both on the computer and on paper to help students evaluate which format (print or screen) works better for them.

Experiments like these can be helpful because they give students experiences to inform their decisions at college about whether to read online or print their readings, as they're likely to have some classes where all of the readings are in digital form. At many colleges, students get a *printing allowance* (sometimes called a *print allotment, allocation,* or *quota*) each term, which means they can use the university printers to print a number of pages for free.[18] They may decide to use that allowance to print readings only for their most challenging classes. Even if they use text-to-speech software, some students may find it helpful to print some readings so they can follow along with them on paper.

What Students Can Do Once They Get to College

Students can select an environment most conducive to reading (dorm versus library, music or no music, etc.). They can incorporate reading time into their weekly study and assignment schedule and figure out how long they can read in one sitting before they begin to lose focus. For some students, this will be a half an hour at a time, whereas others may be able to read effectively for a few hours. Students who have been assigned widely read plays or texts can look online for summaries of these to read before they get started to "prime" themselves by learning what the story is about and what to focus on while they read.[19]

If they haven't been approved by DS for text-to-speech software but are interested in it, they can experiment, too, with free screen readers.[20] Not all of their reading materials may be in a format that is accessible to such programs, but it could be worth trying to see if they like it.

Writing Assignments

What's Challenging

In college, students may be required to write essays that are more sophisticated than those they wrote in high school. Students may have to use primary sources or express their own opinions rather than just repeating what another author thinks. Like the exam schedule, writing assignment due dates are often included in the course syllabus, and a student's progress on these assignments is not typically monitored by the professor, who may only expect to see the final product on the due date. Colleges expect students to write in a way that avoids plagiarism, citing sources using the course's required format (e.g., Modern Language Association style). Some colleges require a long term paper or thesis as part of a concentration for a major, and some courses require students to prepare a paper as a group.

There are a number of aspects of college writing assignments that students may find challenging, including:

- knowing when they have gathered enough research and should start writing
- integrating large amounts of information
- formulating a central idea or thesis
- devising a plan that allows enough time for the actual writing

How High Schools Can Help Students Prepare

Districts can make sure the curriculum requires all students to complete a long-term research paper. Teachers can model how to create interim deadlines and break projects into smaller tasks or steps, and to teach effective research and notetaking skills.

They can also ask students to look online for an assignment calculator, into which students plug in their starting and due date for an assignment. The program produces a schedule for them to follow, with interim deadlines built in.[21]

At college, students are expected to cite their sources and avoid accidental *plagiarism* (failure to give credit to someone else's work). Teachers can explicitly teach and model how to use primary sources and contrast examples where sources have been cited correctly with others where they haven't, helping students to effectively recognize the difference. When students submit drafts of their work, teachers can point out any instances of plagiarism and show students how the text could be written (or how students could provide citations) to avoid it. If the district uses a plagiarism-checking program such as Turnitin, they should make sure every student takes at least one class where they use this so they get accustomed to it.

Sometimes, students struggle to get their ideas on paper/computer screen. Teachers and case managers can present students with examples of different graphic organizers that aid in arranging their ideas.[22] Students can experiment with different ones to find what works best for them. Teachers may also suggest that students try using the dictation feature built into their word processing program to talk their ideas out.

What Students Can Do Once They Get to College

Students can create a plan for approaching long-term writing assignments. If they want to get started but the professor hasn't addressed the assignment in class, they can make an appointment during office hours to ask for guidance on beginning their work. They can seek out an assignment calculator that suits their preferences. If they struggle with breaking a long-term assignment into steps or tasks, they can seek assistance from the college tutoring or writing center. For students who think better while they're moving, they can use dictation software or a built-in accessibility feature on their phone or computer to record their ideas while they walk around their room.

Developing effective writing strategies can be beneficial across multiple academic disciplines. Even so, districts may want to choose a particular subject area that all students take (such as history or English) to serve as the primary provider of direct instruction in some of these strategies. However, many of the preparatory strategies, such as planning and time management, should be included across the curriculum.

Although it should benefit students in the general population, this emphasis on preparation is especially important for students with disabilities that affect learning, as they will be completing these tasks without the kind of support they may have been receiving in K–12.

Notetaking

What's Challenging

Although some professors use whiteboards or have slides to accompany their lectures (and some will post their notes online), others simply talk for the duration of class. Students must find ways to capture information so they can study it before exams or use it to inform their papers.

How High Schools Can Help Students Prepare

High schools can provide all students with explicit instruction in a variety of linear and visual notetaking strategies and skills. Ideally, though, such instruction would take place while students are in middle school, so that they could practice with different techniques and decide what suits them best. Content-area teachers can reinforce these skills so that students see how to apply strategies across different topics.[23]

What Students Can Do Once They Get to College

If approved for accommodations, students can use the tools made available to them. If they are approved for copies of a classmate's notes, they should make sure they actually review them and either update their own notes with the things they missed or highlight those points in the peer's notes for later review.[24]

When granted permission to record lectures, students can use those recordings to fill any gaps in their own notes. They don't have to listen to the whole lecture again—they just need to skip to the places where they missed something.

Students should try using their own personal shorthand, abbreviating frequently used words, just as they might do when texting their friends. They should try not to worry about whether they are following every word the professor is saying during lectures—they may find that later on, their brain has processed the material and that they understand it better than they did during the lecture.

Addressing Challenges Specific to Students with Disabilities

In addition to the adjustments that all students must make in the transition from high school to college, there are two other points about the college environment that may require special preparation for students with disabilities. One is that students may have to choose classes without the advice of someone who knows how to help them figure out what kind of schedule and class setup might work best for them. They also have to make sure they meet all of the requirements for graduation. They may have some flexibility in the way they structure their schedules, and awareness of these challenges may give them some things to consider as they make their choices.

Course Selection

What's Challenging

College courses differ from high school classes in a number of significant respects, which makes choosing wisely even more important.

Their frequency and length may be different. Although college courses may meet only once, twice, or three times a week, they will often meet for a longer amount of time than the typical high school class (e.g., once-a-week classes may run for 3 hours). Introductory classes that freshmen take may be large and held in big lecture halls, and the professor may lecture the whole time without providing any visuals. Required classes may only be offered in the morning or in the evening, and a student's course schedule may have large time gaps between classes.

Talking with instructors may be more challenging. Professors may only teach once or twice a week and be available for conversation only during scheduled office hours on those days. Although they may be experts on their course topics, not all professors excel in explaining things in different ways. In addition, their course sections may be taught by teaching assistants (TAs) who also grade papers and exams and hold review sessions. This means students may have fewer opportunities to get assistance directly from the person running their class.

For many students, the setup of classes can also require some adjustments. For some students, their disability may add an additional element of challenge. Students have to adjust to the fact that:

- classes may cover a lot of topics and provide little reinforcement of ideas covered
- it can be hard to concentrate during long classes
- professors may not cover everything they expect students to know for exams (which means that they expect them to do some of their learning on their own from the readings)
- for students whose disability makes mornings challenging (e.g., if they have a personal care attendant who comes to get them ready for the day), classes they need may only be held then; or classes may only be held at night (a challenge for those whose disability causes fatigue at the end of the day or who take stimulant medications that could interfere with sleep onset)
- a student's classes may be scheduled for different times of the day with big gaps in between (making it difficult for some students to use the time between classes effectively)

How High Schools Can Help Students Prepare

During a student's senior year, case managers can provide tips in a meeting and handout.[25] These can cover things not typically included in a college freshman's meetings with their academic advisor, including how it might be helpful for students to:

- meet with their college academic advisor to ask what core requirements they need to fulfill and then start by making a rough plan for that (which can be adjusted over time)[26]
- seek advice from upperclassmen on which professors are more engaged and more likely to make themselves available to students
- stay engaged by taking at least one class per term that truly interests them, rather than loading up on challenging classes in one term to "get them over with"
- (if a student's disability makes early or late classes problematic) request priority registration as an accommodation when they register with their college's DS office, to give them a chance to create a schedule that works well with their medication or attention span[27]
- when possible, choose classes where factors such as format are best suited to their particular learning strengths and weaknesses and/or time of day best meets their needs.

What Students Can Do Once They Get to College

Students can do their research, looking at course selections as soon as they are available in order to have adequate time for reviewing possible class choices. Again, they can request priority registration if they think they'll need to schedule their classes to capitalize on times of day when their medication will be at peak effectiveness. Students with physical/medical disabilities who work with a personal attendant who gets them showered/ready for the day or who need time to get from building to building should ask for this, too, so their assistant doesn't have to arrive very early.

Students can also try to balance their course load each semester—meaning they can try to choose a mix of challenging and easier classes, depending upon their learning strengths and weaknesses. For instance, if reading is a challenge, students should try mixing required literature classes with math, science, or other elective courses that may be less reading intensive.

In seeking this balance, students should remain mindful of the college's *core* or *general education* requirements as well as the requirements for their major.[28] As early as freshman year of college, students can create a rough plan for meeting the college's overall graduation requirements, seeking help from their academic advisor in plotting this out. It doesn't matter if a student hasn't yet identified a major. The plan can and should be adjusted as needed; the important thing is to create a plan that enables the student to be more strategic in choosing courses.

Students should be aware of different options for fulfilling graduation requirements. For example, a computer-programming course might satisfy a math requirement for all students, not just those approved for a substitution as a disability accommodation.[29] By doing a little research, students may be able to find classes that both meet overall requirements and are more interesting or better suited to them.

Just as several different classes may fulfill the same graduation requirement, some core classes (such as Freshman Writing) will likely have numerous *sections* (classes teaching the same content, but offered at different time blocks and usually with different instructors). Talking to other students who have taken a course with a particular instructor can also inform students' decisions. Students can ask whether DS might be able to refer them to others with disabilities who've done so; there's a chance they may be able to find someone.

Online sites such as Rate My Professors (www.ratemyprofessors.com) can be helpful tools, although students should assess the information there critically, understanding that some students post negative reviews for personal reasons, e.g., because they didn't do well in the class, or because the class was more difficult than they anticipated. What students should look for in these reviews is information about teaching style, workload, professors' willingness to meet outside of class time, and so on.

For especially challenging courses they need for their major or to fulfill the college's general requirements, students can consider registering during a winter or summer session. Registering for just a single course during one of these between-term periods can give them the extra time and energy to focus on that single class. However, they should be aware that classes held during these sessions may involve long days of class time and that a lot of material may be covered in a short amount of time. This can be too much for some students. Moreover, for students who struggle with time management, process slowly, or have conditions that cause them to miss classes at times, these classes may not be good choices, either.

Another alternative is to take challenging required courses at a local community college, where instructors may have more experience working with a lot of students with disabilities. (In the National Longitudinal Transition Study-2, a large, longitudinal study, the rate of enrollment for students with learning disabilities was highest in two-year schools.)[30] Before registering for a class at any other college than their own, students should check with their college to make sure that the community college credits will transfer.

Sometimes, students may have no choice but to take classes that meet only once a week for an extended period of time because it's the only time a class they need for their major is offered. They may find it helpful to:

- turn their phone off and put it in their bag (if they use an insulin monitor connected to their watch, they can turn off all other notifications)
- use an internet- or site-specific blocking program or app to help avoid any temptations to get off task if they take notes on their laptop
- bring a caffeinated beverage or chew gum
- take a walk outside to get some fresh air if professors give the class a break (setting a timer to ensure they return to class on time)

Students with big time gaps between classes who are worried they'll be tempted to skip their later classes can arrange to meet a classmate and walk to class together to create a sense of accountability for themselves. They can also set a recurring electronic reminder to pop up on their phone flashing a "go to class!" message. If students don't find these strategies helpful, they can keep trying new ones until they find what works for them.

Choosing classes isn't the only part of the college experience where students will be on their own. When it comes to academic tasks, students accustomed to a lot of adult assistance may find it helpful to engage with technology to provide the help they used to receive from a teacher, aide, or parent.

Technology
Students may be happy using technology for social and entertainment purposes but may not see its value when it comes to academic tasks. Since colleges don't have to provide "personal" services, though, students may find that they're expected to use electronic tools to do things adults used to do for them, such as reading assigned texts.

What's Challenging
Colleges are increasingly using assistive technology (rather than human assistance) to accommodate students with disabilities. For instance, as already noted, some colleges accommodate students with reading disorders by making sure that they have their texts or exams in an accessible electronic format (e.g. Word, EPUB, HTML, tagged PDF, etc.) so that they can be read by text-to-speech software, screen readers, or apps. While some colleges

provide the text-to-speech software, others don't. If this is the case at their college, a student who wants to use it will have to buy it.

Notetaking is another area where more and more colleges are accommodating students with technology in the form of notetaking software instead of providing them with copies of notes from a classmate. Students attending one of these schools may have no choice but to get comfortable with it.

The absence of modified grading standards, combined with the reduction in the amount of help students receive, may also necessitate that students engage with technology. For instance, a student who didn't get penalized for spelling or grammar errors on high school exams may instead find themselves accommodated at college with permission to take tests using a computer so that they can check their grammar and spelling before submitting their exam. And they'll be expected to check any papers they complete outside of class for proper form.[31]

Even when colleges do provide students with access to tools such as text-to-speech software, they don't have to provide those students with instructions on how to use it effectively. For this reason, it's a good idea for students to get used to using these tools before college, so that they feel comfortable and confident with them.

How High Schools Can Help Students Prepare

It's ideal when districts employ an assistive technology (AT) professional who can assess a student's needs and pair them with technology that suits them. To maximize chances that a student will use the technology, they can provide regular check-ins with students to troubleshoot and check to see whether students actually find the tools useful.

If there isn't a specially trained AT specialist, high schools can designate a special educator to research tools. Korey Singleton, ATI Manager at George Mason University, suggested teachers look online to connect with AT professionals from other districts who may offer learning tools. He added that teachers could look at their state's Board of Education website to see if it links to assistive technology tools. And he noted that each state has a Tech Act Project, where individuals can learn about AT, receive an AT assessment, borrow AT, or acquire AT by way of low-interest loans.[32]

But not all of the technology needs to be specialized. Singleton said high school special educators can introduce students to the tools that are already embedded in the devices and programs they use all the time.[33] Singleton added, "Too many students are unaware of what resources are native to the operating systems they use every day, such as notetaking, text-to-speech and speech-to-text capabilities. They're not perfect, but they can still be helpful."[34]

What Students Can Do Once They Get to College

They can request certain kinds of tools as accommodations, such as text-to-speech software (and their texts in a format that can be read by it).[35] If they're approved, they may find that the programs their college offers them aren't the ones they were accustomed to using in high school. Colleges don't have to provide students' preferred program, so students in this position can either adjust to the program the college offers or they'll have to buy their own copy of the software they like.

If their college offers tools that are different than what students are used to, they can still try them out before giving up on them. If the DS office has an AT specialist, students can make an appointment to learn how to use the tools effectively, and then check in with that person a week or two later to troubleshoot any challenges they've had. (A benefit of using the college's tools in these situations is that the specialist will be familiar with them.) In cases where the student finds the tool to be difficult or ineffective, the AT specialist may have a strategy to suggest. Students can also search groups on social media or look for YouTube videos that might provide helpful tips for how to use the software.

Getting Academic Help at College

If they are having trouble in their classes, students can usually get help on individual subjects (such as physics or art history) at a campus tutoring center. Some schools also have writing and math centers or "help rooms." Typically, the tutors will be other undergraduate students who do well in those particular classes. In some cases, they may be graduate students.

DS may offer access to learning disability specialists, and some college counseling centers run workshops on time management.[36] Students struggling to establish a weekly schedule for themselves can ask their DS coordinator for assistance, or ask the tutoring center if someone can help them. If they are worried about their ability to keep up with work, they can start the semester by setting up weekly appointments. Even if the tutoring center normally offers help on a walk-in basis rather than by appointment, students may still be able to check with DS to see if it's possible to schedule an appointment ahead of time. And although colleges aren't required to do this, students should also ask DS whether they can get more tutoring sessions than are typically allowed. (It never hurts to ask.)

Addressing College Readiness in High School Accommodation and Modification Decisions

Students have to be ready to handle a lot of academic tasks at college and do so without a lot of the human help they may have been accustomed to in high school. Additionally, they'll likely find that they have to meet the same performance standards that their peers do.

It's a good idea for the high school team to think about accommodations a student is receiving. Is there skill instruction the school could provide that might eliminate the need for some supports and accommodations that aren't likely to be available at college?[37] For instance, if the student is used to having an adult review their papers for errors, can they be taught to use proofreading software?

When it comes to modifications, it's unlikely that students will receive these at college. Offering students different types of exams from the ones their peers are taking—for instance, providing a word bank for fill-in-the-blank tests—can leave them unprepared for the college environment. Again, the team should consider whether the student needs instruction in study strategies so that they can get accustomed to taking all kinds of exams, something they'll likely have to do at college.

Of course, the team may be focused on helping the student get through high school. Defining what success looks like in that context may lead the team to decide that modifications should stay in place. As always, the student should be well-informed about what they'll have to do at college and what supports are unlikely to be available, so they can make a decision about whether they want to use modifications and accommodations they're unlikely to get in college while they're still in high school.

Another way that students may get a good sense of what colleges' demands will be like is to take some college classes while they're still in high school. They may be able to do this in a dual-enrollment program.

Dual-Enrollment Programs

An increasingly popular way some students are preparing for the shift to college is by taking college classes through what's called a dual-enrollment program held at either their high school or a local college. This kind of program can offer them a chance to get a sense of what the academic demands at college are like. And it may also give them some practice self-advocating for their accommodations.

There's no one rule for schools across the country dictating whether a student enrolled in college classes in a dual-enrollment program will get to use the accommodations listed in their IEP or 504 plan for the high school, or whether they'll have to register for accommodations through the sponsoring college's DS office. If the student does have to go through the DS office, this means that they may not get all of the same accommodations they receive through their IEP or 504 (as explained in step 1). In some states, the rule centers on whether the classes students are taking will count toward their high school requirements or earn them college credits. Before committing to a class, the high school student should ask their case manager about the *memorandum of understanding* (i.e., agreement) their district has with the college around these questions regarding dual enrollment.

As an additional bonus, the decision about whether to take dual-enrollment classes is a great opportunity for students to practice their self-determination skills. They may decide that if they can't have their high school accommodations in place, they don't want to take the college classes, or they may decide to challenge themselves and see how things go.

Summary

All students will need to make adjustments to the college environment, where the expectations are more sophisticated. High schools can help by making sure classes embed direct instruction in the areas where they'll need skills to function independently. They can provide additional instruction for students with disabilities and suggest strategies to bypass any areas of weakness. IEP teams should consider whether the supports the student is receiving can be pared back after some direct instruction that develops the student's skills, to make them college-ready. And students may want to try out the college environment by taking dual-enrollment classes.

All of this instruction should position students to be successful at college. The next step is for them to identify some schools that will be a good fit.

Notes

1. Grace L. Francis et al., "Student Perceptions of College-Readiness, College Services and Supports, and Family Involvement in College: An Exploratory Study," *Journal of Autism and Developmental Disorders* 48 (2018): 3573–85. http://dx.doi.org/10.1007/s10803-018-3622-x

2. Paul A. Verrell and Norah R. McCabe, "In Their Own Words: Using Self-Assessments of College Readiness to Develop Strategies for Self-Regulated Learning," *College Teaching* 63, no. 4 (2015): 162–70. http://dx.doi.org/10.1080/87567555.2015.1053046

3. Robert A. Bjork, John Dunlosky, and Nate Kornell, "Self-Regulated Learning: Beliefs, Techniques, and Illusions," *Annual Review of Psychology* 34 (2013): 417–44.

4. Learn more in step 7.

5. Some students get to use a notecard on high school exams when their peers can't. This isn't commonly approved at college. See step 7 to learn more.

6. See appendix C for an article offering instructional strategies.

7. Bjork, Dunlosky, and Kornell, "Self-Regulated Learning," 417–44.

8. John Dunlosky et al., "Improving Students' Learning with Effective Learning Techniques: Promising Directions from Cognitive and Educational Psychology," *Psychological Science in the Public Interest* 14, no. 1, (2013): 4–58. https://doi.org/10.1177/1529100612453266

9. See appendix C for an article offering strategies to teach these to students.

10. And a request to receive a study guide as an accommodation isn't commonly approved. See step 7.

11. Find examples online, or find a link to one in appendix C.

12. The Learning and Study Strategies Inventory, or LASSI, is a published questionnaire, but professionals can look online for an informal one.

13. 2 hours of studying x 3 hours per class a week = 6 hours of study time per class per week.

14. Find a link to an explanation of this strategy in appendix C.

15. See appendix C for a link to an example of a college study scheduling tool.

16. Survey, Question, Read, Recite, Review.

17. Jill Barshay, "Evidence Increases for Reading on Paper Instead of Screens," *Hechinger Report*, August 12, 2019, https://hechingerreport.org/evidence-increases-for-reading-on-paper-instead-of-screens/

18. They can use the double-side setting to get the most out of their allowance.

19. SparkNotes and CliffsNotes offer these.

20. See a link to one in appendix C. https://www.naturalreaders.com/online/

21. Find a link to an example in appendix C.

22. See appendix C for a link to free downloadable graphic organizers. There are also programs for mind-mapping, such as MindMeister.

23. See appendix C for teaching resources.

24. As step 7 will explain, many DS offices expect most students to take some notes even if they're being accommodated with copies of someone else's notes.

25. This could be part of the transition packet suggested in step 3.

26. Some colleges have online tools to help students map this out. They may be called a "degree audit" or "degree progress report" or "degree evaluation."

27. See step 7 for more on this accommodation.

28. As step 1 discussed, many colleges require students to take classes in a variety of areas in addition to the classes they need for their major.

29. See step 7 for more on this.

30. See appendix A to learn more from this research.

31. Many colleges offer writing help, but some writing centers don't help with grammar and spelling. As students add colleges to their list, they can research the policies at those schools.

32. Korey Singleton (ATI Manager at George Mason University), in communication with the author, September 16, 2021.

33. Singleton, interview.

34. Singleton, interview. Read more from Singleton's interview at https://ldadvisory.com/blog/assistive-tech/

35. They'll have to be found eligible for these. See step 7 to learn more.

36. See step 5 for more on sources of support on campus.

37. See step 7 for a discussion of these.

Identifying Colleges
That Are a Good Fit

What You'll Learn in This Step

- Elements to look for in any college
- The levels of supports available at colleges
- How to research schools, degree programs, and supports
- Special considerations for students with mental health disabilities and physical/medical disabilities
- Programs for students with intellectual disabilities
- Resources for college searches

For many students, the college search represents a chance to make so many exciting decisions—what they want to study, the geographical region where they want to go to school, the size of the institution—even the kind of peer group around whom they'd feel most comfortable. There is a wide range of colleges to choose from, so they should be able to find a good match. Visiting the colleges on their list—either virtually or in person—can make their decision a little easier, as can assistance from their parents in the overall search process.

Finding the Right Overall Fit

Now that you know that colleges don't have to do a number of things for students with disabilities but that some colleges may choose to go beyond the minimum that's required of them, you may think that students should start by finding colleges that do so. You may be surprised to hear that the DS directors interviewed for this book instead recommended that students focus first on the considerations that any student's search would, and then explore the accommodations and services that each college provides.

Indeed, rather than focusing first on services, it makes sense for students with disabilities to narrow their college choices the same way everyone does: by selecting a college that is a good fit and that matches their goals, abilities, finances, and interests in terms of course and graduation requirements. Only then should they consider what the DS office is like, because—as the directors said, based on their experiences—no matter how supportive the office is, it won't make a difference if a student is unhappy at their school.

A good place to begin is by narrowing their list of "wants" so they can figure out what they should look for.

Components of a Good Fit

The elements of a "good fit" for any student include the general characteristics of a college, such as:

- location (urban, suburban, rural)
- size (of the school overall, and class size)
- cost
- faculty-to-student ratio
- how classes are run (i.e., are they mostly large lectures, small discussion groups, etc.?)
- whether group work is integrated into a lot of classes
- how students are assessed (is it mostly papers, exams, etc.?)
- choice of majors
- program structure (does it include practical experiences along with academic programming?)
- term length (does the student prefer longer terms where they study a few subjects at a time, or short ones where they study one or two for a brief period?)
- social environment (if it's centered on fraternities and sororities, is that what they want? Are there clubs that interest them? Does the university sponsor activities for students not interested in parties?)
- housing choices (are there quiet dorms? Single-gender dorms?)
- a career services office
- (for students interested in this) living and learning communities for certain majors (e.g., nursing) or interests (e.g., focused on spiritual life or environmental sustainability)

These facets of a college can help to make it a good general environment for the student.

One thing students may not be thinking about when they imagine themselves at college is that they might need help—with academics, with their mental health, etc. But it's a good idea for them to know what each college might offer in case they do need assistance.

General Support Services

Students may want to look at what supports colleges provide to the general student body. Because of their disability-related needs, these may be important. They can look to see if there is:

- free tutoring. If so, who does it, and how often can students come? Is it by appointment or drop-in only? Does it cover all subjects?
- mental health counseling. If so, do they limit the number of visits students can have each term before referring them to a private provider? Who provides the counseling?
- a campus health center. If so, can they provide daily/weekly treatments/infusions? Can they refill prescriptions? Do they administer medications?

Thinking about all of these points can help a student get started creating their list of colleges to apply to.

Requirements for Graduation and Specific Courses

Another important consideration is the college's requirements for graduation. Although these requirements apply to all students, they may be even more important for students with disabilities. Schools may vary in the core or general education classes they require each student to take in addition to the required classes for their major. Some may require two years of foreign language and/or math. Students should remember that although substitutions may be available, that doesn't mean every student who asks for them will be eligible to receive them.

Students should also check the course requirements for any majors that interest them. Again, colleges may vary in what they require, which may help them decide which schools they want to add to their list. Even if no classes are a particular worry, a student may simply decide they like (or dislike) the requirements at some schools more than others.

The list of items to consider is long, but it can help students narrow the field. And all of these points are important, since they'll spend a few years of their lives studying at the school they choose, and many students will live there, too. The college a student chooses should suit their needs as well as possible.

Once they've decided which colleges might be a good match, then it's time to think about how well the college can meet the student's disability-related needs.

Researching the Disability Services Office Online

What if a student finds a college they really like and it doesn't have a disability services office? They need not worry about this. Again, as explained in step 1, very few colleges will meet all three criteria to be exempt from following federal disability law, so it's likely that any school they want to attend will provide at least the minimal accommodations and necessary services the law requires.

Knowing this, you may be wondering—how much energy should students spend looking at each college's DS office? The degree to which the office figures into a student's search depends on their level of interest and what their needs are. If all a student wants is to receive their accommodations each term, they may not think it's worthwhile to look over the site in detail (or at all).

But even if a student knows that the accommodations they'll request are pretty standard and widely available,[1] there are some things they may not be thinking about that might make them decide against a college. For instance, some schools may implement accommodations in ways that don't appeal to the student (e.g., their peer notetaking accommodation isn't anonymous, so notetakers know the identity of the student for whom they're taking notes). Also, some colleges' course substitution policies are quite strict and may even require students to take the course in question before the school will consider a substitution. For these reasons, it's a good idea (even for a student who isn't interested in much interaction with DS) to at least review the sites at their target colleges briefly.

Navigate to the Right Page

They can start by searching in their favorite browser using the name of the college and the phrase "disability services." (They can also use the search feature on the college's website.) They may get results that show offices that have names including words such as:

- equity
- access/accessibility
- diversity
- ability
- learning or academic resources
- success

These are likely to be the correct office; some schools don't use the word "disability" in their name.

Know What They Might Find on DS Sites

Contrary to what you might expect, the laws don't provide a lot of specifics telling colleges how they must provide students with disability accommodations and services. As a result, a student may find there's a lot of variation in the way this is done at the schools on their list. It may help to know what those differences might be, so that they know what to look for.

There May Not Be a Dedicated DS Office

Colleges only have to make sure that there's someone in charge of accommodations and services; there's no mandate for them to set up an office. At College X, the person in charge might be the dean of undergraduates; working with accommodations and services for students with disabilities may only be part of what they do.

Sometimes, DS falls under the "umbrella" of the academic support center. In these situations, it may be the director of that center who decides on and coordinates accommodations.

A Dedicated DS Office May Have Only One Staff Member

Even if a college establishes an office just to serve students with disabilities, the laws don't dictate staffing levels. This means that a college DS office's single employee may be in charge of coordinating accommodations, hiring sign language interpreters, etc., and have to answer the office phone and emails, too. The college doesn't have to provide them with any support staff or increase the number of coordinators working with students if the number of students registered with the office goes up.[2]

Staff Working with Students with Disabilities May Not Have Specialized Training

The laws in place don't say anything about what degree or background people have to have to work in college disability services offices. State laws don't typically address this, either, so colleges get to decide on the requirements for anyone hired for DS positions. This means that the person making decisions about a student's accommodations may be someone with no disability-related background. They might have a degree in higher education administration or another field that isn't related to special education, vocational rehabilitation, or other areas that would give them relevant experience.[3] If attending a college where the people working in the DS office have a certain kind of background matters to a student, it's something they can research while looking at schools.

As students look at different colleges' DS sites, they may be surprised by what they find if they've been led to expect DS offices at private colleges to have more staff than those at public colleges. (Presumably, the thought behind this myth is that because private colleges charge more in tuition, they provide more staffing for their DS office.) In fact, some private colleges might not have a dedicated office, and some public colleges may have a well-staffed one. Each college individually decides what the budget and staffing will be for the DS office; institutional priorities will determine that. It's important not to make assumptions.

Basic Points to Review

Again, even if a student wants minimal contact with DS, it's a good idea for them to navigate around the DS site to get a general sense of what it offers and the processes it uses to coordinate accommodations at services.[4] They may want to think about categories of items to review.

Office Setup and Staffing

Again, if a student is interested in attending a college whose DS office has a large staff, this is something they should check. Some colleges have a single staff person, while others have coordinators who specialize in working with students with different disabilities (e.g., physical disabilities). A student who is curious about the background of DS staffers can see if the office site provides their bios.

Looking at staff lists may give a student some ideas for what positions offices might have that they hadn't thought of. For instance, there might be a learning disability specialist who works with students on strategies. This is something they can look for at other colleges, too.

Processes

Students can review the information on a college's DS site to get a sense of how they would register with DS and how long it would take. Also, they might want to look to see how they would renew accommodations after their first term.

This is a good opportunity for them to check each college's documentation requirements so they have a sense of what they may need.[5] They can also see whether they'll be required to update documentation after their initial registration.

Additionally, students can get a sense of how accommodation information is communicated to professors. They can see whether they'd have to email the information themselves or if their coordinator would send it through the office's system.

If they are interested in a course substitution, a student can see what the approval process entails. It might be less involved at one school than at others.

They can see how accommodations work, too. If they get accommodated with permission to record classes, will they have to sign an agreement about what they will and won't do with the recordings? If they get test accommodations, will they have to complete a form before every test?

Accommodations

Some DS offices list accommodations they commonly approve.[6] Students may be pleasantly surprised by what they find there; they may even learn about some accommodations they didn't know were possible. Sites may also list accommodations they don't commonly approve. Students should keep in mind these lists may just provide some examples; they likely aren't meant to be *exhaustive* (meaning they don't include every single accommodation the office provides).

A student might be put off by DS sites that state that because the law doesn't require them to make modifications (see step 1), they don't. While this may seem harsh to some students, they should be wary about reading too much into the presence of such a statement. It doesn't necessarily mean that the staff isn't friendly or supportive of students with disabilities. Some offices might state this up front because of previous experiences with students who didn't know about the exemptions and were disappointed when such requests were rejected. As one director said, "We don't want the first thing students hear from us to be 'no.'" Stating this up front might be seen as a way to avoid that.

Extras

It can help to know what kinds of services some offices provide that go beyond the minimum that the law requires of them. Some may provide tutoring, academic coaching, weekly check-ins, mentoring, or executive functioning help. Students may be able to get academic advising from someone in the office. An office might have a full-time assistive technology specialist who can teach students to use the tools for which they've been approved. (This isn't the case everywhere.) Some have special orientation experiences for students with disabilities. If it's of interest to them, students can see if there's a campus disability cultural center that organizes events to actively cultivate a community.

Contact DS to Get Answers

Be aware that DS offices may not have control over how much information they can offer on their site, or how it is presented. (The university site may have a template that isn't flexible.) Students shouldn't assume that what's on the site represents everything that is available; an office might not have a chance to showcase some of what it does.

If a student doesn't see answers to their questions, or if they just want to know what might be available that they don't see on the site, they can contact the DS office (or person in charge of accommodations). And they shouldn't be worried. Despite what they may have heard, DS doesn't take down the name of any student who calls seeking information and send it to the college's admissions office. Presumably, the idea behind this myth is the mistaken notion that colleges don't want to admit students with disabilities and that they make notations in a file somewhere to ensure that these students will be rejected. Both DS directors and admissions directors interviewed for this book were unanimous and adamant in saying this doesn't happen. Knowing this, the student should feel very comfortable seeking the information they need without wondering how it might affect their chances at admission.

Knowing how variable the offerings can be from college to college, students may be wondering how to decide how much support they'll need. It can help to have a sense of what the bare minimum looks like, and what might constitute "enhanced" services.

Choosing the Right Level of Support

One challenge for students composing a college list is that schools may vary widely in the level of support they provide for students with disabilities. It can be hard to differentiate one college's offerings from another.

They shouldn't make assumptions. Just as private colleges don't necessarily have more DS staff people, they also may not offer more numerous or more supportive accommodations than public schools. Students need to do some research.

You may have heard that some colleges offer fee-based programs for students with disabilities that go beyond the minimum the law requires. Well-meaning adults may point a student toward these schools, assuming that they are a good match for everyone with a disability, and that they all need such a program. Or they may suggest a student apply to Beacon or Landmark, two colleges that are just for students with LD, ADHD, and autism. But many students will be able to get the support and services they need without attending a special program or school. Students should figure out what services they need before opting for fee-based services or applying at one of the two special colleges. They can use this information to guide their search.

Again, getting a sense of the differences between schools' services can be challenging. Although there is no official system for categorizing them, it can help to think of DS offices as falling into one of three categories of service. Beyond schools that can be identified in this way, there are those two specialized colleges.

Level 1 Services

Level 1 offices comply with what the law requires but don't go beyond that. These offices (or the designated person, if it's a dean of students or someone similar) make decisions about accommodations and coordinate those for students. Even within this range, there can be differences. These offices provide the required accommodations but don't offer additional services that aren't mandatory.[7]

Level 2 Services

Level 2 offices usually provide more staff and services than the minimum, but like Level 1, they do so for free. Level 2 offices may:

- have a large staff
- have staff members who specialize in working with students with different kinds of disabilities
- offer students copies of useful software for their personal computer
- have a special lounge where students can study
- offer *free* structured programs for students with specific types of disabilities (such as autism spectrum disorders) that might offer career counseling or skill development

However, at Level 2 schools, there may be some limitations on the services. For instance, a student might only get to meet with a learning disabilities specialist for their first year.

It can take some time to learn to identify Level 2 services, since these are not set off from the workings of the DS office in official "programs," and there are no official guidelines to distinguish them from Level 1 services. Like beauty, the difference between Level 1 and Level 2 services may be "in the eye of the beholder." For this reason, students will have to do their research.

Level 3 Services

Schools at this level charge a fee to provide a variety of different services on a regular basis through a structured program. These programs may have limits on how many students they serve each year. A student may have to complete the application to the university and to the program at the same time, or they might not be able to apply to the program until they have been accepted to the university; it varies from program to program.

The case manager should help each student figure out what kinds of services they need; many won't need what a Level 3 program offers. For a high school student who works with a tutor or coach a few times a week, receives a lot of support during school, and/or whose family provides them with a lot of structure at home, Level 3 services may be a better choice than the others, at least when they start college.

In their interviews, directors of several Level 3 programs listed the kinds of services they provide, including:

- weekly meetings with someone they call an academic specialist[8] or counselor who might help with organization, accountability for schoolwork, problem-solving with nonacademic topics like roommate troubles
- instruction in study and organization strategies
- tutoring in academic subjects
- labs equipped with assistive technology
- special study sessions for particular classes
- writing help
- progress reports from professors
- tiers of support so that students have choices in what they receive (and pay for)
- regular communication with parents (usually students are looped in on this)[9]
- mental health counseling (beyond what the campus's center for this offers)
- career counseling (beyond what the campus's center for this offers)

For students seeking these services, a Level 3 program can be a great option. While it's good to know the benefits, they should also be fully aware of some of the limitations. They can do some research on their own and ask questions.

Compare Level 3 Programs to Other Levels

Students interested in Level 3 programs can research them thoroughly to see what they offer; they shouldn't assume each provides similar supports. They should also compare any Level 3 services to the Level 1 or 2 services offered at these same colleges, as well as at other schools they're considering that don't offer a special program. They may find that they'd be paying for a program that doesn't provide much more than they could get for free, or that DS offers everything they need.

Even Level 3 Programs Have Limits

There are some frequently requested services that Level 3 programs don't always provide. These include instructing students in social skills, having program staff contact professors, or providing assignment modifications. Students considering a fee-based program should ask a lot of questions to make sure they know what is and isn't offered.

Level 3 Program Costs

One reason it's important for a student to consider whether they need Level 3 services is that the costs can be significant. The program directors said their fees ranged from $4,050 to $8,170 per year, depending on the degree of support students used. Some schools may offer financial aid for these fees. Students should ask about this.

Fee-Based Programs May Have Caps

It's important to note that many of these fee-based programs have caps on how many students they can serve, and admission to programs may happen on a first-come, first-served basis, though one director interviewed said her program doesn't limit participation. Leann DiAndreth-Elkins, EdD, Executive Director of Disability Resources Services at Muskingum University, said the school's special PLUS program will hire any additional staff needed to support students who demonstrate college-ready skills and the motivation to participate in the program.[10]

Program Application Timelines May Vary

The timelines for submitting applications for Level 3 services may be different from college to college. Students interested in using a program should pay attention to the application process at each school.

At some colleges, students can complete both the application to the college and to the Level 3 program at the same time. What happens next may vary. Gabrielle Miller, Assistant Vice Provost and Executive Director of the

University of Arizona's SALT (Strategic Alternative Learning Techniques) Center, said that her staff doesn't review students' applications until they are admitted to the university.[11] This is true at some other colleges, too.

At some colleges, students can't apply to the special program until they have been admitted to the college. However, these schools' admissions applications may have a box students can tick to indicate that they're interested in the special program. Colleges typically add this to their application just so that they can follow up with any student who expresses such interest and provide them with further information.

Indicating interest on the application doesn't obligate a student to apply to the program later, so they shouldn't feel pressured to do so. And a student also doesn't *have* to indicate interest in the Level 3 program on their college application in order to be able to apply to it later.[12]

No Guarantees

Colleges don't have to guarantee that students get admitted to these programs, even if the only reason students applied to those schools is that they want to access these programs. They can set their own eligibility requirements and don't have to admit a student that doesn't meet them.

Even students who meet the criteria aren't guaranteed a space in their college's Level 3 program. Many accept students on a first-come, first-served basis, and they're not required to hold a space or add capacity for students who applied at a later date, after program slots were filled.

Also, students shouldn't assume that getting admitted to the program guarantees them admittance to the college, if those applications get reviewed at the same time.

Sometimes, a student isn't just looking for a lot of support for their learning—they're looking for a community. They may find it at one of the two colleges that specialize in serving only students like themselves.

Colleges Just for Students with Disabilities

Beacon and Landmark are colleges dedicated just to serving students with LD, ADHD, and autism. Their offerings include faculty trained in learning strategies, use of assistive technology and training in how to use it, ADHD coaching, and more. A student may appreciate the positive culture of these special environments. As with any other school in their search, students should consider whether these colleges are a good match for them on all of the usual points, and then consider whether they are looking for the level of support Beacon and Landmark offer.

Many students don't need the level of support provided by Beacon, Landmark, or Level 3 programs and will do fine with basic accommodations (or some of the extras offered at Level 2 schools). Directors of Level 3 programs commented that the students who get the most out of these programs tend to be those who have a level of self-knowledge about their disability and are comfortable with it. They said those who tend not to benefit are students who don't have that level of self-understanding and comfort, and who, frequently, are in the program because their parents pushed it.

Special Considerations for Searches

Many Level 3 programs are focused on students with LD, ADHD, and/or autism. Students with mental health disabilities, physical/medical disabilities, or with autism may find that the services they offer don't address their needs. A student with an intellectual disability may want to continue their education after high school. Experts who work with these students offered specialized advice and information for these students

Mental Health Disabilities

For students with mental health disabilities, academics may not be a primary area of challenge. But even if learning itself isn't a worry, the academic environment of a college may have an effect on their mental health. And if they're going to live on campus, the dorms and social environment will have an influence, too. They should think about how to find a school that meets their needs across all facets of the college experience.

Laura DiGalbo, an experienced consultant who specializes in working with students with mental health disabilities, uses the image of a three-legged stool to help people visualize the equal importance of a college's learning environment, overall campus environment, and interpersonal atmosphere. She suggests adults helping a student with their search ask them how they learn best and how much support they are currently receiving. Once they identify colleges that can provide that level of support, they can further assess the "three legs" by thinking about:

- whether the setup of classrooms at each college makes them feel comfortable
- how they feel about the dorms
- whether having classes taught by teaching assistants (instead of professors) would be less intimidating
- whether students are enmeshed in academics all the time
- how the social environment feels to them

DiGalbo suggests that giving serious consideration to each facet of a college may help a student identify their best match.[13]

Physical/Medical Disabilities

Similar to those of their peers with mental health disabilities, the needs of students with physical/medical disabilities and sensory disabilities may not center on academics. The recommendation of Annie Tulkin, Director of Accessible College, echoes DiGalbo's suggestion that a student think about all aspects of their daily life and how colleges can meet their needs. Students can ask about what colleges provide to meet their transportation or dietary needs. They can inquire about workout facility accessibility and classes, as well as student union/student center accessibility—every part of the college environment that they will engage with. Tulkin says that students with physical/medical disabilities should plan to engage with the disability support office as soon as possible in the college search process—prior to applying and absolutely prior to committing.[14]

Tulkin recommends students consider their needs holistically. Some questions to help guide the conversation for students with physical disabilities may include:

- Is the campus navigable for the student? If not, can accommodations be made in order to assist the student?
- Does the student need a personal care attendant for daily living needs such as dressing, bathing, eating, etc.? If so, how will this be funded, since colleges don't have to provide this kind of assistance?
- Does the student need access to specialists, physical therapy, etc.? Is that available on campus or in the area?[15]

A few questions for a student with a health condition may include:

- Is there a hospital on campus or nearby?
- Will they be able to manage independent living (medication, laundry, academics) by themselves? If not, what support do they need?
- If they experience fatigue, how will they navigate campus? Does the college provide transportation? Do they need a mobility device?[16]

By thinking beyond academics to their day-to-day experience, a student can identify all of the areas where they may need supports at college.

Autism

Some of the Level 3 programs already described do serve students with autism, but several of the directors interviewed for this book specifically said that some of the supports that a student may seek aren't offered in their programs. Programs that focus just on serving students with autism do offer these other services, so students might want to look at them, too.

Jane Thierfeld Brown and Lorraine Wolf, cofounders of College Autism Spectrum and coauthors of *The Parent's Guide to College for Students on the Autism Spectrum*, said families need to ask questions about what any program provides; some are more focused on social activities, not social skills.[17]

Brown and Wolf said many colleges don't offer social skills training because they've found students don't want that once they get to college—they feel they've had enough of it by that point. They said programs often focus instead on planned social activities that students can participate in so that they can practice social interactions. (These events are usually smaller than what a student would experience in a typical university event.) Some programs offer academic supports and some teach self-advocacy.[18]

Brown and Wolf suggested some questions for families to ask about these programs, including:

- How many students are in the program?
- Is the assistance offered in groups only, or is one-on-one help available?
- How often can they have contact with the professionals running the program?
- How many graduate students are employed in the program?
- How long has the program existed?
- Do people stay in the program if they sign up for the first year? If not, do they come back?
- Do they graduate? If so, how long does it take?[19]

Brown also recommended inquiring as to how many of a program's graduates are employed, as one of the challenges she and Wolf see is that academic success doesn't translate into strong employment numbers for these students.[20]

Options for Students with Intellectual Disabilities

Students with intellectual disabilities (ID) who are interested in attending college can apply just like their peers do. Like their peers, they will have to meet the requirements for admission. If admitted, they'll take the same classes and will have the right to request accommodations (or not). And if they do register with DS, they'll likely find that they receive similar accommodations to their peers with LD and other disabilities, but not modifications or personal aides. For some, this may be an appealing option.

Some students with ID may want to continue their education after high school but may not have an interest in pursuing a two- or four-year degree. Think College (www.thinkcollege.net) maintains a public directory of colleges and universities offering dedicated programs for students with ID, searchable by state, financial aid and residential offerings, and other program characteristics. The admission requirements and processes for these may vary from program to program.

According to Meg Grigal, Senior Research Fellow at the ICI/UMass Boston and the principal investigator of the Think College National Coordinating Center (a project of Transition and Postsecondary Programs for Students with Intellectual Disabilities [TPSID]), Think College programs focus on building academic and employment skills as well as strengthening independence and campus membership.[21]

Most offer students a nondegree credential that can support future employment or further education. Some may provide access to on-campus or off-campus housing, though this is not true for all programs. Grigal said financially eligible students with ID attending programs called comprehensive transition programs (CTPs) are able to receive grants (Pell/Supplemental Educational Opportunity) and work-study funds to help with expenses.[22]

Grigal's suggestions echo the guidance offered for any student pursuing postsecondary education:

- Explore the student's level of interest and goals for attending a program. (This can help narrow the range of programs being considered.)
- Consider whether the location and cost are a good fit.
- Visit the programs in person, as what is shared on a program website might look different in person.[23]

She suggests asking a student about what they want in a program, e.g., inclusive academics, emphasis on paid employment, and/or availability of residential experiences. And she noted that programs offer varying levels of support, so families need to have honest conversations with program staff about a student's needs and the family's expectations for how programs will meet those, to make sure the fit is a good one.[24]

For ID students and their families who have received very little information about college options during transition planning, Grigal recommended that school staff and other related professionals introduce them to existing resources that can help guide the student's next steps.[25] Think College offers college search tools, frequently asked questions, and a family support group.[26]

Once a student has identified colleges that are a good match, they can learn more about them by visiting.

Paying a Visit to Campus

Although thorough online searches (and follow-up phone or Zoom calls) can provide a lot of answers about prospective colleges, one of the best ways to get a true sense of a college's atmosphere is to visit it—either virtually or in person—and, if possible, to stay overnight.

Virtual Tours

Even before COVID-19, a number of schools offered virtual tours; these may be available for even more schools now as a result of the pandemic. They can be one way to get a sense of different schools, too. There may be breakout rooms where students can talk to current students, or where they can pose questions to DS staff and staff at other campus offices. Students may also want to search for sites that offer them other views of their college rather than just those that colleges themselves offer.

On-Campus Tours

Students who travel to schools on their list may want to know how much information they can expect to get about the workings of the DS office from a campus tour. Answers from admissions directors interviewed for this book typically indicated that tour guides are trained to answer a few basic questions, but if students have questions beyond that, at the end of the tour, the guide may connect them with a member of the admissions staff. If they can't answer, they'll connect the student to the DS office.[27]

A student may think that what they see (or don't see) on tours speaks to a college's view of students with disabilities. Deciding for or against a college on this basis can be a chance for them to exercise their self-determination. But there are reasons to be cautious in deciding how much weight they assign to how DS is or isn't featured on a tour.

Location of the DS Office

A student may think that if the DS office isn't housed in the center of a college's campus, that's a bad sign about how the administration views the students who utilize that office. But the determination of where DS is located may involve a lot of factors the student hasn't considered.

Sometimes, the DS office isn't centrally located for positive reasons. It may be placed in a building that's easily accessible. A DS office may have been moved to a space that isn't centrally located because the university expanded the staff and it needed more space (which is positive); there simply may not have been a closer building with enough room to accommodate it.[28]

That said, if students just don't like the vibe they get from DS being located away from the campus's center, that's something they can use to help them narrow their choices of schools to which they want to apply. It's another way in which they can exercise their self-determination skills.[29]

Inclusion of the DS Office on Tours

A student may see the inclusion of the DS office on a college tour as a positive indication of how that school views students with disabilities and, perhaps, as a signifier of the importance of the office to the school community in general. DS might be included on a tour route because it's housed in a building where a lot of other student services offices (e.g., financial aid) are housed, or it may be housed within the tutoring center. If so, DS may be mentioned in the list of resources there. But if a college tour doesn't pass the office, the student shouldn't assume the opposite, that is, that it's a negative sign. Again, the office may be a bit out of the way for positive reasons.

The student should remember that colleges serve many kinds of students (e.g., first-generation students, LGBTQ+ students), and tours may not have time to walk by all relevant resources in the limited amount of time they have. Again—they can decide that inclusion of DS in a tour is important to them; that's a great decision for them to make. They should prioritize what's important to them.

Other Admissions Events

Tours aren't the only event where students may be able to get some basic information about what DS offers, and especially if the tour doesn't pass the office, they and their family may want to see whether DS is represented at other events they attend while on campus.

For example, an important indication of the importance of the DS office may come in general overview sessions run by admissions staff. Do they mention DS? Or if representatives of different offices get to speak during those sessions, does that include someone from DS? If there is a "tabling event" where students can talk to representatives from different offices or campus services, does DS have a table? These may be better indicators of how DS is viewed at a college.

Overnight Visits

If a college offers overnight visits, students may want to consider taking them up on the invitation. A benefit of such an opportunity is the chance it gives students to get a sense of the campus during nonacademic times; as DiGalbo noted, it can often be this unstructured time that some students find most difficult. They can see whether dorms are noisy, the college environment is social or studious (e.g., are there parties on a Wednesday night? Are people studying in the library on Saturday night?), and whether the dining arrangements are comfortable for them. They can also see what kinds of structured activities the school offers (e.g., movies on campus, concerts). Students who have needs that will require support during such a visit should mention this to the admissions office arranging it, to make sure they are accommodated.[30]

How Parents Can Help

Parents may be concerned that the extra research suggested will add stress to an already labor-intensive college search and application process. Knowing the role they can play in supporting their student's development of self-advocacy and self-determination skills (which include information-seeking and decision-making), they may wonder if there's a way to help out with this research. DS directors interviewed for this book said that while it's their preference that a student contact them with questions, they are happy to talk to parents as well.

Two ways parents can assist their student in their college search are by aiding them in composing a requirements list and by providing tour and visit feedback.

Assist in Composing a Requirements List

There are a number of ways parents can help their student while teaching them some skills along the way.

They can start by working with their student to compose a list of things the student wants to know about DS offices and what accommodations they might want to request there.

By doing so, parents can model the research process, having the student observe while they:

a. search one college's DS site and take notes on what's there that answers the student's questions
b. contact that school's DS office to set up an appointment (by phone or email) to get further information
c. send an email containing questions that they and their student hope to have answered in that appointment
d. have a conversation with the DS staff and take notes on their responses for later reference

Parents can set an example and provide a template for their student's search process. They can divide up the list of colleges to contact; they can research some of them themselves and have their student research the rest. They can offer additional assistance and encouragement by creating scripts for emails and phone calls that their student can use in that research.

Provide Tour and Visit Feedback

Parents can also help their student by discussing their own impressions from college tours and DS visits. They should consider asking for their student's reactions first. If parents feel strongly that a college isn't a good match, they can share their thoughts with their student.

In order to keep the conversation objective, it can help if parents focus on their student's anticipated need for accommodations and how each college meets—or fails to meet—those needs. If their student has their heart set on a school that doesn't meet their accommodation needs, parents can encourage them to work without such accommodations in a high school setting as a "test drive" for the college setting.

Available College Search Resources

Do students engaged in the college search process need to start from square one—or are there resources, such as a list of the "best" schools for students with dyslexia, that can help to jumpstart their search?

There are some resources available, including lists, a book, and online databases. Each has its limitations, so a student should consider them a helpful starting point in composing a list of schools but recognize that they'll have to go beyond the information they provide in order to fully research their target colleges.

Lists of "Best" Colleges

There are a number of "best" lists available online, but they may be too broad to be helpful and their criteria for ranking schools isn't always transparent.

An online search is likely to turn up some lists created by consultants, parents, students, or online platforms. One benefit of these lists is that they may introduce students to some colleges they've never heard of.

The challenge with trying to use one of these "best" lists is that each student has their own individual needs, and what makes some colleges better than others for them (or "best") will vary. Students should look to see if the compilers of any of these lists explain how they decided to put a college on the list. Do they explain what these do better than other colleges?

Also, most of these lists don't specify what kinds of disabilities the colleges serve well. What a student with a physical/medical disability needs will be very different from what a student with ADHD needs. Lists found online may not make these distinctions.

Students may also find that some lists only include schools with fee-based programs. Again, this can be helpful if they learn about schools and programs that weren't on their radar. But as already noted, a lot of students don't need such programs, so they shouldn't assume from these lists that they need to attend one of those schools.

Perhaps the best way for students to use these lists is to find colleges that are unknown to them and then probe them (as discussed in the beginning of this step) to see whether they're a good match. But they should be wary of assuming the colleges included in them are an appropriate fit for them and their individual needs. To help them, they may want to seek a well-researched, comprehensive guide.

The K&W Guide

The only consistently updated published guide available is *The K&W Guide to Colleges for Students with Learning Differences*, currently in its 15th edition.[31] In an interview for this book, Imy Wax said that she and coauthor Marybeth Kravets collect information from schools every two years through use of a questionnaire sent to several thousand two- and four-year schools.[32]

Wax noted that—given how many colleges exist—this book could not possibly include all of them. This means that a college's absence from this guide doesn't mean that it doesn't provide accommodations. She said that she and Kravets sort through the responses they receive and try to pick colleges representing a wide range of school types and offering a range of services and accommodations. But Wax said the book can't be seen as a be-all and end-all.[33]

The K&W Guide presents each school's information according to the same template. Wax commented that some colleges may interpret the same question differently, so answers may not be directly comparable from school to school. Also, sometimes the services a college lists on its profile may be offered specifically for students with disabilities by the DS office, or they may be offered to all students at the general campus tutoring center, counseling center, etc., but that won't be clear from the way the college answered the question. Also, because the surveys are collected every two years, specialized programs may open (or close) between one edition and the next. Wax said that K&W readers should consider the information there as a starting point, and verify the information they see there by contacting the schools.[34]

Also, the fact that a college is listed in the guide as offering certain accommodations doesn't necessarily mean those accommodations are available to all students. As always, they have to be found eligible. And Wax added that the fact that a college is listed in the guide doesn't mean that students should take that to mean they'll get admitted.[35]

The K&W Guide can be helpful to students who like to have a print resource. But others may prefer to find information online. There are two resources they can explore.

The NCCSD Database

Campus Disability Resource Database (CeDaR), the free database from the National Center for College Students with Disabilities (NCCSD), presents information about each college's DS office, gleaned from questionnaires it sent to nearly 4,000 colleges in 2021. (Not all responded.)[36] Students can search the site by state or refine their search to include items like size, degree type offered, and three types of special supports for students with disabilities.

If a college didn't respond to the questionnaire, that school's page in the database will simply provide a link to its disability services office on the college's own page. When a student clicks through to a school's page, they'll find the information on the school's page is organized in a template, similar to the way K&W Guide presents it. A student can see some information about the kinds of disabilities the DS office had served in the previous three years, some accommodations they had commonly provided, as well as additional details. This site can be a starting point to gather some basic information, and then students can contact these offices with their follow-up questions.[37]

CollegeWebLD.com

An additional online resource is CollegeWebLD.com, a site created and run by Judith Bass, a college consultant who has specialized in working with students with learning disabilities and ADHD for decades. The information provided is gathered through questionnaires and the data Bass and her colleagues have gathered over time. At the time of this writing, users can access some of the information about each college for free; with a paid subscription they can access narratives the team has written reflecting their impressions of the schools.[38]

It's important for students to research the on-campus support options available to students with disabilities at colleges they're interested in attending. But they don't have to limit themselves to what the college offers. If a college they like overall doesn't have the services they need, they may be able to find them elsewhere.

Seeking Off-Campus Supports

A student may find that the colleges that seem like the best fit for them overall lack the enhanced services they need. Even so, they may not have to cross those schools off their list. Instead, they can look for supports available off-campus that can provide what they require to be successful.

For example, a student may realize they'll need help with their executive functioning skills once at college. If the schools on their list don't offer this, they may be able to get this help from a tutor or coach who works remotely. This isn't currently an area where someone can earn a degree, certification, or licensing, so families may want to ask questions about any consultant's training and how this person would work with the student. For instance, they may want someone who at least has some experience working in special education. (This may not matter to the student.)

A student who been working with a coach, tutor, or therapist during high school may want to continue with them in order to ease the transition into college. When it comes to some kinds of professionals, such as psychiatrists and therapists, licensing requirements may restrict them from offering telemedicine or teletherapy. The student should ask about this before they leave for college.

Online assistance may prove especially helpful for a student planning to attend a college in a rural location without easy access to public transportation and without a high concentration of relevant professionals working nearby. If this is the case, they may want to make sure they've found someone to work with remotely before they make their final college decision.

It's important to note that outside consultants do not have any standing to interact with the college on a student's behalf. DS staff members and professors aren't required to confer with an outside professional about a student client, even if the student wants them to. That said, some college staff members and professors may be amenable to this.

Beyond learning and mental health needs, some students may require support for their medical needs but find that the colleges on their list don't have a health center, and some may be in remote locations where the nearest pharmacy isn't close by and access to public transportation is limited.[39] They might want to check with their insurance company to see whether they can get a 90-day supply of their medication and/or receive their medication by mail.

A student with medical or other kinds of needs may get approved for an aide, but since colleges don't provide those, they'll have to find one on their own. They may be able to connect with the local vocational rehabilitation office to locate a helper. (This may be more of a challenge for students attending rural schools.)

Seeing what is and isn't available to them in the way of supports, and understanding the demands of the college environment, a student might decide that immediate transition to a traditional four-year school after high school isn't what they want to do. There are many different pathways they can take.

Exploring Alternatives to a Four-Year College

The focus of postsecondary transition planning should be on what a student's goals are and what they need to achieve them. Moving directly from high school to a four-year college won't be every student's goal.[40] If a student's desired career doesn't require a four-year degree, they might prefer to attend a career and technical education (CTE) school or earn a two-year degree or certificate at a community college. They'll finish more quickly, spend less money, and be ready to start their career sooner.

One commonly heard piece of advice is that a student with learning disabilities and/or ADHD or a student with autism should start their postsecondary education at a community college. Hopefully, this book has made it clear that immediate transition to a four-year environment can be an appropriate choice for many of these students. There are accommodations and supports available there. If a student shows the necessary amount of independence by the end of high school, there isn't a reason to hold them back from attending a four-year school, assuming that this is their preference and that it would advance their goals for their future. (The same advice applies to their neurotypical peers.)

Attending a Community College

A student may have a desire to attend a four-year school but may not feel ready to go immediately after high school. They may not feel prepared for the level of self-management they'll need and may need time to develop the skills they'll require in the absence of supports and modifications they've received in the past. (Again, this applies to many neurotypical students, too.) They may want to start by studying at a community college.[41]

Easing Into College Life

Starting at a community college can allow students to adjust to the demands of the college environment by working up to the academic expectations there. And if they live at home (the community college may not provide housing), they can adjust to the academic demands alone, rather than also having to adjust to the social demands of the on-campus living environment at the same time.

A Stepping Stone to Four-Year Schools

Success at a community college can provide an inroad to state schools. In many states, students who successfully complete their two-year degree at a community college are automatically eligible for admission at some or all of the state's public four-year institutions. They should also be aware of what are commonly called *articulation agreements*, which usually indicate which of the classes that a student takes at the community college will count for credit for certain requirements at the four-year schools—both for the general education requirements and toward certain majors. Students who hope to go on to a four-year school from a community college can ask their academic advisor about these agreements and use them to guide their course selection.

It's not just public institutions that open their doors to community college transfers. Many private universities do, too. A student who didn't get into the four-year college they hoped to might take classes at a community college so that they can reapply to their target school, hoping success at the community college will show the four-year school that they're ready.

Students interested in this should check with their target college about how many openings they typically have for transfer students. If those slots are limited, they may need to limit how many credits they earn before applying, as it may make the difference between applying for admission later as an incoming freshman (for which there are many more openings) versus as a transfer student. And some private colleges have special programs or schools for students who started college and then stopped going to college for at least a year (the reason why doesn't matter). Examples include Temple University's Bachelor of General Studies program and Mount Holyoke's Frances Perkins Program.

Some students might decide that they need a break from school before starting college. They may decide to work for a time. Or they can explore a gap program.

Taking a Gap Year

A student may be feeling burned out (especially post-pandemic) and feel that attending any kind of school immediately after high school isn't the right choice for them. If they've been accepted to the college they want to attend, they can ask to defer their enrollment. They may want to take some time to learn some skills they'll need at college, engage with therapies that may be time-consuming, or they may want to travel. There are gap programs that offer a lot of different options.

What Students Should Ask

Students with a disability may be interested in traveling, interning, or doing something different as part of a structured gap experience, just as their neurotypical peers do. Jane and Jason Sarouhan, cofounders of J2Guides, offer some advice for what they should ask about gap programs they're considering:

- What is your experience with how your program has impacted students and their ability to manage their disability?
- What are the qualities of students who do well in your program?
- What can students expect from their relationships with program staff?
- (After the student has described themselves and their disability), do you think this program is a good fit for me? Can you support my needs? (Parents may wish to offer their view of their student's needs, too.)
- What are the ground rules for the program?
- How do you choose your leaders? What training does your program provide them in working with students with medical, mental health, and/or learning issues?
- Is it possible to have weekly contact with their therapist during this particular experience? (Families will need to make sure that any professionals students work with are allowed to do telemedicine or teletherapy according to state laws where they're licensed.)
- If a student takes medication, how is that handled in this program?
- What happens in minor or major medical situations?[42]

Jane Sarouhan commented that they have seen students with sensory disabilities (e.g., students who are legally blind) go on gap experiences, and at the time of her interview, she was exploring options for a student who used a wheelchair. Students who are interested should see what's possible! And they should ask specific questions about how such programs can meet their needs.[43]

For students seeking one, there are a few programs designed just for students like them.

Gap Programs Just for Students with Disabilities

Jason Sarouhan reported that there are some gap programs designed just for students with learning disabilities or ADHD, though there aren't many. They include Ingenuity Year, SOAR, and Inventive Labs. He said some of these programs focus on building executive functioning and/or other skills. A student can find out what kinds of activities these programs offer, and they should ask about items like housing, if they don't live nearby.[44]

What about Accommodations?

It's important to keep in mind that the disability laws discussed in this book apply only to the United States; if students choose to go abroad, they should know each country will have its own laws. Also—gap-year experiences aren't covered by the parts of Section 504 or the ADA that apply specifically to colleges. There's no specific language around them, so families shouldn't assume they will provide similar supports.

Jason Sarouhan said, "Students who have been on an IEP or 504 plan for a long time may assume they'll need accommodations on a gap experience. But that may not be the case because many programs' fundamental function is to help students 'step up into' themselves. Many of these gap experiences will be able to support these young adults."[45]

Jane Sarouhan added, "Families need to ask these kinds of questions early in the process, before a student falls in love with a particular program that won't be able to meet their needs. This is why being transparent with a program from the beginning is so important. Gap-year programs and families have the same goal: being sure that the programmatic experience can truly support that student."[46]

Final Thoughts on Postsecondary Choices

Jason Sarouhan made a comment about choosing a gap program that may prove apt when thinking about a student's college choice. He said:

> Gap time is about students stepping out of their comfort zones, but there's a difference between *stretching* them and *stressing* them. Choosing gap experiences that a student is ready for takes into account identifiable areas where a student will be stretched but successful, and balances those with areas that feel easy and comfortable.[47]

This could prove to be a good rule of thumb for decisions about colleges, too.

Additional guidance comes from Jennifer Walker, Dean of Admissions and Financial Aid at Brandeis University. She encouraged students to find a college "that feels like home, academics that challenge them appropriately, and a community and services that will support them as they grow into an adult."[48]

Summary

Choosing a college can be exciting, but it's important that a student fully explores any school they're considering to make sure it will suit them in every way. The amount of time they spend researching supports will be guided by the level of involvement they hope to have with DS, but any student should at least look at what different colleges offer. They can find information online and in person, and parents can help them throughout the process. For those who aren't ready yet, there are other great postsecondary options. And for those ready to go straight to college, their next step will be applying for admission.

Notes

1. See step 7 to learn which ones are, or aren't.

2. This is true at colleges where there isn't a dedicated DS office, too. Going back to the example, College X wouldn't have to provide the dean of undergraduates with support staff to assist in the coordination of services and accommodations even if the number of these students kept growing.

3. This doesn't mean they can't be very helpful and supportive. But this is why it's so important for students to have self-knowledge of their needs and accommodations and strategies that work for them.

4. Find the link to a video demonstrating how to do this research in appendix C.

5. See step 7 for more on this.

6. Students should remember that they would need to be found eligible for any accommodation they request. See step 7 to learn more.

7. See step 7 for a discussion of commonly approved accommodations and those that aren't commonly approved.

8. Be aware that colleges can call anyone they want a "specialist." This person doesn't have to have any particular educational or professional background.

9. Some directors said that they didn't communicate with parents regularly.

10. Leann DiAndreth-Elkins, EdD (executive director of Disability Resources Services, Muskingum University), in conversation with the author, March 17, 2022.

11. Gabrielle Miller (assistant vice provost and executive director of the University of Arizona's Strategic Alternative Learning Techniques Center), in conversation with the author, November 12, 2021.

12. DiAndreth-Elkins, interview.

13. Laura DiGalbo (consultant), in conversation with the author, January 6, 2022.

14. Annie Tulkin (director of Accessible College), in conversation with the author, January 5, 2022.

15. Tulkin, interview.

16. Tulkin, interview.

17. Tulkin, interview.

18. Jane Brown and Lorraine Wolf (cofounders of College Autism Spectrum and coauthors of *The Parent's Guide to College for Students on the Autism Spectrum*), in conversation with the author, December 6, 2021.

19. Brown and Wolf, interview.

20. Brown and Wolf, interview.

21. Meg Grigal (senior research fellow at the ICI/UMass Boston and principal investigator of the Think College National Coordinating Center), in conversation with the author, January 6, 2022.

22. Grigal, interview.

23. Grigal, interview.

24. Grigal, interview.

25. Grigal, interview.

26. See appendix C for a link to the site.

27. Admissions directors interviewed for this book said that they don't keep a list of students who ask about disability services for the purposes of rejecting them when they apply. See step 6 to learn more.

28. One admissions director interviewed for this book spoke with pride about how DS is located in a revered building in the center of campus; to him, it *was* representative of how the college values its students with disabilities.

29. Again, this said, for students with physical disabilities, the location of an office could be a deal breaker, especially if that office itself is inaccessible to them.

30. DiGalbo, interview.

31. Imy Wax (coauthor of *The K&W Guide to Colleges for Students with Learning Differences*), in conversation with the author, December 15, 2021.

32. Wax, interview.

33. Wax, interview.

34. Wax, interview.

35. Wax, interview.

36. Richard Allegra (director of information and outreach, Association on Higher Education and Disability), in conversation with the author, March 1, 2022.

37. Find the link to CeDaR in appendix C.

38. Find the link to Bass's database in appendix C.

39. Colleges don't have to provide students with transportation off campus to allow students to get to medical or therapy appointments or to pick up medication.

40. Community, family, and cultural norms may inform students' choices. See appendix B to explore how professionals can examine their own cultural lens when working with CLD students and their families on a student's postsecondary goals.

41. Note that in step 6, a DS director from a community college reported that they don't modify assignments and tests, so going to a community college likely won't be a way for students to receive supports they wouldn't typically get at the four-year level.

42. Jane and Jason Sarouhan (founders of J2 Guides), in conversation with the author, January 4, 2022.

43. Jane Sarouhan, interview.

44. Jane Sarouhan, interview. For a link to the Gap Year Association's site, which contains a list of programs, see appendix C.

45. Jason Sarouhan, interview.

46. Jason Sarouhan, interview.

47. Jason Sarouhan, interview.

48. Jennifer Walker (dean of admissions and financial aid at Brandeis University), in conversation with the author, September 20, 2021).

~

Applying for College Admission

What You'll Learn in This Step

- What the law says about disability disclosure in the admissions process
- Information that may be included in paperwork the high school sends to colleges
- Advice on disclosing a disability—how to decide and what to say
- What the law says and doesn't say about college admissions requirements
- How some colleges show flexibility in their admissions policies
- Advice on submitting SAT or ACT scores

When students apply to colleges, it's their chance to paint a picture for the admissions office. Through their essays, their history, and other information they provide, they'll show colleges who they are and who they hope to become.

It can be an exciting time, but it can also be a time of anxiety, not just for students with disabilities but for all students. Colleges can't admit everyone who applies for attendance, so students may work hard but not get into some of the schools they like.

For students with disabilities, their concerns may be raised or worsened by things they hear from others about the admissions process and how colleges view applicants. They may also be concerned about what information the high school will provide about their disability and wonder whether they should say anything about it. They may wonder what role their disability

127

plays (or doesn't) in admissions reviews if they do decide to disclose or if information provided in the school paperwork does this.

All team members should have facts at hand to make sure students have accurate information guiding them through the process.

Facts about Disability Disclosure in the Admissions Process

A student may hear all sorts of things about the admissions process and wonder where their disability comes into it. They may wonder what colleges are allowed to ask them, what information their high school might share, and whether they have to disclose their disability if they hope to receive support for it once they enroll.

Disability Inquiries Are Not Allowed

Disclosure of a disability is totally voluntary in the college admissions process. Colleges can't ask students about this, except in a very rare situation.

At § 104.42(b)(4), Section 504 says colleges "may not make preadmission inquiry as to whether an applicant for admission is a handicapped person but after admission, may make inquiries on a confidential basis as to handicaps that may require accommodation." This means that colleges can't ask an applicant whether they have a disability before they are admitted, but once a student gets in and enrolls, their college can contact them to let them know about the availability of disability accommodations.

There is one kind of circumstance where a college is allowed to ask students if they have a disability at the point that they are applying. At § 104.42(c), the law says colleges that are "taking remedial action to correct the effects of past discrimination" can do this. A college that has previously gotten in trouble for excluding students with disabilities and is now trying to make up for that past discrimination can ask students if they have a disability, presumably so that it can make sure it admits some students who do. Examples of colleges being found to have discriminatory admissions practices are so unusual it's not worth diving into the details.

School Documents May Disclose Information

As part of the application process, the high school guidance department will send a copy of a student's *transcript* (list of courses the student took and grades earned each year) to each college to which they apply. They'll also send a high school profile or description. Students should know what these documents might or might not reveal.

Transcripts

When admissions staffers look at a student's application, they review the transcript the high school has sent. What can it say about them and their disability?

The U.S. Department of Education says that "it would be a violation of Section 504 and Title II for a student's transcript to indicate that a student has received special education or a related service or that the student has a disability." It does say, though, that "a transcript may indicate that a student took classes with a modified or alternate education curriculum. This is consistent with the transcript's purpose of informing postsecondary institutions and prospective employers of a student's academic credentials and achievements."[12]

What this means is that parents shouldn't keep their student from having an IEP or 504 plan in high school, preventing them from having the accommodations and services they need, for fear that this would be noted on their transcript. If the team is considering placing a student in a modified class that would be noted on the transcript, they should make sure the student understands this.

This information about what transcripts don't say also counters another myth you may have heard that is a variation on this idea—that a student who has an IEP should be moved to a 504 plan before their senior year because (as the thinking behind this seems to be) colleges view 504 plans more favorably. Admissions directors interviewed for this book were unanimous in saying they'd not seen transcripts indicating that students had had IEPs, 504 plans, or used accommodations, and they're not allowed to ask about disabilities in the process, so the kind of plan students had wouldn't even be a consideration.

Even so, students who don't want to disclose their disability might wonder how admissions staffers would respond to the appearance of a learning disabilities support class on their transcript.[3] Admissions directors insisted that they do not use information about a student's disability to include or exclude them.

What they said is that their primary focus in looking at transcripts is to check whether a student took the courses that would give them the preparation needed to do well at their college. Rick Clark, Assistant Vice Provost and Executive Director of Undergraduate Admission at Georgia Tech, remarked that because his is a *STEM* school (meaning it's focused on science, technology, engineering, and math), the admissions process focuses on the student's performance in classes they took related to those areas.[4]

Directors emphasized that when they do take note of classes where students receive support, admissions reviewers just see this as part of a larger picture. Mike Langford, Director of Undergraduate Admissions at Western Carolina University, said, "To me, it would be no different than if you took Chorus or Band. Even if it was listed as Study Skills—to us, that says students are serious about their academics and are trying to get ahead. It would not be a deterrent for us."[5]

The transcript will tell admissions staffers about what classes a student took and how they did in them. To provide some context to what the transcript shows, reviewers will typically reference the school profile that accompanies it.

High School Profile

Along with a student's transcript and application, the high school will also send a school *profile*, or description, to each college to which a student applies. This profile may include some information about the demographics of the community where it's located, the curriculum of the school, admission or state testing score averages of a recent graduating class, and more.

Admissions staffers may look to this profile to see how students have challenged themselves, given the opportunities for this at their high school. For instance, they may look at whether a student took Advanced Placement (AP) classes. Certainly, some schools don't offer all of the same courses others do. The profile helps admissions staffers understand this.

If a student attends a school just for students with disabilities, they should know that the school profile will likely state this fact. This may cause them to worry about how their transcript will be evaluated alongside those of their peers who attend different high schools. When asked about this, directors were unanimous in saying that they look at those transcripts through the same lens they use for transcripts from other high schools—they're looking at a student's preparation for the academic environment at their college, and how they challenged themselves given what they *could* study.

Knowing that the profile of a school will state that it serves students with disabilities, parents may wonder whether sending their student to a specialized school could affect their college admission chances. They may be reassured by something Vice President for Enrollment Management at Xavier University of Louisiana Keyana Scales said in her interview: "There are many situations where high schools that specialize in serving students with learning challenges and learning differences position them much better to master academic concepts than more mainstream high schools. I don't know of any institution that thinks about these specialized schools in a negative way."[6]

For some students, the paperwork sent by the school will not indicate that they have a disability. But students who want to use accommodations through the DS office or access a fee-based program may wonder whether they have to disclose their disability in order to do this, and whether applying for a special program will result in the admissions office knowing about their disability.

Disability Documentation Shouldn't Be Included with the Admissions Application

High schools won't send a student's disability documentation (e.g., testing, IEP or 504 plan, SOP) along with the transcript and school profile. No matter what decision they make about disclosure, the student shouldn't send these materials either, unless they're required to do so as part of the application to a fee-based program (where it will go straight to the program staff). If a student does send documentation to a college, the admissions office will likely set it aside without considering it in their review of the student's application. And there is very little chance admissions will send it to the DS office should the student eventually be accepted and enroll, as it's unlikely staffers will note in their records that they have that information so that they can later send it on. Students should be aware that the time for sending documentation is once they've enrolled at the college they'll attend.

Disclosure Is Not Required for Students to Later Seek Services

Students should know that they don't have to disclose their disability anywhere in their college application in order to register for accommodations once they are admitted and enroll. Colleges can't preclude a student from registering with DS if they didn't mention their disability before they were admitted.[7] They shouldn't feel any pressure to disclose before that time.

Admissions Doesn't Review Applications for Level 3 Programs

As discussed in step 5, colleges have different timelines for when a student can complete the application for a Level 3 program. They may have to wait until they're admitted to the college, or they may be able to complete it at the same time they submit their application for admission to the college. If they can apply to the college and the special program at the same time, the disability paperwork will likely only go to the program; admissions staff won't review it. This means that a student could apply to a Level 3 program without indicating in their application to the university that they have a disability.

Disclosure Will Not Give the Student an Advantage

In their interviews for this book, admissions directors encouraged students who want to disclose their disability to do so. This may cause a student to wonder whether there's an additional incentive to do this beyond allowing admissions reviewers to get a full picture of who they are. They may have heard a myth that students *should* disclose their disability when applying to college because it will put them at an *advantage* in the admissions process. Admissions directors all said this wasn't true.

Clark expressed things this way—"There's no formula being used where we put an asterisk next to a student's name if they do or don't have some kind of background that puts them in a special category for admission. That's not the way this works."[8]

Still, students applying to colleges that have fee-based programs might wonder whether disclosing their disability could boost their admissions chances, on the assumption that the college will want to make sure all program slots are filled. Directors of such programs who were interviewed for this book said that neither applying to the program at the same time they apply to the college nor ticking a box on the application that indicates their interest in their program provides students with a "leg up" in the admissions process.[9] Their response also echoed what admissions directors said—that colleges can't consider disability as part of their admissions decisions, even if it's to the student's (perceived) advantage.

Disclosure Won't Put a Student at a Disadvantage

One commonly shared myth says that students shouldn't disclose their disability when they apply to college because doing so will put them at a disadvantage in the admissions process. This myth assumes colleges seek to exclude students with disabilities and that disclosure would give them the chance to reject these students.

One source of encouragement refuting this myth comes from Jeremiah Quinlan, Dean of Undergraduate Admissions and Financial Aid, who said in his interview—"Yale welcomes students representing a wide range of diversity,"[10] a sentiment echoed in the comments of other directors. When asked about this myth that disclosure would negatively affect a student's admissions chances, all of the directors said they understood the anxiety the admissions process can cause for any student, and that it might be even more anxiety-provoking for a student with a disability, but that this statement about disclosure was false and was based on a misguided idea of how the admissions process actually works.

No Data is Publicly Available on Admission Rates for Students with Disabilities

You may wonder whether there are statistics showing the college acceptance/ rejection rates for students with disabilities that might help them decide whether to disclose. While colleges may publish these rates for their overall pool of applicants, none publishes specific rates for students with disabilities (and it's unlikely that they privately analyze their data for this kind of specific point). Even if a college did want to look at this, remember that *they could only count the students who disclosed their disability in their application.* They would have no way of knowing whether some of the students who applied had a disability they didn't disclose; they could only count those who did.

Given all of this information, and knowing it's up to them to decide whether or not to disclose, students may wonder what they should do. Comments from a variety of admissions directors may be helpful to them.

Advice from Admissions Directors

Students thinking about disclosing may know the facts but still have trouble deciding whether it's a good idea for them. In their interviews, admissions directors and college admissions consultants who specialize in working with students with disabilities shared their thoughts.

Disclosure Helps to Complete the Picture

A common thread running through comments from directors was that they wanted to have a full picture of a student, and that disability is included in that. Gregory Moyer, Assistant Vice President for Enrollment and Director of Admissions Recruitment at Dickinson College, said, "They should give us the complete sense of who they are. If they choose to discuss their disability, it could add important context that helps us understand them in a different or deeper way, and in that way, it could add value to their process."[11]

Some reiterated their suggestion that students disclose. Quinlan said, "It helps us get a better understanding of you as an applicant."

Directors were also unanimous and adamant in stating that it was illegal for them to consider disability as part of their decision-making.

All encouraged students to share this information in some way but they also emphasized the importance of a student's deciding for themselves what they wanted to do. If a student does choose to disclose, directors noted they could use either the essay or the section that asks if they want to include additional information—it was up to the student to make that choice.

All of the directors said their school uses a *holistic* admissions process, meaning that they don't just look at scores and grades but consider the full picture of a student created by all parts of their application. Information about a student's disability can be a part of that.

Disclosure May Explain Anomalies in Test Scores and Grades

Sometimes disclosure can fill in certain gaps that transcripts alone are unable to explain. In their interviews for this book, college admissions consultants said that they encourage students they work with to disclose when there is something on their transcript that they want to explain. For instance, if a student's learning disability isn't identified until later in high school, and their grades go up as a result of receiving accommodations and learning helpful strategies, students might want to explain that. If a student applies to colleges that require scores and their math score is low because of their learning disability, they might want to explain that. And of course, if a student simply wants to tell colleges about their disability, they can.

One admissions director who works at a school in a state university system said that if a student's transcript didn't show all of the courses that system requires, an admissions counselor would reach out to them to ask why. If the student hadn't already disclosed their disability and chose to do so at that point, this director said that their application might get moved forward for review, but they shouldn't assume it would mean they were guaranteed admission.

Other universities might not reach out to a student in this way, but if they do, this director encouraged students to respond. This is an opportunity for them to provide more information that could help round out a college's view of who they are.

Understanding that disclosure is voluntary and may help colleges to have a better understanding of them, a student may decide to do it. What they may want to know next is the best way to provide information about their disability.

How to Disclose

Students who plan to disclose may get advice from people they know about what they should say and how they should say it. Admissions directors and experienced college consultants gave their advice on how to disclose in an effective way.

Keep It Simple

No matter which section of the application students use to discuss this, the directors recommended that they be matter-of-fact in talking about how their disability impacts them and what strategies they use in response. Several directors suggested that students avoid being dramatic in their descriptions. Clark said, "If students talk about it in a way that discusses a challenge they've overcome or adapted to, or even if they mention it matter-of-factly, it may be something admissions considers as adding value to the community they're attempting to create."

Directors also recommended they ask a trusted advisor to look over what they've written before submitting their application. Sacha Thieme, Assistant Vice Provost and Executive Director of the Office of Admissions at Indiana University Bloomington, said "I always advise students to think about the fact that this information will be read multiple times by multiple people, including school admissions committees and (if they apply for them) scholarship committees. I suggest they provide context to their application with their disclosure, but they don't have to feel compelled to share every detail in their application that they might with someone they know well."[12]

"Own" the Disclosure

Students who choose to disclose their disability should address it head-on. Comments from Belinda Wilkerson, independent educational consultant and founder of Steps to the Future, LLC, reflected another theme in the consultants' recommendations. She said, "I find it really effective when they're talking about their disability that they really 'own' the conversation. They can talk about their disability. They know what they need. They're fully immersed in what their disability is."[13]

Accentuate the Positive

Asked what approaches students should take in disclosing, advisors recommended emphasizing the positive. "The key is for students to present themselves as someone who's adaptable or resilient," said Eric Endlich, founder of Top College Consultants.[14]

Provide Disclosure in a Recommendation

When a student applies to college, they typically have to ask one or more teachers, a coach, or another adult who knows them well for a letter of recommendation. Their school counselor also typically includes a letter they've written about the student when they forward the application to a college.

One way for a student to make sure their disability is disclosed is to ask their school counselor or teacher to mention it in the letter they write for them. The student can politely request that the writer not make the disability the sole focus of the letter and that they emphasize the positive. On the other hand, if students prefer that these letters not reveal their disability, they might find it helpful to mention that to any well-intentioned counselor or adult writing a letter about them.

Once students learn that they don't have to disclose their disability, and nothing in their admission packet will do this, they may still be looking for information to help them decide what to do. What they may want to know is this: if something in their application, accompanying letters, or other paperwork discloses their disability, what does the law require in terms of how the college treats them?

What the Law Says about Admissions Policies and Disabilities

You already know that disclosing a disability in their application neither provides a student with an advantage nor puts them at a disadvantage. But even though admissions directors said they see a disability as part of the whole picture of who a student is, a student may wonder if that disclosure means colleges have to treat their application differently than they do other students' applications. It can be helpful to know what the law says about college admissions policies. Does it require different admissions standards for them? Does it allow colleges to place a cap on how many students with disabilities they admit or require that they admit a minimum number of these students? Does it allow colleges to require that students take admissions tests like the SAT or ACT?

Colleges Don't Have to Alter Their Admissions Standards

Colleges can't refuse to admit students just because they have a disability. At §104.42(a), Section 504 says, "Qualified handicapped persons may not, on the basis of handicap, be denied admission or be subjected to discrimination in admission or recruitment." This means that if a student discloses their disability in some way in their application, a college can't refuse to admit them *simply* for this reason.

But an important word there is "qualified." As discussed in step 1, the definitions provided in a different part of the law at § 104.3(l)(3) provide clarification that "qualified" means that the person "meets the academic and technical standards requisite to admission or participation in the recipient's education program or activity." So any applicant also has to be *qualified* for admission, according to a college's requirements. There isn't an exception for students with disabilities.

While the law doesn't say so explicitly, this means that a college doesn't have to make any exceptions to its admissions requirements for students with disabilities. It just has to make sure that its admissions requirements aren't designed to screen out students with disabilities. If University X requires applicants to have a 4.0 GPA and to be a state-ranked athlete and first chair in the state youth orchestra, it does not have to admit a student with a disability who doesn't meet all of those standards. Since many students who didn't have a disability couldn't meet such requirements, they likely wouldn't be seen as discriminatory.

Colleges Can Require Certain Classes for Admission

Since colleges get to determine their "academic and technical standards," this means that a college *can* require students to have taken certain classes in high school in order to be considered eligible for admission, and it doesn't have to make exceptions for students with disabilities. For instance, a college that requires applicants to have taken foreign language in high school isn't required to admit a student who didn't, even if the reason they didn't take it was their disability. Remember that there could be other reasons why a student who doesn't have a disability didn't take those classes (e.g., their high school didn't offer foreign language). So a requirement that applicants take certain classes likely wouldn't be considered discriminatory.

Colleges Can Require Admissions Tests

You may wonder whether colleges can require the SAT or ACT, given that test-taking is something that many students with disabilities struggle with. Section 504 says that colleges can't use tests that have a "disproportionate, adverse effect" (§ 104.42(b)(2)) on students with disabilities and that measure their impairments instead of their ability (§ 104.42(b)(3)(i)). The boards that administer these tests address these mandates by providing accommodations. For instance, a student with slow processing speed might get accommodated on the ACT or SAT with extended test time. This way, their score would reflect what they know and can do, rather than how quickly they can respond to test items.

The law goes on to say that admissions tests should reflect a student's aptitude instead of their "impaired sensory, manual, or speaking skills (except where those skills are the factors that the test purports to measure)." For instance, a student found eligible to use a calculator on an admissions test wouldn't be able to use it on any parts of the test that measured calculation skills, but they could for other portions of the math section.

While you may think that the ACT and SAT have a "disproportionate, adverse effect" on students with disabilities (and you wouldn't be alone in thinking this), there isn't currently anything preventing colleges from using these tests in admissions decisions. This means that colleges can require them.

There Is No Admissions "Disability Cap"

Students don't have to worry that a college will only admit a certain number of students with disabilities. Section 504 says colleges can't have such a limit (§ 104.42(b)(1)). This means that a student doesn't have to worry that, for instance, if College A has *rolling admissions*,[15] it might run out of slots for students with disabilities if the student applies in the second half of their senior year of high school.

Remember that colleges can't ask about disabilities in the admissions process. So even if College A was trying to keep out students with disabilities (in violation of the law), it would only be able to count the number of students who mentioned their disability in their application.

What the Law Doesn't Say

Given that colleges can't cap the number of students with disabilities they admit, you might wonder whether the law *requires* them to admit a certain number of them. In short, it doesn't, so students shouldn't expect that simply by saying they have a disability in their application, they might have a better chance at admission because colleges have to meet a certain quota.

To return to schools with rolling admissions, they don't have to set aside a certain number of admissions slots for students with disabilities who apply later in the year. Every student gets the same chance at admission, and those with and without disabilities who delay applying may find there aren't any spaces left for them.

Some Colleges Are Flexible with Their Admissions Policies

It may seem disappointing that colleges don't have to make any exceptions to their admissions requirements for students with disabilities. One thing to keep in mind is that they can always choose to do so. In fact, colleges may admit students who don't meet their requirements, but they may not make this information public. Some colleges publicly show flexibility by establishing an alternative admission process for students who don't meet their state requirements. And others leave it up to the student to decide whether or not to submit their admissions testing scores.

Admission By Exception

Some colleges have a formal application process for students who don't meet their stated requirements. For instance, the University of California system's schools offer "admission by exception" for students who don't meet the minimum GPA or haven't taken the required classes in high school. This policy applies to all students in this situation; it's not just for students with disabilities. At the time of this writing, students who want to try this can either write about their unique circumstances or answer some supplemental questions the system provides.[16]

Other colleges may offer a similar policy. Students should ask about this at colleges that interest them.

Test-Optional Policies

Colleges are allowed to require that students take admissions test, and a number of schools do. But at the time of this writing, more than 1,800 colleges currently have adopted *test-optional policies*, meaning that they "do not use the SAT or ACT to make admissions decisions about a substantial number of their incoming freshmen classes."[17]

This means it's up to the student to decide whether to send their scores or not. (Their high school doesn't do this.) College admissions consultants interviewed for this book suggested that students look at the range of data colleges post showing where previously admitted students' scores fell and—if they find themselves at or above the 50th percentile—submit their scores.

Joan Casey, founder and lead consultant at Educational Advocates College Consulting Corp., added one additional consideration. She remarked that SAT/ACT score ranges for the previous year's graduating class may be included in the high school profile sent to colleges along with the student's application. If a student's score is at the top of that range for their own school, Casey suggested they submit their scores, because admissions offices evaluate students within the context of their own high school.[18]

Summary

When applying for admission, students should be aware of what colleges can and can't require from them according to the law. In addition, they should separate the facts about disclosure from the various myths that swirl around this decision and consider the recommendations of experts before making their own personal choice as to whether to disclose their disability or not. And for those who aren't ready yet, or who would rather do something else, there are other great postsecondary options. For those who are ready, the next and final step will be to assess the accommodations they will need in college and to understand how to request them.

Notes

1. "Questions and Answers on Report Cards and Transcripts for Students with Disabilities Attending Public Elementary and Secondary Schools," U.S. Department of Education, 2008, https://www2.ed.gov/about/offices/list/ocr/letters/colleague-qa -20081017.html

2. "Questions and Answers on Reports Cards and Transcripts," U.S. Department of Education.

3. An example of such a class might include a period each day where students earn credit by working with a special educator on developing learning strategies or getting pre-teaching or supplemental instruction for their general education classes.

4. Rick Clark (assistant vice provost/executive director of admissions, Georgia Tech), in conversation with the author, August 19, 2021.

5. Mike Langford (director of undergraduate admissions, Western Carolina University), in conversation with the author, August 10, 2021.

6. Keyana Scales (vice president for enrollment, Xavier University), in conversation with the author, November 2, 2021.

7. Remember that disclosing their disability in their application doesn't equal registering with DS, so even if a student does this, they still must follow the registration process anyway once they enroll (if they want to use accommodations).

8. Clark, interview.

9. If the student ticks a box on the application, directors said this simply functions as a trigger for admissions staff to send the student's name to program staff so they can follow up and provide information about the program.

10. Jeremiah Quinlan (dean of undergraduate admissions and financial aid at Yale University), in conversation with the author, November 8, 2021.

11. Gregory Moyer (assistant vice president for enrollment/director of admissions recruitment at Dickinson College), in conversation with the author, January 25, 2022.

12. Sacha Thieme (assistant vice provost/executive director of admissions at Indiana University), in conversation with the author, November 2, 2021.

13. Belinda Wilkerson (independent educational consultant and founder of Steps to the Future, LLC), in conversation with the author, January 4, 2022.

14. Eric Endlich (founder of Top College Consultants), in conversation with the author, December 21, 2021.

15. This means they review applications at the time they come in throughout the year, rather than making all of their decisions at the early and regular admission deadlines.

16. For details, go to https://admission.universityofcalifornia.edu/admission-require ments/freshman-requirements/admission-by-exception.html

17. "Test Scores Do Not Equal Merit: Executive Summary," FairTest, August 22, 2007, https://www.fairtest.org/test-scores-do-not-equal-merit-executive-summary

18. Joan K. Casey (founder and lead consultant at Educational Advocates College Consulting Corp.), in conversation with the author, September 21, 2021.

~

Requesting Accommodations

What You'll Learn in This Step

- What documentation requirements may be
- How the DS registration process works
- What documentation students will need
- What accommodations are commonly approved, and some that aren't
- Students' options if their accommodation requests aren't approved
- What students can do if their needs change
- How professionals can help students in thinking about accommodations

Once students are accepted to and enrolled at the college they'll attend, their attention may turn to exciting tasks like shopping for the items they'll need for their dorm room and completing a roommate compatibility questionnaire. One of the things that may not be on their mind at this time (unless they plan to request a housing accommodation) is getting registered with the disability services office. But at a lot of colleges, this is something that can and should be done before they start at college, whether it's move-in day for students living on campus or before the first day of classes for students who will be living at home.

As already discussed, students will need lots of different kinds of skills to be successful. Accommodations alone are not enough to help a student do well in the college environment, but they can be a helpful tool, and registering for and using them should be part of a student's plan.

It's important to remember that:

- Students have to register with DS if they want to receive accommodations; this is true even if they disclosed their disability in their college application.
- If a student doesn't want to use accommodations, no one will (or can) "make" them register with DS.
- If a student does register and finds they don't need their accommodations, no one will (or can) "make" them use them.

You may have heard that if students didn't disclose their disability when they applied to college, they can't register for accommodations once they've enrolled. This is false. Make sure students know that it is their right to apply for accommodations at any point, and that no prior notification to the school is required.

The DS Registration Process Step By Step

As already noted, colleges don't ask students directly if they have a disability. Information about how to register may be included with other paperwork or emails a student receives when they are first accepted, or after they enroll. The process is fairly straightforward. Typically, the student has to:

1. Complete a form, which may ask them what accommodations they hope to receive.
2. Submit their documentation showing they have been identified as having a disability.
3. Meet with someone at DS to discuss their requests (this is sometimes called an *intake meeting*).

Sometimes they'll get DS's decision during the intake meeting. Sometimes, they'll hear afterward. (Processes vary. Students should ask how long they can expect to wait for a response.)

As noted in step 1, students are responsible for all of the parts of the process. Students in some studies said they didn't register upon first starting at college because they thought the process was too time-consuming, or they didn't know what to do.[1] Giving students a few details about the process may make it seem less onerous and may help encourage students to follow it.

When to Register

When should students register? The DS directors agreed that students should contact the office as soon as they are enrolled and have a student ID number. (This is necessary at some schools, since students go through an online system for the DS process.) Some directors said that no matter how early students register, though, they don't conduct intake interviews until closer to the start of school, sometimes even after students have registered for their classes. This way, DS can see what complications might be involved in some of their accommodations (such as requests that might be seen as fundamental alterations). One director said they prefer to have these meetings closer to the start of school because they explain the DS processes at that time and have found that when they've done the meetings earlier, they have to review everything for students again later.

Remember—a student can register at any point they want. However, accommodations begin the day they're approved; they're not *retroactive*, meaning the college doesn't have to allow "do-overs," a grade adjustment, or the dropping of a grade if a student who registers after classes have begun thinks they might have done better if they had used their accommodations.

If they didn't see the information about how to register in the materials they received when they were accepted or enrolled, students can do a search using the name of the college and the terms "disability services" and "registration." Or if they prefer to start right on the college's site, they can type those terms into the search window there.

Once they get to the right page, students can look for something that directs them to the process in a clear way. If they don't see it, they can try clicking on anything that says "new students"; this typically means students recently admitted to the college or who have already been attending classes and are not registered with DS yet. They'll likely find the process there. If they can't, they should call the office for help. (Sometimes, students will see a tab or link for *prospective* students. This usually refers to students who are just looking at the college or who have applied but not yet been admitted. The information they seek might be there, too.)

Completing the Registration Form

At some colleges, the form students have to complete will be a PDF that they can either fill in online or print out, complete, and then scan and upload (or they can mail or drop off the physical copy). At some schools, they'll need their student ID number to log into a system, and they'll complete the form there.

These forms typically ask for some basic contact information. Additionally, they may ask students:

- what specific accommodations they want to request
- how their disability affects their schoolwork and other activities of their daily life
- how the accommodations they're requesting help them
- what accommodations they've received in the past (and what helped or didn't)

It's important to stress that there are no "wrong answers" to these kinds of questions. DS offices are trying to get a sense of a student's awareness of their needs and maybe get some additional information about why they are requesting specific supports. As noted in step 2, the team can help students prepare to answer these questions. And again, the student should ask for whatever they want.

At the time they upload or complete the form online, students will likely be asked to submit disability documentation. They can prepare this ahead of time.

Scheduling and Attending the Intake Meeting

Students typically have to attend a meeting with someone from DS. Answers from DS directors interviewed for the book indicated the scheduling process for this varies. At some colleges, students need to set the appointment up on their own at the time they submit their registration form, while at other colleges, DS will contact them to set up that appointment once they've received a student's form.

How Long Will Students Wait to Get DS's Decision about Their Requests?

Asked how long it takes them to tell students whether they've been found eligible for accommodations and—if so—which requests were approved, DS directors gave a range of answers. Some directors said that they have already reviewed and decided upon the student's accommodations before the intake meeting, and they give them their NOA (notification of accommodations) during it. Others said that they like to get more information from the student during these meetings to help inform their decision. For those who said they didn't give students their answer in the meeting, the range of responses indicated it could take anywhere from a day or two to two weeks from the intake appointment for the student to learn what DS has decided. A student who is curious about this can ask at the time they submit their registration form.

Even if a student learns of DS's decision through a discussion in the intake meeting, they should ask for this information in writing (they'll likely get an email) and retain it as a formal record in case any questions or problems should arise.

Clearly, the overall DS registration process isn't time-consuming, and students shouldn't see it as an intimidating experience. DS staff is trying to get as much information as they can so they can determine what students need.

Before they sit down to initiate the registration process, students should gather what they'll need. An important part of the paperwork will be their disability documentation.

Gathering Required Documentation

As part of the DS registration process, students will likely be required to provide documentation to show that they have a disability and require accommodation. This might seem strange, especially when most were identified as having a disability early in their education and received services without question throughout their K–12 years. While a history of having received accommodations may help to support students' requests, colleges still get to decide how much weight they'll give that history in deciding whether a student is eligible for the accommodations they've requested.

Contrary to what you may have heard about documentation:

- Colleges don't have to accept a student's IEP, 504 plan, or SOP as stand-alone documentation; they can require testing;
- Testing for learning disabilities may not need to be less than three years old;
- Students with learning disabilities or ADHD likely won't need to have a neuropsychological evaluation instead of a psychoeducational evaluation.

The truth is that the laws in place don't say anything about documentation. Students may find one of the above statements is true at the college they attend, but that would be because that's what that college decided their requirements would be, not because of anything said in the laws. As a result, requirements can vary widely from school to school. For example, College A may rely solely on students' self-report to determine their eligibility for accommodations, while College B might require (for LDs, most commonly) testing that was done in the last three years, and College C might require testing for students with LD that was done in the last five years. A recent study looked at the DS sites of almost 300 colleges and found that 10 percent said that a 504 plan, IEP, or SOP was sufficient as stand-alone documentation. (The review didn't report on schools that didn't require *any* paperwork.)[2]

Students shouldn't assume they know what a college will require. They must look up the documentation requirements for the college they'll be attending. It's a good idea for them to do this as soon as they enroll.[3] In that way, if they need to gather information from their high school for that purpose, they can reach the people they'll need to talk to before everyone is off for the summer break.

All students should be able to find their college's documentation requirements by going to the college's website, typing "disability documentation" in the search window, and following a link from the list of results. If they don't see a direct, obvious link there, they should click on any link that appears to be for the disability services office. As mentioned in step 5, the office name may not include the word "disability." They'll know for sure once they click through.

Once they get to the right page, students may see a list of general requirements for documentation. In addition to (or in place of these), they may also see specific requirements for different kinds of disabilities.

General Requirements
On the DS sites for some colleges, students may see a list of requirements for any and all documentation. It may contain the following elements:

- age of the report/letter/information
- qualifications of the evaluator
- clinical interview
- history
- testing scores and narrative
- clinical summary
- conclusion/diagnosis (some schools may require a code for this) or rule out of a disability
- recommendations for accommodation

A lot of these elements won't apply to all kinds of diagnoses. Here's what you should know about each:

- Age—The requirement for the age of documentation is one of the things that may worry team members most, and it may be the subject of the majority of myths you may hear.

As they look at their college's DS site, students may see very specific requirements (e.g., testing that is less than three years old). This may vary by disability type, i.e., a student with LD may be required to have documentation that is "fresher" than a student who is Blind/VI.

Sometimes, DS won't provide a specific number to indicate how old documentation can be; they may just say that they want "current" documentation (with no further specifics provided). The definition of "current" can vary from college to college, too, and from one disability to another. Some DS directors interviewed for this book said that for students with medical or mental health disabilities that might change over time, "current" may mean within the last few months or year. When it comes to documentation for LD, ADHD, and autism, the directors generally just said that it needed to be "current." Only one specified that they wanted to see something completed within five years of a student's start at college (for students coming right after high school).

Many directors said they don't commit to a number to define "current" because they want to be able to be flexible on this point, and they may find that the entirety of the information they get about the student (between the intake meeting and the paperwork) is sufficient to help them make a decision.

- *Qualifications of the evaluator*—Colleges may specify that the person writing the report must have a PhD (not just a master's degree). However, if the people doing assessments in a school district have a master's and are licensed/certified by the state to do evaluations, this is unlikely to be a problem.

  Some colleges may also stipulate that any person writing a report for a student must have training in assessing adults. It's unlikely they will ask to see a report writer's background. Also, even if their requirements say that the person doing the evaluation has to have experience in assessing adults, colleges are unlikely to reject a school district's (or private examiner's) testing if they don't have it.

  Additionally, some schools may require that a medical doctor provide documentation of certain conditions; they won't accept paperwork from a nurse or a related professional, such as a therapist or nutritionist.

  Colleges may also require that the person providing documentation be qualified in the appropriate area of expertise. For instance, a college might not accept an ADHD diagnosis from a podiatrist.

  One additional common point students may see in lists at a number of colleges is that they don't accept documentation from a member of the student's family or a family friend.

- *Clinical interview*—This won't be appropriate for all types of disabilities, though it should be part of any evaluation for a learning disability, ADHD, autism, or mental health disability.
- *History*—No matter what the disability, any good report should have this.
- *Testing scores and narrative*—Testing won't be appropriate for every kind of disability Testing is typically only required for students with LD, but students with ADHD and autism can check with the college they'll be attending. It's possible they may need this if they are asking for academic accommodations.
- *Clinical summary*—Again, any good report should have this. Any professional should provide an overview of the history and how they weighed this along with their own findings to reach a conclusion.
- *Conclusion/diagnosis (or rule out)*—Any letter or report should be clear about what the examination or testing found, or if it failed to find something. When it comes to the conclusion/diagnosis, some schools may require a code from the *Diagnostic and Statistical Manual of Mental Disorders-5 (DSM-5-TR)* or International Classification of Diseases 11th Revision (ICD-11). School district evaluations may not contain such a code, and private ones may not, either. If students are worried, they can contact DS at the college they'll be attending and ask how strict they are about this. The college is likely be flexible about this point.
- *Recommendations for accommodations*—The person writing the report should support their recommendations by relating them to the impact of the student's disability.

Although team members may worry because many reports from school districts don't contain some of the points in this list of requirements, this should not be a cause for concern. Colleges are unlikely to reject a student's school district documentation because it lacks elements such as a clinical interview or history.

DS offices are accustomed to receiving documentation from school districts, and staff members are likely aware that school evaluations don't include all of the points in their list of requirements. For instance, because a student likely would have had to go through some kind of referral process before being evaluated by the district (including observations/comments from teachers, some attempts at intervention before testing, a review of their history, etc.), they may decide that they don't need to see the student's history. Colleges may also assume that anyone doing evaluations in a public school district has the necessary licensing/certifications, since the state likely requires this. If students are worried, they can contact their college's DS office.

Independent evaluations students pursued outside of the district may be held more strictly to the list of requirements because a history of documented issues isn't presumed. Even so, colleges are unlikely to reject reports from privately done evaluations that don't contain every item on that list.

That said, families who pay for an evaluation on their own *should* expect to see all of those elements in a write-up they get from a professional they hire independently. In order to make sure they receive a high-quality report, a family can ask anyone they're thinking of hiring for a *redacted* report (where the personal information about a student is taken out). They can review this sample of the person's work to make sure that the evaluation write-up they would get for the student would be a quality one.[4]

One thing you should note about this list of requirements—it applies mostly to students who have a learning disability (and it may be relevant for those with ADHD and/or autism). Students with other types of disabilities may find that their treating professional simply has to fill out a form or write a letter that includes certain information. All students should check the requirements for the college they'll be attending.

When it comes to requirements for students with learning disabilities (and possibly ADHD and autism), colleges may have additional specifications for what testing should include. It may be helpful to know what those are.

Requirements for Students with LD

If a college requires testing for a student's evaluation, the DS site may state what kinds of testing should be in a student's documentation. Across schools, students may see the same three components listed: tests for cognitive ability or aptitude, achievement, and information processing.

1. *Cognitive ability or aptitude*—This includes testing of a student's reasoning, working memory, processing speed, and verbal comprehension.
2. *Achievement*—This includes testing of a student's reading, writing, and math skills, and sometimes their oral language skills.
3. *Information processing*—This includes testing of a student's memory, auditory and visual perception, and processing speed.

Colleges may provide lists of different tests that are commonly used to test these areas, too. Anyone providing evaluations for students with LD should be familiar with these.

Item 3 can cause team members to worry unnecessarily. Even though information processing is listed as a separate area to be tested, these skills are typically assessed with the kinds of tests used for item 1, so as long as a student has been tested with one of the testing *batteries* (groups of subtests) or a similar one, it's very unlikely the college will not accept their report.

In addition to listing the testing DS requires, an office might also list reasons why a student's report might not meet the requirements. These include limited testing and use of tests that aren't meant for adults.

One reason a college might not find a student's report meets the requirements is that the *examiner* (person who did the testing) didn't administer all of the tests that make up the standard battery for one or all of the measures administered. Most test batteries have a certain number of subtests that have to be given in order to calculate certain scores. If an examiner skips some of these, the report may not meet the college's requirements.[5]

The same may be true if the examiner used what's called a "brief" battery. Publishers put out versions of their main tests that include only a few subtests. If an examiner used one in a student's evaluation, the college might not accept the report.

One point some DS sites mention is that they require that students be assessed with tests normed on adults. This is typically only a problem if a student was evaluated with the Wechsler Intelligence Scale for Children–5 (WISC–5) which can be used up until a student turns 17.[6]

Sometimes, a DS site will list certain tests they don't accept—typically because they're not comprehensive enough. As long as a student's testing also contains other measures that test the same skills, it's unlikely that a college would reject their testing simply because it *contained* one of those tests. If a student's documentation contains any of the tests that their college's site says it doesn't accept, they shouldn't panic. They should contact DS and ask what they recommend. DS may suggest they submit the report anyway and they may accept it. A student shouldn't seek out new testing until they are sure their college won't accept what they have.

Requirements for Other Disabilities
For students with ADHD or autism, or with a physical/medical, sensory, mobility, or mental health disability, their college might require a letter from the person who diagnosed/identified the disability or from the current professional treating the student (if applicable). Or the college may require that the appropriate professional complete a form that asks specific questions about a student's functioning (e.g., "How does the student's disability affect him or her in the classroom?"). Again, students should be able to find this information online.

As suggested in step 2, schools can prepare students for the DS registration process by helping them put together a transition packet before they graduate. Documentation is one of the items to put in there. The other is a list of accommodations students want to request at college.

Making a List of Accommodations

As step 1 discussed, colleges have to provide accommodations for students with all kinds of disabilities, and they have to do so across all aspects of their programs—not just in the academic setting. It's impossible to know how many different accommodations are offered at colleges across the country. DS directors interviewed for this book mentioned several accommodations they do and don't commonly approve, and those are represented here, but their lists weren't exhaustive.

Ideally, high school case managers will help students prepare a list of accommodations they want to request before they graduate from high school and help them take notes they can use explaining why these accommodations are appropriate for them. Students can use this list and their notes as a resource to complete the registration form and/or in their intake meeting. (They won't just hand the list over to DS.)

If students and/or team members want to go beyond the list provided in this book, they can look at a few DS office websites; some offer lists of accommodations they approve, and these may provide ideas for accommodations they didn't know were available.

A little research will show that many of these lists look similar to each other in what they include. Some DS sites may group accommodations by setting, meaning that they list accommodations they provide in the classroom, testing situations, housing, etc.

Lists aren't typically divided up by disability category (e.g., a student with ADHD gets *this* specific list of potential accommodations), though some may be. This is because two students with the same disability aren't likely to have identical needs, and the college will match each student's accommodations with what they see as their needs.

If a college's DS site doesn't list accommodations, that doesn't mean it doesn't offer any. It may simply mean that the amount of content the office can post is limited by the site's template.

If the college's DS site does provide a list of accommodations they offer, the student shouldn't take this to mean that these are the *only* ones available, either. The office may have decided to highlight just a few accommodations—perhaps the ones commonly requested by their students.

When they make their requests, students should know that there are no "wrong" answers to the question of what accommodations they want. They should ask for everything they think they need, even if they are aware that an accommodation isn't commonly granted at the college level. They also shouldn't hesitate to ask for accommodations they haven't received in the past. Their college won't necessarily reject an accommodation simply because their high school did; they'll make their own decision about whether it seems appropriate to the student's disability and is appropriate at the college level.

For any accommodation they request, they should be ready to explain why it's appropriate for them, given the specific way their disability affects them. In other words, just saying "I have ADHD" likely won't be sufficient to support their requests; they'll need to say specifically how their disability affects their everyday functioning.

Also, students don't have to worry that if they make one request that DS doesn't think is appropriate for some reason, DS will also reject all of their other requests on that basis. And they shouldn't be concerned that if they request numerous accommodations, DS will say no to everything because they asked for too many. DS will consider each accommodation a student requests individually.

Students do need to remember that even if the accommodations they want are listed on the DS site, this doesn't guarantee that *they* will be found eligible for those specific ones. And even if they are found eligible for something by DS, in some classes or programs of study, a specific accommodation might represent a fundamental alteration. This said, they should ask for whatever they want! It's possible they'll get it.[7]

The list that follows includes accommodations commonly granted for academic settings, as these were the kinds mentioned by the directors, likely because students with a variety of different kinds of disabilities request them. It is by no means complete, and it doesn't cover accommodations for other parts of a college's programs like dining services, so don't worry if you don't see a particular accommodation here. (Contact a few colleges' DS offices to see if they offer the one you're curious about.) There are accommodations that are more procedural, and then others that are specific to what happens in the classroom and on tests.

General Accommodations Related to Academics

When a student considers what they'll need in college, they may envision themselves completing academic tasks, which may cause them to focus their attention on accommodations they'll need in class and on exams. They should know about some other accommodations that relate to academics but may not be obviously academic in nature. These include a reduced course load, priority registration, course substitution, text and materials in alternative formats, and flexibility with attendance.

Reduced Course Load

This can be an appropriate accommodation for students who are concerned about handling their academic workload. Federal grant money (e.g., Pell Grants) is linked to how many credits a student is taking, so that may be reduced. The student can speak to the financial aid office about how this could affect them. It's possible that the college might offer some private aid to make up the difference, though they aren't required to do so.

Priority Registration

Colleges may deem this appropriate for students who take medications that have peak effectiveness at certain points during the day, those whose medications may interfere with getting to sleep if they take them late in the day in order to focus in night classes, or those who have medical issues that necessitate a certain kind of daily schedule. Depending upon the college's policy, a student may get to register before the entire general population of the college, or they might get to register before others in their graduating class (e.g., before the rest of the sophomores). But even if they receive this accommodation, the student should know that colleges don't *guarantee* that students will get the classes they want. (Such a guarantee is not an accommodation.)

Course Substitution

Although colleges may argue that making substitutions would result in a fundamental alteration to their programs (see step 1), all of the directors interviewed for the book who work at colleges that have a math and/or foreign language requirement said they have granted substitutions. Some said they don't see a lot of requests, while others noted that they have had to say no to some because of a student's chosen major.

Remember that colleges aren't required to grant this just because a student received a waiver at their high school. Students have to be found eligible according to the college's standards. This may be more challenging at some colleges than at others.

When it comes to substitutions, DS usually serves in an advisory role; at many colleges, they aren't the body that makes the decision. A number of colleges have committees or administrators who make the decision about a substitution, guided in part by DS's recommendation.

And even if a substitution is approved, a student's major might require the courses in question anyway. For instance, a DS director at an arts school said that a voice performance major might have to take a foreign language because many operas are not written/performed in English. And some science majors will require students to be able to complete some levels of math. Students in these situations might decide to choose a different major if they don't think they can complete the requirements.

If a student is granted a substitution, the college will probably have a list of approved courses they can take to satisfy the school's requirement. As noted in step 4, the student approved for a substitution should research their options to make sure the class they take won't be more challenging than the class for which it will serve as a substitute.

Texts and Materials in an Alternative Format

There is a variety of formats colleges will offer to students who are Blind/VI, such as Braille and electronic text (also called *e-text*). If DS can get an electronic copy of the texts a student needs directly from the publisher, they'll do that. (Remember that students have to purchase the copy of the text they need; DS's job is just to facilitate that purchase if they can't get the electronic copy on their own.) If the readings students have to do aren't available as e-text, DS will scan and convert them into e-text that can be read by text-to-speech software.

Students with reading disabilities can request e-text, too. As noted in step 2, if DS finds them eligible for this, the student will be required to purchase the same books or packets as their classmates, but DS won't charge a fee to make them accessible. And some colleges will offer a student a copy of a text-to-speech program to load to their personal computer, but they don't have to.

Flexibility with Attendance

DS directors said that they typically only approve this for students who have a mental health or physical/medical disability that causes severe, brief episodes where they can't attend class as a result. If approved, a student may have to follow some sort of protocol about communicating with professors or DS about this. Colleges may have policies dictating how much time students must be in a class in order to earn credit for it; professors may set their own requirements.[8] If a student exceeds the number of absences approved, they may have to take an incomplete and finish the class within a certain amount of time after the term ends, or they may have to withdraw and take the class again if they need it to graduate.

These accommodations might be seen as being focused on general processes where a student's disability may create a need for accommodation. Since college is an academic setting, schools provide a number of accommodations in the classroom.

Classroom Accommodations that Are Commonly Approved
There are a number of ways that students with disabilities can be accommodated in a classroom setting. These include being granted permission to record classes and/or to use a laptop for notetaking, and to receive copies of notes from a classmate.

Permission to Record Classes

When they approve this accommodation, DS offices don't expect a student to listen to an entire lecture over again (unless the student likes to do that). Instead, they may advise the student to use a strategy of making a mark in their notes when they miss something the professor said (or noting the number on the counter, if their recording device has one). Later, when they go over their notes, the student can scan to that part of the recording to catch what they missed.

Students may be able to use their phone as a recording device. Some colleges loan out "smart" pens that have digital recorders in them; these devices track the recording to a student's handwritten notes with use of a special notebook. (Students have to buy their own notebooks, as these are their own school supplies.) Because that smart pen would be a personal device, colleges can choose to loan these out, but they don't have to provide these or any other device, even when they approve a student to record lectures as an accommodation. Some DS offices also offer software that helps with notetaking (such as Glean or Otter AI). The accommodation is the permission to record, not the device or software with which a student can record.

Students may need to sign an agreement if they are approved to record a class. This may require them to agree that they won't share the lecture recordings or post them to the internet.

Sometimes, a professor will tell a student that even though DS approved them for permission to record, the student can't do this because the lectures are the professor's intellectual property. But Section 504 specifically says colleges "may not impose upon handicapped students other rules, such as the prohibition of tape recorders in classrooms" (§ 104.44(b)). Even though the technology has changed, the idea is still the same. Students should alert their DS coordinator immediately if a professor raises this kind of objection.

Permission to Use a Laptop for Notetaking

At some colleges, using a laptop to take notes in class is not something students will need permission to do. But some professors have no-laptop policies for their own reasons. Again, if DS has approved this and professors object, the student should not assume professors will contact DS to discuss their objection. They should contact their coordinator immediately.

Permission to Receive Copies of Notes from a Classmate (Peer Notes)

When asked about commonly approved accommodations, the DS directors interviewed for this book didn't indicate this was something they approved frequently. Some said they approve it occasionally for students who physically can't take notes, not for those with LD, ADHD, or autism. Some directors said that they accommodate students who have asked for copies of someone else's notes with one of the notetaking programs already mentioned. Policies will vary from college to college.

If a student is approved for copies of peers' notes, it may not be an anonymous process. In other words, notetakers may email the notes directly to the student (meaning they'll at least know the student's email address, which may include that student's name). At some colleges, notetakers upload their notes to a system, and the students approved for them download the notes. Processes vary.

Commonly, notetakers are identified by having professors read a statement to the class asking if anyone wants to do this. (Some schools offer compensation to notetakers; others don't.) If class has gone on for more than a week and no one has stepped up, students should contact their DS coordinator. They shouldn't assume the professor will do so, or that DS is aware they don't have a notetaker yet.

Also, many DS offices view the purpose of the designated notetaker's notes as being to supplement or fill in the gaps in the student's own notes. At the time they are approved for notes, students should ask their coordinator whether they are expected to take their own notes. They'll likely be told that they are.

Whether classes are based on lectures, discussions, or labs, students with all kinds of disabilities will be accommodated for in-class activities. The same is true for exams.

Exam Accommodations that Are Commonly Approved

Classroom accommodations are intended to help students have access to class content. Often, students will have to demonstrate the knowledge they've gained in class by taking exams. Students found eligible may receive accommodations such as extended test time, the use of text-to-speech software, a reduced-distraction site, the use of a laptop and/or a calculator, and permission to take breaks during the course of the exam.

Exam accommodations tend to be worded in a specific way. This is because the wording used is intended to specify details about how those accommodations look. It can be helpful to introduce high school students to the specific vocabulary college DS offices use as you work with them on the list of accommodations they want to request. This way, they'll get the sense of what they can and can't expect.

Extended Time

Students coming out of high school may request "untimed" exams or "unlimited time for exams" because that's what their IEP or 504 plan says. But most colleges won't agree to either of those specific requests because if they approve one and a student wants a week to take each exam, they'll have to provide it.

Again, that doesn't mean that if a student asks for untimed exams, their college won't give them any extra testing time simply because they didn't use the appropriate wording. Instead, DS will substitute an appropriate accommodation.

The college may give a student what's called 1.5 times (maybe listed as 1.5x or 150 percent time), meaning that if the class gets two hours to take an exam, the student approved for this would get three hours. Students may also request double time (2x or 200 percent), but at some colleges, the bar to receive that might be high. For students requesting double time (or more), DS may instead provide other accommodations (such as use of text-to-speech software) that could help the student finish more quickly. (Spending a lot of time on exams isn't fun for anyone.)

Sometimes, students request extra time for exams because they use strategies to calm themselves or refocus, but their documentation doesn't support the approval of extra time because their processing speed, academic fluency, and other relevant scores aren't weak. These students might instead be accommodated with breaks during testing.

Breaks

Sometimes a student doesn't need more time to work on exams but needs to regroup mentally for a few minutes without worrying about running out of time as a result. Or they may have a physical disability whose management requires a break. In these cases, they may get a short break in the middle of testing. If a student is allowed to leave the room for these breaks, they might get only get a few pages of the test at a time that they must turn in before exiting, and they may not be allowed to revisit those pages when they return.

Use of Text-to-Speech Software

Rather than giving them a human reader, a college is more likely to accommodate a student who has a reading disorder or who is Blind/VI with a laptop loaded with text-to-speech software that will read them the exam. However, for some kinds of exams that the software doesn't handle well (e.g., math), DS may assign a reader.

Reduced-Distraction Site

In high school, a student might be accommodated with a private room for testing. Some colleges have testing centers where students can take their tests in a private carrel or booth, which can help to reduce distractions. This typically means they'll be in a room where they'll be aware of other students also taking tests at the same time. At some colleges, the student may take their tests in a small space that is totally enclosed and where they can't see or hear others. In these settings, a proctor may observe them through a window or by video camera.

But some colleges don't have a testing center, and many don't have enough room to provide every student who's eligible with a private testing space. Instead, a student may be allowed to take their exam in a different room from the rest of the class along with a small number of peers and a proctor. Students who are very distractible can request to use noise-canceling headphones (which the college would provide).

Even if they don't think they need a private testing room, a student might request a "distraction-free" testing environment. Instead, they're likely to be approved for an accommodation that's worded to say they'll have a "reduced-distraction" testing site because it's not possible to guarantee that students won't be distracted, no matter how quiet DS tries to make the environment.

Students who ask to be tested in a separate room because they *subvocalize* (meaning they read or think aloud while problem solving) should note this in their request so that DS knows this is why they want it.[9] A student approved for this may be put in a room away from others, or they may be provided with use of a device that allows them to speak aloud without disturbing anyone. For those who need this accommodation because of a reading disorder, they may instead be granted use of text-to-speech software for exams and headphones so the sound doesn't disturb others.

Use of a Laptop

If a student is approved to use a laptop during an exam, they'll likely have to use one provided by the college, unless they have a specially adapted one to accommodate a physical disability. If a student asks to use this because their spelling skills are weak, they may encounter situations where correct spelling of terms is part of what the professor is measuring, so use of the laptop with spellchecker would be a fundamental alteration. But this isn't likely to be a problem.

Use of a Calculator

In many college math classes, students *have* to use a calculator, so this is unlikely to be an issue, unless a professor is assessing a student's basic math skills, as they might do for teachers in an elementary education major who will be expected to complete calculations on the board for their own students. Otherwise, this is unlikely to be an issue for most students.

Again, there are many more accommodations that colleges grant than are discussed here, and for all kinds of disabilities. The accommodations discussed here are presented simply to provide a sense of what is commonly approved for students with a variety of kinds of disabilities. As already noted, though, there are a number of accommodations that aren't commonly approved. Students should ask for whatever they want, but it's a good idea for them and members of the team to know which ones aren't typically granted so that they can help students prepare for that before they graduate from high school.

Accommodations Not Commonly Approved

Because of the changes in mandates and expectations, there are a number of accommodations students commonly request that DS offices don't often approve, though they might do so for a very small number of students who request them. Those include modifications to tests or assignments, certain exam accommodations, requests for extended deadlines for assignments outside of class, copies of a professor's notes, and advance copies of PowerPoint slides. There are likely a number of requests that get denied each year that aren't included here. Those that appear below are the ones commonly mentioned by the directors interviewed for this book.

Modifications

As discussed in step 1, colleges don't have to approve anything that would "fundamentally alter" a class or program. In high school, students may be accustomed to writing shorter papers than their classmates, having alternative assignments (such as creating a video instead of writing a paper), having to complete fewer math problems, etc. In colleges, these are very unlikely to be approved.

Similarly, alternative forms of testing aren't commonly approved. For instance, a student may ask to take a fill-in-the-blank test instead of an essay test, or to be allowed to write fewer words for an essay test than their peers. If they took multiple-choice tests in high school, they might have had some of the possible answers omitted by the teacher so they'd have fewer to choose from. This isn't typically approved at the college level. Sometimes students want to be able to give their answers orally to the professor instead of taking the paper-based exam. Again, this isn't often approved. (Students who have physical difficulty with writing are likely to be accommodated with a laptop instead, or a scribe, if they have a physical disability.)

Memory Aids for Tests

In high school, students might have had "open book" exams where they were allowed access to their text and notebooks. Some professors may have exams where all students have this kind of access. Sometimes they allow the whole class to bring in one notecard or sheet of paper with whatever notes students want to include on it. (No one has to help a student with a disability put together such a tool.) But if they don't, it's very unusual for a student to be approved to bring a formula card or other kind of memory prompt, because often what professors are measuring with their exams is mastery of material. Similarly, sometimes students ask to be accommodated with a word bank on fill-in-the-blank tests. The issue of mastery is likely to be an issue for this, too.

Students with severe memory deficits may get approved for one or all of these; eligibility will vary from college to college. But the directors interviewed for the book didn't mention any of these being accommodations they commonly approve.

Someone to Explain Exam Questions

As already noted, students who request a reader for exams are more likely to be accommodated with the use of text-to-speech software. Sometimes, students ask for a reader because they want someone to explain the test questions to them. Any student with or without a disability should be allowed to ask a question during an exam (though policies may vary, and the number and length of questions may be limited). But college students are generally expected to be able to understand their exams (when their reading disability has been accommodated) without having someone else talk them through the questions.

Extended Deadlines for Assignments Completed Outside of Class

This is a commonly requested accommodation that directors said that they grant *only* for certain students who are in certain situations. As with attendance flexibility, this group includes students with physical/medical or mental health conditions that are experiencing a severe, brief exacerbation of symptoms at the time an assignment is due. If this happens and the student wants an extension, they may have to communicate with the professor or DS about this and work out what their new deadline will be.

You may be surprised to learn that this accommodation isn't commonly granted to students with LD, ADHD, or students with autism. Directors explained that students typically have a few days to complete assignments, and they are expected to manage their time and complete them. (If students have a 24-hour turnaround for something significant, they may get approved for that particular assignment.) Directors said often the problem isn't the amount of time students have to complete assignments, but rather that they don't start them until the last minute and moving a deadline doesn't typically change this, so all it does is extend students' procrastination. They noted that when students fail to meet their original deadlines, they often fall further behind the class. This can increase their anxiety, which can further hamper their ability to complete their work, which may cause them to miss the next deadline. Students who struggle with time management and other elements of executive functioning may find a number of resources on campus to help them, including those mentioned in steps 4 and 5.

One of the DS directors who works at an arts college and sometimes approves extensions said that for students involved in an upcoming performance who are tied up in rehearsals and performance several hours a day for several days in a row, they might grant an extension for assignments due at that time. But the other directors, who work at a range of universities, said they typically don't.

Copies of a Professor's Notes

Colleges have a variety of ways to accommodate students who have trouble taking notes because of their disability. Some professors may not even use notes when delivering a lecture, and DS can't require them to create notes just for students with disabilities. DS would instead provide one of the other notetaking accommodations. Even when professors do use lecture notes, they may not make sense to anyone else, and DS doesn't have to require them to edit their notes so they can be read and understood by someone else.

Advance Copies of PowerPoint Slides

Some professors will provide their slides to their whole class on their own ahead of time, but DS directors interviewed for the book said that others don't like to do this for a variety of reasons. One of these is that they make edits to slides after class based on the discussion that happens in class.

Students' reason for requesting this accommodation may be that it allows them to use strategies like previewing material (which is a good practice). Remember that the goal of accommodations is to "level the playing field," not help students achieve success. Some DS directors don't think that giving students with disabilities access to the class content ahead of their classmates is necessary to achieve this goal. And they point out that neurotypical students would benefit from the early access to slides, too. While students might *like* to print the slides out before class so they can write directly on them, some DS offices consider that a preference, not a need.

Private Dorm Room

Since this list only discusses academic accommodations, you may wonder why a housing accommodation is included here. It's because several directors interviewed for this book mentioned that some students with LD or ADHD request this so that they can have a quiet place to study. The directors said that their college doesn't see dorm rooms as serving this purpose, and they refer students to libraries and other study lounges to find the quiet setting they seek. A student may get a single for this reason—it depends upon their school's housing supply and the way DS views the student's eligibility, but this accommodation isn't granted as commonly as students may hope and expect.

Requests that Aren't Really Accommodations

As already discussed, sometimes students request services or modifications colleges don't have to provide. Sometimes students make requests that don't even fall into those categories—they're just things colleges don't have to provide or things students have to seek for themselves. When recommending these in their reports, professionals who provide documentation for college-bound students should be clear about the fact that these really aren't accommodations, but rather things students can seek out on their own to support their own needs. They include:

- Small class size—if this is important to students, they can look for this as they research and visit colleges.
- Extra time with professors—students who want to meet with professors can attend office hours; they may have to sign up for a slot or wait in line like everyone else.
- Quiet study space—students can find this at the library, and some dorms may have quiet study rooms. (Students may be able to reserve certain spaces; if not, they'll have to secure space on a first-come, first-served basis.)
- Advance notice of assignments—course syllabi generally indicate deadlines for assignments as well as exam dates. Students who want more specific information about assignments should ask their professors directly.

Accommodation Requests Arising from COVID Experiences

During the pandemic, some students found aspects of taking classes remotely to be beneficial. As classes at brick-and-mortar schools have returned to being held on-campus, some students have requested that they be allowed to attend classes remotely. Others have asked that their in-person classes be video-recorded (and captioned) so they can watch them again later, as they've become accustomed to doing. Some students have requested permission to take exams at home, where they feel less anxiety. While colleges have likely fielded these kinds of requests before, they may be seeing more requests now that students have had a chance to experience them.

As they do with other requests, colleges must give each one individual consideration. And they may be granting them for individual students based on their specific situation. But at this time, professionals in the field don't interpret the law as requiring colleges to transform in-person classes into ones where students can either come in person or attend by Zoom in order to accommodate students who can't come to campus because of their disability. And while some students have found that they *prefer* captioned video recordings or find they aid their concentration, it is unlikely that colleges will be required to provide such recordings or make sure they're captioned for students who aren't Deaf/HOH. Instead, they're likely to grant the other notetaking accommodations already discussed so that students who struggle with concentration can catch what they missed in class later.

As with anything they hope to receive, students should ask for whatever they want. Doing so might help them to better understand the circumstances under which colleges usually grant such requests (or don't).

- Study guides—the expectation at college is that students will figure out for themselves what they need to study. DS offices and professors aren't required to create guides for students who request them. Instead, students can seek assistance at review sessions (if the professor or TA holds them), the tutoring center, or from peer mentors or academic coaches on campus.
- Information about exam format—students who want to know in advance whether they will be taking an essay or multiple-choice exam can ask their professors, though it is likely that professors will give the whole class this information ahead of time anyway. If not, professors are not required to do so exclusively for students with disabilities, as this is something that would be seen as helping them be successful, not simply providing access.
- Progress reports—many colleges use a course management system, where students log in to find their assignments and view their grades. If a student sees that their grades haven't been entered, they can directly ask professors about how they're doing in their class.

As with anything else students want to request, they should still ask for these things; it's always possible their college will say yes.[10] But the likelihood is low, which is why previous steps have laid out strategies for preparing them to do a lot of things independently in the college environment.

Again, case managers can help students create a list of accommodations and take some notes to help them explain why they need them. Hopefully, they'll get approved for everything they requested. However, if they don't, they should know what they can do.

Learn What DS Decides and Know What to Do If Requests Aren't Approved

Many students will have all of their requests approved. Sometimes, though, a student's college won't find them eligible for any of the accommodations they requested. DS directors interviewed for this book said they will tell a student why they made that decision and typically suggest other information the student might gather that could help to support their requests (unless they're accommodations the college just wouldn't grant). Sometimes, additional or updated information is needed. In other cases, the documentation is thorough but doesn't demonstrate the student's eligibility. Although students can choose to appeal the decision without gathering additional information, doing so may improve their chances.

Sometimes DS will approve different accommodations than a student requested. This may be because they don't think the requested adjustments are appropriate for the student based on the information they have. It may be because they're just not appropriate at the college level, or they seem designed to help the student achieve success (e.g., permission to retake tests for a better grade). Or they may fall under the four exceptions carved out in the law, as discussed in step 1.

Students can and should file an appeal. They should pay attention to whatever DS told them about why they were turned down; they may need to gather additional information, or they might need to provide further explanation about their reasons for requesting a particular accommodation, or about their history.

Students who have been granted accommodations that are different from those they requested don't have to try them before appealing DS's decision. For example, a student isn't required to try using notetaking software before appealing DS's decision not to grant them copies of a peer's notes. However, it might strengthen their case if they try the alternative accommodation first and can explain to DS why it wasn't effective.

Students who aren't found eligible for any of their requested accommodations can ask DS whether they could have basic accommodations on a temporary basis (e.g., during their first semester) while they gather whatever information is needed to support their eligibility. The laws don't require a college do this, but some may choose to.

Even when students are granted whatever they initially request, they might worry that they underestimated their needs and are stuck with those accommodations for the rest of their time at college. But they can always ask for more or different accommodations if they find their needs change later in their education or that what they requested just wasn't sufficient. Although colleges expect a student to have a sense of what adjustments they will need when they start school, they also know that the environment may prove challenging in ways students didn't anticipate, and that accommodations may need to be added or tweaked.

How the Team Can Help Students Prepare for Working with College Accommodations

As already discussed, it's important that the student's high school plan incorporates helping them to develop compensatory strategies so that they will feel comfortable about their ability to succeed, even if they do not receive their ideal accommodations. As already discussed, once a student has had some direct instruction in such strategies, the team may consider scaling back accommodations they're unlikely to get in college so that everyone has a sense of how the student functions without them, which they may have to do in college.

In a large, longitudinal national study, some students received modifications, so there is always a chance that students will receive those. But the data showed that, for example, less than 1 percent received modified or alternative tests, 3 percent received shorter or different assignments, and 1 percent received modified grading standards, showing the chances are very small. That said, what the data can't tell us is how many of the students in the study *asked* for those modifications, so perhaps the possibilities are better than they seem, though DS directors interviewed for this book said that they don't typically grant modifications.[11]

As already discussed, the research reveals the variety of reasons students have said they delayed registering for accommodations. Sometimes, it is because of a lack of understanding. It may be helpful to see some specific comments students have made, to make sure that the way you speak to students doesn't interfere with their ability to advocate for their needs.

One student remarked that no one ever told them they had an LD or counseled them about how it could affect them in the college environment. "The only advice I had was, 'Don't take too many courses with a lot of writing in them.' What's too many? What kind of writing?"[12]

Another student had a similar experience. "No one ever used the term 'learning disability' to me, ever, in high school, so I certainly never discussed how my learning disability would affect me in college."[13]

One student said, "I'd read somewhere that LDs go away in some students when they reach adulthood. I was crossing my fingers that I was one of those people."[14] Because of their lack of knowledge about their disability and its impact on their performance, one student at first attributed their difficulty to typical freshman year adjustment problems (which may have been a factor, but may not have been the sole explanation).[15]

This information is provided here with the understanding that some families may prefer to approach conversations with students about their disability in a way that differs from the way the school proposes. School staff should be sensitive to how families wish to approach this topic. And professionals who use "learning differences" to avoid saying "learning disability" should understand how that could affect the student's understanding of themselves. If families are open to using accurate terminology, then professionals should honor their desire for transparency, especially since self-knowledge will be important for students' futures, whatever they decide to do after high school.

A different study also holds implications for discussions of accommodations, and even for the recommendations professionals make for students. It asked students which of the accommodations written into their plans were ones they didn't use, and why. Students commented that they didn't use some of the recommended strategies or accommodations because they:

- weren't interested
- thought they would be a waste of time
- had tried the recommendation before and it didn't work
- were overwhelmed by the number of recommendations

The researchers commented that the accommodations that got the least usage were those that required time and effort, and in some cases, money.[16]

Professionals preparing students for transition to college can discuss with them what they've used that they found helpful (or not) and talk to them about accommodations they plan to use so that they don't overwhelm them with suggestions. (You may decide it's in the student's best interest to make certain recommendations anyway.) More may not necessarily be better in this situation.

It can also be helpful if professionals make a distinction between accommodations students can request from DS and strategies they should use on their own. And it's ideal if high schools and any professionals working with students outside of school can teach students strategies before students make the transition to college so that they are prepared for the college environment.

This speaks, too, to the importance of finding ways to get students engaged in the development of their own IEP or 504 during high school. Asking them questions about what they find helpful (or not) provides opportunities not only to get this valuable information from them but also to give them a chance to reflect upon their experiences and give professionals and parents a chance to see if there are gaps in their self-knowledge that can be addressed before they graduate.[17]

Summary

The college approach to disability services differs from the one in high school and may result in students being offered different (or fewer or more) accommodations than they are accustomed to receiving. If the student's goal is to attend college, the team can consider setting a long-term goal of moving them closer to using only accommodations they are likely to receive at college by the time they're finishing high school, so that they have the confidence that they can be successful with what's available to them.

FAQs

Can a parent complete the DS process for a student?

Strictly speaking, registration is the student's responsibility, not a parent's. As noted in step 2, many colleges will allow parents to send in information students don't have with them at school, but most won't let them complete the process *for* a student. (State laws on legal guardianship or power of attorney vary; parents should check with a qualified attorney about how this does or doesn't affect their ability to complete the registration process for their student.) However, this doesn't mean they can't be helpful to their student during their process.

So, what role can the parents play? Parents can help their student decide what accommodations they want to ask for and what they want to say about why they need certain accommodations, and they can help to prepare their student for their DS intake meeting. If the student agrees, many colleges will let parents attend the meeting. (The laws don't say anything about this, so colleges can make their own decision about this.)

If they do get permission to attend, parents can see their role as providing emotional support and filling in gaps in information when requested by their student or the DS staffer. DS is often using this appointment to get a sense of students beyond what the paperwork says, and to get a sense of their self-knowledge, so they typically want to hear directly from the student. One director mentioned they might decide to add some accommodations to the student's approvals after meeting with them.

Can an outside professional or advocate complete the DS process for a student?

Professionals can't handle the registration for a student, either. Although a student may have worked with a coach from their vocational rehabilitation office or with another kind of professional the family may have hired, colleges don't typically allow any of these folks to register a student. Colleges expect a student to complete the process themselves, though they can utilize supports as they do so.

What if a student's documentation doesn't meet requirements?

Colleges are not required to pay for testing for a student whose documentation doesn't meet the school's requirements. The U.S. Department of Education advises, "If a student with a disability is eligible for services through the state VR Services program, he or she may qualify for an evaluation at no cost. High school educators can assist students with disabilities in locating their state VR agency," but not all students are eligible for such services.[18] (*VR* means Vocational Rehabilitation offices.) And school districts don't have an obligation to do testing for students who have already received their high school diploma.

If their college says their documentation doesn't meet the requirements, the student can ask DS if they keep a list of examiners they recommend who are willing to adjust their fees for students in need. They may also look to see whether their college or a nearby one trains graduate students in School Psychology programs to do testing. They may be able to get testing for a reduced price.

Do most students who register with DS get approved?

The National Center for Education Statistics doesn't have any data on this. And while a college may be collecting such information, it's not likely to make that information public. So no one can reliably answer this question.

In a post for educators on the U.S. Department of Education's website, it says that in order to be eligible for accommodations as a student with a disability, a student must show "that he or she has a disability, that is, an impairment that substantially limits a major life activity and that supports the need for an academic adjustment."[19] What this means is that the student's documentation may meet the technical requirements for what has to be *in it*, but it doesn't guarantee that their college will find the documentation shows (even if they have a disability) that the limitations they experience are sufficient to necessitate accommodations, or at least the accommodations they requested.

It may help to imagine the college accommodations process as two "gates." To get through the first one, a student has to document that they have a disability. It is likely most students will get through Gate 1.

Gate 2, however, may prove more of a challenge for some students. Although this may come as a surprise, as transition expert Joseph W. Madaus noted, "the existence of a disability does not equate to eligibility or need for accommodations."[20] What this means is that if a student's documentation doesn't demonstrate that their disability "substantially limits" their functioning, the college might not find the student eligible for accommodations.

Though it is unlikely to happen to many students, some may find that their college doesn't find them eligible, even though they have been accommodated throughout their education. This can happen because professionals administering testing can have different approaches for identifying a learning disability or ADHD.[21]

For instance, according to the tests used in their evaluation, the difference between Student A's scores that fall mostly above the 90th percentile and another score that falls at the 63rd percentile may be statistically significant. Staff at University B's DS office may acknowledge that the difference is significant. But they may also say that that since the average range in testing falls between the 25th and the 75th percentile, that 63rd percentile score—while weaker than the student's other scores—doesn't demonstrate a need for accommodation. It actually shows that the student's skills are stronger than 63 percent of students their age.

Madaus noted, too, that some students may have been accommodated by their high school because they had difficulty in one particular area (e.g., test taking) even though they were not found to have an LD.[22] These students, too, may be found ineligible for accommodations.

Students who received services solely on the basis of test anxiety in high school may not be found eligible for college accommodations (though they might if they also have generalized anxiety disorder). Even so, a student who has a severe response in testing situations (e.g., vomiting during tests, panic attacks others have observed) and can provide documentation of that can see whether DS would consider an accommodation.

Again, most students who register with DS will be found eligible for accommodations. But team members who are professionals should be sure to review the student's documentation with them and raise their awareness that their college might not find them so. They should encourage students to register anyway, and also point out the numerous other supports they can utilize beyond the DS office, if they find they need assistance.

What does the research on accommodations show?

Several years ago, leaders in the transition field conducted a review of the available literature and identified its numerous limitations in creating a picture of what works. The challenges they noted include that many studies didn't:

- specify what kinds of disabilities students in the cohort had
- provide demographic information about students, including gender, race, and ethnicity
- describe the schools these students attended (e.g., four-year or two-year)[23]

Additionally, they said the research rarely looked at *causation*, meaning that they couldn't say that a variable *caused* the results seen at the end. Some looked at correlation, meaning they looked to see if two things were related (e.g., students who used extended test time had a higher GPA than other students who didn't use that accommodation). And many lacked a control group, meaning they didn't look to see if there were differences between groups of students who did or didn't, for example, use accommodations.[24]

A correlational study with a control group might show that students with disabilities who used accommodations tended to have a higher GPA than those who didn't. It's hard to design a study that would prove that using accommodations resulted in students' having a higher GPA than those who didn't because of all the things that could affect GPA, such as students' class attendance, amount of time spent studying, how well students understood the class content, etc.

Some studies have interesting results but don't probe certain areas that could yield some helpful points for action, perhaps because the relevant data isn't available. For instance, if researchers wanted to see if having a notetaker improved students' test grades, they could pull DS records showing who was approved for a notetaker, but they might not be able to see whether the study subjects got the notes from the notetaker. (Again, one DS director said that at his last job, they found many students didn't download them from where they were stored.) Of course, even in a theoretical study like this, it would be impossible to know how students used those notes in preparing for tests or how good the quality of the notes was, and many other factors would affect test performance, such as sleep. And it would be important to consider differences in disabilities; a student who didn't have use of their arms but had no learning disability might have a higher GPA than a student who did have an LD.

Additionally, the research can't answer a lot of questions that matter in determining whether the accommodations are truly effective. First, studies can typically only confirm that students were approved for an accommodation; they generally can't confirm that students used the accommodation (e.g., notetaking software)—and if they did use it, that they did so consistently. For instance, one study noted that a number of students didn't use their accommodations until they were motivated to by low grades.[25]

The definition of success varies, too. Many studies examine GPA over a term or a longer period, and some studies look at graduation rates. The challenge with using such measures is that so much goes into whether students earn good grades (and finish college). As this book has discussed, students have to get to class, seek help when they're struggling, eat well, sleep enough, study effectively and for long enough, etc. For these reasons, it's hard to pinpoint the actual effect of accommodations on student success, no matter what the measure.

The focus of a recent meta-analysis was on such predictors. Some of the studies it looked at found that particular accommodations were predictors of GPA and graduation. But the researchers concluded that there weren't enough high-quality studies to draw conclusions that should drive planning.[26]

One area where researchers have been able to make sure students actually were using an accommodation is that of extended test time. Several studies have looked at DS records to see how much time students actually used (though they didn't look at GPA or any other kind of success measure). One large study looked at test records from more than 7,000 exams. It found that for all tests for which students had 1.5-time, 37 percent were completed within the *standard time* (i.e., the amount of time a student's typical classmates had to take the same test). Fifty-five percent of tests were taken within 1.25x of the standard time, even though students had been approved for 1.5x. At the same time, some students used more time than they had been approved for.[27] Other recent studies yielded similar results.

None of this is meant to discourage students from using accommodations. Accommodations are their civil right, and they are intended to "level the playing field" for students. But parents and professionals can remind students that accommodations are only one of the tools they'll need for success.

It is important for students to remember that they have the right to make these decisions, but they must take responsibility for them, too. If they choose not to use their accommodations in a certain class and do not earn the grade they desired, it is unlikely that they will be allowed to retake the test or have the grade dropped. Again, colleges don't have to make accommodations retroactive.

Notes

1. Kirsten L. Lightner et al., "Reasons University Students with a Learning Disability Wait to Seek Disability Services," *Journal of Postsecondary Education and Disability* 25, no. 2 (2012): 159–77. https://eric.ed.gov/?id=EJ994283

2. Manju Banerjee et al., "A Survey of Postsecondary Disability Service Website Information," *Learning Disabilities: A Multidisciplinary Journal* 26, no. 4 (2021): 34–42.

3. As noted in step 5, it's a good idea to look at and take notes on documentation requirements as students compose the list of colleges to which they'll apply. That

way, they'll know ahead of time what documentation they'll need once they choose the college they'll attend.

4. Learn how to evaluate a redacted report at https://ldadvisory.com/good-not-just-long-LD-report/

5. Some tests have what are called *extended* batteries, where they provide additional subtests examiners can use to further probe a student's skills. Colleges don't typically require that reports include these additional subtests, so team members don't have to worry about this.

6. Team members considering when to reassess students while they're in high school should pay attention to this and—if a Wechsler battery will be used—consider whether it is a good idea to wait until the student can be assessed with the WAIS-IV in order to give them the best chance their documentation will meet a college's requirements.

7. Appendix A, "A Picture of How the Laws Work at the National Level," compares the accommodations received by students in high school and in college over the course of a large, longitudinal study.

8. As with questions about fundamental alterations, professors' rules for or objections to this accommodation should be reviewed through whatever process the college has for this.

9. DS might only approve this if a student's use of this strategy was noted in their documentation by someone who tested them or by classroom teachers.

10. Class size is an exception. A college won't create a smaller class section in order to accommodate a student with a disability.

11. See "A Picture of How the Laws Work at the National Level" in appendix A.

12. Lightner et al., "Reasons University Students Wait," 159–77.

13. Lightner et al., "Reasons University Students Wait," 159–77.

14. Lightner et al., "Reasons University Students Wait," 159–77.

15. Lightner et al., "Reasons University Students Wait," 159–77.

16. Frances Prevatt et al., "Perceived Usefulness of Recommendations Given to College Students Evaluated for Learning Disability," *Journal of Postsecondary Education and Disability* 18, no. 1 (2005): 71–79. https://files.eric.ed.gov/fulltext/EJ846382.pdf

17. See appendix B to learn how this can be done in ways that align with families' cultural values.

18. U.S. Department of Education, "Transition of Students with Disabilities to Postsecondary Education: A Guide for High School Educators," 2011.

19. Ibid.

20. Joseph W. Madaus, "Let's Be Reasonable: Accommodations at the College Level," in *Preparing Students with Disabilities for College Success: A Practical Guide to Transition Planning*, edited by Stan F. Shaw, Joseph W. Madaus, and Lyman L. Dukes III (Baltimore, MD: Brookes, 2009), 10–35.

21. Jason M. Nelson et al., "How Is ADHD Assessed and Documented? Examination of Psychological Reports Submitted to Determine Eligibility for

Postsecondary Disability," *Journal of Attention Disorders* 23, no. 14 (2014): 1–12. https://doi:10.1177/1087054714561860; Richard L. Sparks and Benjamin J. Lovett, "Learning Disability Documentation in Higher Education: What Are Students Submitting?" *Learning Disability Quarterly* 37, no. 1 (2014): 54–62. https://doi .org/10.1177/0731948713486888; Michael D. Watson Jr., Joan B. Simon, and Lenora Nunnley, "SLD Identification: A Survey of Methods Used by School Psychologists," *Learning Disabilities: A Multidisciplinary Journal* 21, no. 1 (2016): 57–67. https://doi .org/10.18666/LDMJ-2016-V21-I1-6392

22. Madaus, "Let's Be Reasonable," 10–35.

23. Joseph W. Madaus et al., "Literature on Postsecondary Disability Services: A Call for Research Guidelines," *Journal of Diversity in Higher Education*, 11, no. 2 (2018): 133–45. https://doi.org/10.1037/dhe0000045

24. Madaus et al., "Literature on Postsecondary Disability Services," 133–45.

25. Yung-Chen Jen Chiu et al., "Impact of Disability Services on Academic Achievement among College Students with Disabilities," *Journal of Postsecondary Education and Disability* 32, no. 3 (2019): 227–45. https://eric.ed.gov/?id=EJ1236854

26. Joseph W. Madaus et al., "Are There Predictors of Success for Students with Disabilities Pursuing Postsecondary Education?," *Career Development and Transition for Exceptional Individuals* 44, no. 4 (2021): 191–202.

27. Will Lindstrom et al., "Examination of Extended Time Use Among Postsecondary Students with Non-Apparent Disabilities," *Journal of Postsecondary Education and Disability*, 34, no. 4 (2021): 297–306. https://www.ahead.org/professional-resources/publications/jped/archived-jped/jped-volume-34

~

Final Thoughts for Parents

As I noted at the start of this book, I know that some of the information you have read here may be disappointing and perhaps even caused you some anxiety. I am sorry if this book has caused you to worry. Remember that knowledge is power, and that's what I want you to have. It's important for you to know what the college environment is really like, because I want you to feel confident that you have the information you need to give your student the best possible preparation for it.

As I also said, I have presented the information in a straightforward way for the purposes of clarity. I apologize if that has made me seem dispassionate, because that's not how I feel. I want you to know that I've written this book because I care tremendously about students with disabilities and want to do whatever I can to help them pursue their goals.

It is my hope that reading this book has left you feeling empowered. You now have the information you need to help your student plan for their future.

If your student has a lot of the skills discussed in here, don't be hesitant about them moving straight on to college. Like their neurotypical peers, they'll likely encounter some bumps along the way, but they'll figure things out, and they'll be okay. Remind them that they have the skills they need, and encourage them to use the resources available if they experience any struggles.

If your student really wants to go to college, and you don't think they have the skills necessary *yet*, keep in mind that students can start their postsecondary education at any time. Those who take the time they need to mature and develop their skills are much more likely to have a successful experience than those who move straight on to college when they're not ready. I know it's hard for students not to be on the same timeline as their peers, and I empathize with them. Perhaps you can persuade them that it's better to wait until they're fully prepared (which some of their neurotypical peers won't be), giving themselves the best possible chance to make a smooth transition.

Whatever your student decides to do in the future, I know that one asset they will have is your support. That will be of incalculable value to them.

Take a deep breath. Then—knowing what you now know—get out there and take whatever you think should be the next step.

~

Appendix A

A Picture of How the Laws Work
at the National Level

Given all of the points of law that address students with disabilities (see step 1), what really happens at college? Understanding the changes in the laws is vital, but it's only part of the picture.

The best way to get a sense of how things play out is through research conducted at a national level. The National Longitudinal Transition Study (NLTS) has collected data over three different time periods, beginning in the 1980s, to "help in developing an understanding of the experiences of secondary school students with disabilities nationally as they go through their early adult years."[1] As part of the study, data was collected from those students in each cohort who attended *postsecondary* schools (meaning they continued their education after high school).

At the time of this writing, some reports have been published using the data from the NLTS2012. But none has provided the kind of overview on college enrollment and accommodation use that is available from the NLTS2. For that reason, the data from the NLTS will be discussed here.

The NLTS2 followed a "nationally representative sample of students who were 13 to 16 years old and receiving special education in grade 7 or above, under the Individuals with Disabilities Education Act (IDEA) in the 2000–01 school year."[2] It collected information a few times over the course of the study (in what are called "waves") through surveys and interviews with students, their parents, and high school personnel.[3]

The last data collection was done in 2009. Some of the language used to describe disability categories may seem outdated and insensitive; it is included in the tables here because that's how it appeared in some of the write-ups. Even though the data is outdated, because of the study's size, it can provide some helpful insight about the experiences of students.

College Enrollment

Over the course of the NLTS2, 60.1 percent of students in the cohort had ever enrolled at any kind of postsecondary school.[4] Using data for the general population (i.e., neurotypical students) gleaned from other studies for comparison, Newman et al. found that 67.4 percent of that cohort enrolled at any type of postsecondary school.[5]

In their analysis of the NLTS2 enrollment data, Newman et al. found that of the students who attended any kind of postsecondary education:

- 44.2 percent of students with disabilities enrolled at a two-year or community college compared to 20.6 percent in the general population
- 32.3 percent of students with disabilities enrolled at a career and technical education (CTE) school compared to 20.3 percent in the general population
- 18.8 percent of students with disabilities enrolled at a four-year school compared to 40.2 percent in the general population[6]

Newman and Madaus explained that in their analysis of the NLTS2 data, students who attended more than one kind of college were included only once in the overall enrollment number calculated (51 percent), but they may have been counted twice in the enrollment rates for different kinds of schools (36 percent for two-year schools, 23 percent for CTE schools, and 15 percent for four-year schools).[7] This may explain why their overall number for enrollment doesn't align with Newman et al.'s figures.

Students with learning disabilities were by far the largest part of the NLTS2 cohort that attended any kind of postsecondary education. Prevalence rates were:

- 69 percent—learning disabilities
- 9 percent—students with emotional disturbances (that is the wording used in the study)
- 6 percent—intellectual disabilities
- 5 percent—other health impairments (students with ADHD are included in this federal disability category)
- 5 percent—speech/language impairments[8]

The remaining 6 percent of the cohort comprised students in other disability categories (hearing impairment, visual impairment, orthopedic impairment, autism, traumatic brain injury, and deaf-blindness); the researchers didn't provide further breakdown of that number. Thirty-six percent of students had ADHD in addition to another disability.[9]

Receiving Accommodations at College

Even though 98 percent of students in the NLTS2 had had at least one accommodation in high school, only 24 percent did at the postsecondary level.[10] Looking at different school types, the rate of receipt was:

- 25 percent of students enrolled at a two-year college
- 22 percent of those enrolled at a four-year college
- 16 percent of those enrolled at a CTE school

A separate analysis found that of this cohort, those with disabilities that were *apparent* (meaning *visible*), including those with hearing impairments or orthopedic impairments, were more likely to receive accommodations and other disability-related services at two-year and four-year colleges than students with learning disabilities, even though students with learning disabilities made up the majority of students with disabilities at each type of school. At four-year schools, though, students with ADHD were more likely than students with other disabilities to receive accommodations and services. And at CTE schools, students with autism were more likely to receive accommodations than any other group.[11]

Potential Explanations for Lower Rates of Accommodation at the College Level

Why was there such a drop in the number of students who received accommodations in high school versus those who receive them in college? As already noted, students with disabilities who wish to receive accommodations typically have to register with their college's disability services office. This means students have to make a deliberate decision to follow their college's process for registering. It seems likely that they would be motivated to do this by a sense that they would benefit from accommodations.

In what might be relevant to that finding, Newman et al.'s analysis of NLTS2 data found that some of the students in the cohort did not consider themselves to have a disability, even though they had received at least one accommodation, modification, or service for a disability in high school.[12] Echoing Newman and Madaus's analysis of the data on receiving accommodations, this study found that across eleven categories of disability, this was true for 18.5 percent of those with orthopedic impairment at the lowest end of the range and 74.0 percent for students identified as having speech/language impairment at the highest end. In other words, students with apparent disabilities were much more likely to think they had a disability than those with "invisible" ones. The overall rate for this analysis was 63.1 percent—more than half of the students who attended any kind of postsecondary school did not request accommodations because they thought they didn't have a disability.

Interestingly, in this same study, some of the students who attended post-secondary schools *did* believe they had a disability yet didn't request accommodations by telling their school about it.[13] This was true for 3.4 percent of students with multiple disabilities (no specifics are provided) at the low end of the range and 20.7 percent of students identified as having an emotional disturbance at the high end. Overall, 8.5 percent of students thought they had a disability but chose not to disclose it.

Some students did consider themselves to have a disability and did disclose this to their school. This was true for 76.1 percent of students with ortho-pedic impairment on the high end of the range and 16.6 percent of students with speech/language impairment on the low end. Overall, 28 percent of students who attended any kind of postsecondary school thought they had a disability and told their postsecondary school. Twenty-four percent informed their college before they enrolled, and 4 percent did so after they enrolled.

This is where the vagaries of the research can muddy the picture. The data collected doesn't indicate *how* students informed their schools about their disability. As Newman et al. reported, researchers simply asked whether a student's school was aware of their disability before or after they enrolled.[14] As step 2 explains, students who want accommodations have to register for them; this may be represented by that 4 percent.

But it's also possible that some of the 28 percent of students who said they told their college about their disability before they enrolled did so by mentioning their disability in their application, though we can't know this for sure. As this book explains, that doesn't count as notification for the pur-poses of the DS system. If some of that 28 percent did this, and they didn't follow that up by registering with DS, that portion of students likely wouldn't have received accommodations.

What Positively Influenced Accommodation Rates

Newman and Madaus examined whether specific preparation for requesting accommodations after high school influenced a student's receipt of them.

They found that students with disabilities that were apparent (e.g., visual impairments) were more likely to receive accommodations at two-year and four-year schools than their peers with invisible disabilities (such as psychological disabilities), though this wasn't true at CTE schools.[15]

The researchers stated that high schools may need to make sure students have accurate self-knowledge of the way their disability affects them and how accommodations might help. They also noted that students from families with lower incomes and those with less visible disabilities may need more information about the disclosure process and—importantly—chances to learn the skills they'll need in that process while they're still in high school.[16]

In this same study, the researchers also looked at results from a self-determination scale. (See step 3 for more on this important personal skill.) They found that students who attended a two-year school and had greater confidence in their abilities and thought they could make up for their limitations were less likely than students with other disabilities to receive accommodations and disability-related supports there. (Perhaps they didn't request them.)[17]

Relevant to this point, that study also found that students whose high school involved them in transition planning as well as those who had a transition plan that specifically outlined postsecondary accommodations were more likely to receive accommodations at two-year and CTE schools. (The researchers don't explain why this was more likely at these types of institutions than at four-year schools.)[18]

They also noted that only 64 percent of students with disabilities had received transition planning in high school.[19] A separate analysis of NLTS2 data extended the findings of this one, and it showed that not only did students who received transition planning request disability accommodations at a higher rate, they also were more likely to access supports available to the general student body.[20]

What Supports Do Students Receive at College?

When students are in special education in high school, the kinds of supports they receive may vary. They may receive accommodations and/or (less often) modifications and certain kinds of services. As discussed in step 1, the mandates for what colleges have to provide are different than those for K–12 schools. In addition to the fact that students may have decided not to disclose their disability, the reason why rates for receipt of supports at college may have varied from the rates at high school is because the supports students sought were not available there, *or* because students didn't request the *same* accommodations at college that they had received in high

Table A.1. Rate of Receipt of Accommodations in the NLTS2

Accommodation	High School	Any Kind of Postsecondary School
Test accommodations, including more time and/or a different setting	88%	21%
Additional time to complete assignments	72%	6%
Reader for tests or assignments	47%	4%
Use of a calculator for activities not allowed other students*	33%	6%
Disability-related computer use†	23%	4%
Books on tape	15%	2%

*Many college math and science classes actually require students to use a calculator.
†No details are provided on this accommodation, such as whether this applied to tests, notetaking, etc.

Source: Newman and Madaus, "Reported Accommodations and Supports Provided to Secondary and Postsecondary Students with Disabilities" (2015).

school. None of the analyses comment on this; it's possible this information wasn't collected in the study.

One of Newman and Madaus's analyses looked at the specifics of various supports. The overall rate for students receiving any of the adjustments categorized as *accommodations* was 95 percent in high school, while only 23 percent received them in college; rates didn't vary significantly across the three school types. The researchers looked at several specific accommodations and compared the rates at which students received these in high school versus college (see table A.1).[21]

As already discussed, colleges don't have to modify their requirements. This may help to explain why 59 percent of students in the NLTS2 received at least one modification in high school, but only 4 percent received one at a postsecondary school. Newman and Madaus provided specific rates for various modifications (see table A.2); again, rates were similar across institution types.[22]

And, as already noted, colleges don't have to provide personal "services," though few specifics are provided in the laws to help define what these are. Newman and Madaus found that even though 80 percent of students

Table A.2. Rate of Receipt of Modifications in the NLTS2

Accommodation	High School	College
Modified or alternative tests*	37%	<1%
Shorter or different assignments	30%	3%
Modified grading standards*	29%	1%

*Note: No specifics are provided to indicate how tests or grading standards were modified.

Source: Newman and Madaus, "Reported Accommodations and Supports Provided to Secondary and Postsecondary Students with Disabilities" (2015).

Table A.3. **Rate of Receipt of Academically Focused Services in the NLTS2**

Service*	High School	College
A support person to monitor progress and manage school workloads	68%	1%
Assistance with learning strategies	43%	2%
Tutoring	31%	10%
Teacher aid or instructional assistant	26%	3%

*Note: No specifics are provided about whether these supports were actually provided through the disability services office as a formal accommodation or through a different office or department, such as the campus tutoring center.

Source: Newman and Madaus, "Reported Accommodations and Supports Provided to Secondary and Postsecondary Students with Disabilities" (2015).

received an academically focused service in high school, only 12 percent reported receiving one at college. They also provided specifics about those services (see table A.3). Again, rates were similar across institution types.[23]

Use caution in interpreting the data to mean that the services mentioned were provided by DS. For instance, since colleges don't have to provide specialized help, did some students receive "assistance with learning strategies" through the general campus tutoring center and report it as a service? Again, the analysis didn't discuss this. It's possible that this is because the surveys and interviews completed in the study didn't ask these kinds of questions.

Beyond academically focused supports, the mandates covering K–12 also require schools to provide nonacademic services that colleges don't have to provide. Seventy-eight percent of students reported receiving at least one of these kinds of supports, while only 6 percent of them received one at college; rates were similar across school types. Table A.4 shows the different kinds of supports rarely provided at the college level.

As when reviewing the rates for academically focused services, use caution in interpreting the data to mean that students received some of these nonacademic services through DS. For instance, the campus counseling center typically provides mental health counseling, and it's possible some students reported these as services for the purposes of this study even though it wasn't a DS-approved accommodation.

Table A.4. **Rate of Receipt of Other Individualized Services in the NLTS2**

Service	High School	College
Case management	47%	1%
Mental health/behavior management	18%	2%
Occupational therapy or life skills training	13%	<1%
Social work services	11%	1%
Medical nursing for evaluation diagnosis	11%	<1%
Transportation services	9%	1%

Source: Newman and Madaus, "Reported Accommodations and Supports Provided to Secondary and Postsecondary Students with Disabilities" (2015).

Newman et al. didn't provide comparisons between rates of receipt for some supports at high school and college, but they did provide college receipt rates for additional types of assistance not mentioned in the other study, some of which are discussed in step 7. Of the students who attended any kind of postsecondary school and received accommodations, the rates of receipt for those not already mentioned were:

- 37 percent—technology
- 16.8 percent—notetaker
- 10.5 percent—written materials
- 9.7 percent—physical adaptations to classroom
- 3.2 percent—early registration
- 7.5 percent—other accommodations or supports[24]

Again, the data didn't specify what some of these represent. For instance, it's unclear what "written materials" means or what the additional supports or accommodations provided might have looked like.

This analysis does provide some specifics about accommodations students received that weren't provided in Newman and Madaus's analysis. For testing:

- 79.2 percent of students received additional time for tests
- 18.5 percent took tests in a different test setting
- 9.4 percent received other unspecified testing accommodations[25]

It's possible some students received more than one of these testing accommodations.

Other Potential Factors Influencing Rate of Receipt of Accommodations

It's important to remember that these rates of receipt may have been influenced by numerous factors, beyond the shifting mandates, such as:

- how many students requested accommodations, modifications, or services overall;
- which specific accommodations, modifications, or services they requested (it's possible they didn't find their high school supports helpful and therefore didn't request the same ones at college);
- whether some of the accommodations they requested weren't reasonable or available at the college level; and

- their college's decision about their eligibility for the requested supports. For instance, as step 7 discusses, extended time to complete papers and projects is often only granted to certain categories of students in very specific situations.

Because NLTS2 didn't provide these details, it's not possible to know how much any of these factors affected the receipt rates. And as Newman and Madaus show in their analysis, personal characteristics and skills, knowledge, and transition planning activities may have affected whether students chose to self-identify or not and how that process went for them as a result of the influences of these factors.[26]

College Completion Rates

Up to eight years after students in NLTS2 had completed high school, the completion rate for those who attended any kind of postsecondary school was 40.7 percent for students with disabilities in the study compared to 52.4 percent in the general population.[27] Table A.5 shows the rates for completion of programs at the three school types.

The two groups with the lowest program completion rates were students with deaf-blindness (27.7 percent); students with the highest completion rate were those with a hearing impairment (52.9 percent).

Keep in mind that the study spanned eight years, so some of these students may have started college a few years after their high school graduation, while some may have taken more than four years to complete a degree.

Again, the data here is outdated, and it's hard to speculate whether the numbers would look similar currently. But this research establishes the importance of properly preparing students for college so that they have the self-understanding they need (to determine if accommodations would be useful to them) and strategies to use in case some of the supports (accommodations, modifications, and services) they had in high school aren't available to them.

Table A.5. Program Completion in the NLTS2

School Type	Students with Disabilities	Students in the General Population
Four-year college	34.2%	51.2%
Two-year or community college	41.3%	22.4%
Vocational, business, or technical school	56.7%	64.5%

Source: Newman et al., "The Post–High School Outcomes of Young Adults with Disabilities: A Report from the National Longitudinal Transition Study-2 (NLTS2)" (2011).

Notes

1. Lynn Newman et al., "The Post–High School Outcomes of Young Adults with Disabilities Up to 8 Years After High School: A Report from the National Longitudinal Transition Study-2 (NLTS2)," (NCSER 2011-3005) (Menlo Park, CA: SRI International, 2011), iii. https://ies.ed.gov/ncser/pubs/20113005/

2. Newman et al., "Post–High School Outcomes," xiii.

3. No data was collected from DS staff at the colleges students attended.

4. Newman et al., "Post–High School Outcomes."

5. Newman et al., "Post–High School Outcomes."

6. Newman et al., "Post–High School Outcomes."

7. Lynn A. Newman and Joseph W. Madaus, "Reported Accommodations and Supports Provided to Secondary and Postsecondary Students with Disabilities: National Perspective," *Career Development and Transition for Exceptional Individuals* 38, no. 3 (2015): 173–81. https://doi:10.1177/2165143413518235

8. Newman and Madaus, "Reported Accommodations and Supports," 173–81.

9. Newman and Madaus, "Reported Accommodations and Supports," 173–81.

10. Newman and Madaus, "Reported Accommodations and Supports," 173–81.

11. Newman and Madaus, "Reported Accommodations and Supports," 173–81.

12. Newman et al., "Post–High School Outcomes."

13. Newman et al., "Post–High School Outcomes."

14. Newman et al., "Post–High School Outcomes."

15. Lynn A. Newman and Joseph W. Madaus, "An Analysis of Factors Related to Receipt of Accommodations and Services by Postsecondary Students with Disabilities," *Remedial and Special Education* 36, no. 4 (2015): 208–19. https://doi.org/10.1177/0741932515572912

16. Newman and Madaus, "Factors Related to Receipt of Accommodations and Services," 208–19.

17. Newman and Madaus, "Factors Related to Receipt of Accommodations and Services," 208–19.

18. Newman and Madaus, "Factors Related to Receipt of Accommodations and Services," 208–19.

19. Newman and Madaus, "Factors Related to Receipt of Accommodations and Services," 208–19.

20. Lynn A. Newman, Joseph W. Madaus, and Harold S. Javitz, "Effect of Transition Planning on Postsecondary Support Receipt by Students with Disabilities," *Exceptional Children* 82, no. 4 (2016): 497–514. https://doi.org/10.1177/0014402915615884

21. Newman and Madaus, "Factors Related to Receipt of Accommodations and Services," 208–19.

22. Newman and Madaus, "Reported Accommodations and Supports," 173–81.

23. Newman et al., "Post–High School Outcomes."

24. Newman et al., "Post–High School Outcomes."

25. Newman and Madaus, "Reported Accommodations and Supports," 173–81.

26. Newman and Madaus, "Factors Related to Receipt of Accommodations and Services," 208–19.

27. Newman et al., "Post–High School Outcomes."

~

Appendix B

Professionals Working with CLD Students

The goal of this book is to make sure you have the information you need to help your students prepare for a successful transition to college. While the suggestions here are applicable to all of the students you work with, it's important to be sensitive to how students and their families who are culturally and linguistically diverse (CLD) and/or from economically, socially, and politically marginalized communities approach the educational and planning experience. (For this discussion, the term "CLD" will be used to include all of these families.) Their approaches to transition may look different than yours, with respect to their student's goals and how they will achieve them. Because you want them to feel that you are all working as a team, it can help to do some perspective-taking.

Developing Self-Awareness and Cultural Awareness

As a professional, it can be helpful to be aware of how the American educational system's approach to transition reflects the dominant culture's values. These may also be your values and those of others in the district.[1] These values can shape the way that all of you work with students and their families.[2]

The approach taken in the U.S. educational system is very individualistic. It places an emphasis on the student's taking responsibility for many things, including setting their own goals. However, in collectivist cultures, the ways that decisions are made about what a student's goals will be and who speaks about them may be different. These differences may also affect a student's level of comfort with meeting some benchmarks that are usually included in transition planning, such as running their own IEP meetings.[3]

While your job is to prepare students for postsecondary success, and you are aware of the skills students will need (whether they're attending college or going to work), the approach you take with families can show respect for their values. Working with cultural brokers is one way to educate yourself and build effective two-way communication.[4]

Be aware, too, of how your cultural lens affects the way you think about postsecondary goals for students and how those might not align with their family's values. A student may not view living away from home at the most selective college they can attend as the most desirable goal. Remember, too, that students from low-income households may need to work after high school to help contribute to their family, and this may preclude full-time (or any) college participation. Planning should be respectful of their needs and their desires.

Perspective-taking can be helpful in thinking about how to solicit a family's input in transition planning. You can try to put yourself in family members' shoes to see how they experience the process. In a recent study, both students and parents in CLD families reported feeling that they were told what the student's goals would be, rather than being asked for their input. One parent reported that because they had to communicate through a translator, they didn't feel the professionals gave their input as much consideration as they should have.[5] Think about how your district conducts meetings and whether you need to make adjustments.

Of course, college may be the student's goal, and their family may support it. It can help to know what enrollment rates look like and what you and your colleagues can do to improve them for CLD students.

Rates of College Enrollment for CLD Students

Rates of college enrollment vary by race/ethnicity. The most recent data that takes into account both race/ethnicity and disability status dates from the 2015–2016 academic year. American Indian/Alaska Native students had the highest enrollment rates, followed by (in descending order) Pacific Islander students, White, Hispanic, and Asian students, something of a reverse of the rates in the general population.[6]

It likely isn't a surprise to you that socioeconomic status affects college enrollment rates. A large study looking at predictors of college enrollment of students with disabilities found that students whose family made less than $25,000 were less likely to attend college than those whose family income was $25,000 to $50,000. But you may find it interesting that the effect was small, and it was mediated in part by students' having earned credits in general education academic classes and by parental expectations that students would graduate from high school.[7] Consider this information in your planning process for students.

This book is focused on *preparing* students with disabilities for college, not directly on addressing enrollment disparities, so you may wonder why they're mentioned here. Throughout the planning and transition process, there are things you can do that might help students and their families feel more comfortable in considering college as a postsecondary goal.

Think about students from CLD families and from families where parents either haven't attended college or did so in another country. Given the complexity of the processes (taking SAT or ACT, applying early decision or early action or not, completing financial aid forms) and the unique vocabulary used at the college level, it's not hard to see how "college" as a concept can seem intimidating. You can address this by sharing general knowledge about the college environment as well as the search and application process to give CLD students and their families a sense of comfort and empowerment. By doing this, you'll increase their access to all kinds of *capital*.

Sharing Capital

Throughout this book, you'll see terms used at the college level loosely defined. These explanations have been provided to make sure parents with no experience of college (or who don't have experience with the American college system) have the knowledge they need to understand the environment. This kind of information is a form of *cultural capital*.[8]

Trainor discusses the importance of this and of *social capital*, which "embodies cultural goods that contribute to the reification of status and power on the basis of accumulated capital that is highly valued in the larger society"[9] and consists of "networks of people and relationships that contribute to the garnering of capital in its other forms."[10] Put more simply, when people are in a certain position in society, they possess certain kinds of capital, and they are plugged into their society's dominant culture, where they learn and acquire things that help them maintain that social position.

Trainor uses college entrance exam practice and preparation as examples of how this works, pointing out that families with *economic capital* have the money to pay an SAT tutor. Students who get this kind of preparation may do better on those tests, which could result in their receiving scholarships (another form of economic capital) and/or entrance to colleges where they can network with professors and classmates whose parents might provide them with good career opportunities. (These relationships are a form of social capital.) These career opportunities may provide a good salary, which might allow them to, for instance, join a tennis club, where they may meet others with whom they create business opportunities, which contributes to their increased economic capital. CLD families often lack access to all these kinds of capital, which may deprive them of the ability to create opportunities for their children.

You can be a source of capital by sharing what you know. Consider how much terminology is used in talking about the college environment that may be unfamiliar to families who haven't had any interaction with it and how that environment can often seem foreign and intimidating. This could dissuade students from pursuing a degree.

Think, too, about the ways that social capital plays into your district's college planning process. Students whose families are more plugged into the system may know about the resources available to them, such as SAT practice classes, help with financial aid forms, etc., while families of CLD students may be intimidated by the system and either not know about those resources or not feel comfortable accessing them. Make sure your district reaches out to all families to let them know about the supports it offers.

College Planning Considerations

Through the lens of capital, think about the experiences of your students and where changes can be made. This can include looking at their educational programming and at their college planning process.

Research shows that being educated in general education settings is a predictor of college participation. This may be explained in part by something Trainor et al. point to, namely that capital and an individual's "experiences and expectations mutually contribute to one another."[11] In other words, not only does being in general education classes provide a student with the skills they'll need at college, it may also raise that student's expectation that they'll attend college.[12]

And the reverse may be true, too—a student's goals may also influence their high school class placement. If a student expects to attend college, they'll improve their chances of getting there and being successful if they are placed in general education academic settings. Their thinking may be influenced by their parents, so it's important to engage parents in planning and learn how they envision their student's future.

Make sure the systems in your district that provide students with college planning support are talking to each other so that CLD students get support in achieving their goals. One study found that even though the majority of English language learners (ELLs) with disabilities expected to continue their education after high school, only a third or fewer of them reported receiving help with college application–related activities, such as signing up for college entrance exams, completing financial aid forms, and comparing aid packages. Although help rates were similar among the three groups, the only area of significant difference was on financial aid–related help: 11 percent of ELLs with disabilities received this assistance compared to 22 percent of their neurotypical peers.[13] Consider whether your students need more support for the college search and application process than they're currently receiving and, if so, what needs to change in your district in order to provide it.

Summary

Recognizing your perspective on transition goals and learning more about the cultures of your students and their families can shape the way you work with them on transition, making them feel heard and respected. It can also help students who wish to attend college, if they feel that their family supports that goal (perhaps as a result of their transition planning experiences). Given that individuals who earn a college degree earn more over a lifetime than those with a high school diploma,[14] and that they may also develop cultural and social capital through their experiences, the work you do may have positive long-lasting effects on the prospects of those students and their families.

Notes

1. Rudolph L. Valenzuela and James E. Martin, "Self-Directed IEP: Bridging Values of Diverse Cultures and Secondary Education," *Career Development for Exceptional Individuals* 28, no. 1 (2015): 4–14. https://doi.org/10.1177/08857288050280010301

2. Dawn A. Rowe and Grace L. Francis, "Reflective Thinking: Considering the Intersection of Microcultures in IEP Planning and Implementation," *TEACHING Exceptional Children* 53, no. 1 (2020): 4–6. https://doi.org/10.1177/0040059920952007; Audrey A. Trainor, "Using Cultural and Social Capital to Improve Postsecondary Outcomes and Expand Transition Models for Youth with Disabilities," *Journal of Special Education* 42, no. 3 (2008): 148–62. https://doi.org/10.1177/0022466907313346; Valenzuela and Martin, "Self-Directed IEP," 4–14.

3. Valenzuela and Martin, "Self-Directed IEP," 4–14.

4. Kathryn Torres, Nathanie Lee, and Christine Tran, "Building Relationships, Bridging Cultures: Cultural Brokering in Family Engagement," The Equitable Parent-School Collaboration Research Project, 2015. https://education.uw.edu/sites/default/files/programs/epsc/Cultural%20Brokers%20Brief_Web.pdf

5. Wendy Cavendish and David J. Connor, "Toward Authentic IEPs and Transition Plans: Student, Parent, and Teacher Perspectives," Learning Disabilities Quarterly 41, no. 1 (2018): 32–43. https://journals.sagepub.com/doi/10.1177/073194 8716684680#

6. National Center for Education Statistics, "How Many Students in Postsecondary Education Have a Disability?" https://nces.ed.gov/fastfacts/display.asp?id=60

7. Mary M. Wagner, Lynn A. Newman, and Harold S. Javitz, "The Influence of Family Socioeconomic Status on the Post–High School Outcomes of Youth with Disabilities," Career Development and Transition for Exceptional Individuals 37, no. 1 (2014): 5–17. https://doi.org/10.1177/2165143414523980

8. Trainor, "Using Cultural and Social Capital," 148–62.

9. Trainor, "Using Cultural and Social Capital," 151.

10. Trainor, "Using Cultural and Social Capital," 151.

11. Audrey A. Trainor et al, "Postsecondary Education-Focused Transition Planning Experiences of English Learners with Disabilities," Career Development and Transition for Exceptional Individuals 42, no. 1 (2019): 52. https://journals.sagepub.com/doi/full/10.1177/2165143418811830

12. Jay W. Rojewski, In H. Lee, and Noel Gregg, "Causal Effects of Inclusion on Postsecondary Education Outcomes of Individuals with High-Incidence Disabilities," Journal of Disability Policy Studies 25, no. 4 (2015): 210–19; Wagner, Newman, and Javitz, "Influence of Family Socioeconomic Status," 5–17.

13. Rates were similar to those for other students with disabilities who weren't ELLs. Trainor et al., "Postsecondary Education-Focused Transition Planning." 43–55. https://doi.org/10.1177/2165143418811830

14. In 2020, they earned 60 percent more than those who had only completed high school. Elka Torpey, "Education Pays, 2020," Career Outlook, U.S. Bureau of Labor Statistics, June 2021.

Appendix C

Additional Resources

Resources Mentioned in Steps (In Order of Appearance)

Step 1

"Auxiliary Aids and Services for Postsecondary Students with Disabilities," OCR post. https://www2.ed.gov/about/offices/list/ocr/docs/auxaids.html#skipnav2

Step 2

"Students with Disabilities Preparing for Postsecondary Education: Know Your Rights and Responsibilities," OCR post. https://www2.ed.gov/about/offices/list/ocr/transition.html

Step 3

"Age Appropriate Transition Assessment Toolkit 3rd Edition," National Secondary Transition Technical Assistance Center. https://www.nsttac.org/content/age-appropriate-transition-assessment-toolkit-3rd-edition/

"Self-Determined Learning Model of Instruction," curriculum available from the University of Kansas. https://selfdetermination.ku.edu/homepage/intervention/

Christine Y. Mason, Marcy McGahee-Kovac, and Lora Johnson, "How to Help Students Lead Their IEP Meetings," *TEACHING Exceptional Children* 36, no. 3 (2004): 18–24. https://doi.org/10.1177/004005990403600302

Alison Myers and Laura Eisenman, "Student-Led IEPs: Take the First Step," *TEACHING Exceptional Children* 37, no. 4 (2005): 52–58. https://doi.org/10.1177/004005990503700408

Jessica Lahey, *The Gift of Failure: How the Best Parents Learn to Let Go So Their Children Can Succeed* (New York: HarperCollins, 2015). Advice for parents on how they can support their students in developing their independent skills.

William Stixrud and Ned Johnson, *What Do You Say? How to Talk with Kids to Build Motivation, Stress Tolerance, and a Happy Home* (New York: Viking, 2021). Advice for parents on how to help students develop their own internal motivation.

Step 4

Jessica Monahan, Allison Lombardi, and Joseph Madaus, "Promoting College and Career Readiness: Practical Strategies for the Classroom," *TEACHING Exceptional Children* 51, no. 2 (2018): 144–54. https://doi.org/10.1177/0040059918802579

Jennifer Gonzalez, "Note-Taking: A Research Roundup." https://www.cultofpedagogy.com/note-taking/

Hamzeh Dodeen, "Teaching Test-Taking Strategies: Importance and Techniques," *Psychology Research* 5, no. 2 (2015): 108–13. https://www.researchgate.net/publication/348207908_Teaching_Test-Taking_Strategies_Importance_and_Techniques

John Dunlosky, "Strengthening the Student Toolbox: Study Strategies to Boost Learning," *American Educator* 7, no. 3 (2013): 12–21. https://eric.ed.gov/?id=EJ1021069

Time Management Calculator, Study Lab, University of Pittsburgh, Dietrich School of Arts & Sciences. https://www.asundergrad.pitt.edu/study-lab/time-management-calculator

Pomodoro Technique, a strategy for managing blocks of time by Francesco Cirillo. https://francescocirillo.com/pages/pomodoro-technique

Time Management—College Study Scheduling Tool, tips on the author's webpage. https://ldadvisory.com/time_management_tool/

Natural Reader, a free screen-reading program. https://www.naturalreaders.com/online/

Assignment Planner, University of Toronto, Scarborough. https://digital.utsc.utoronto.ca/assignment-planner

Free Graphic Organizer Templates, provided by Houghton Mifflin Harcourt. https://www.hmhco.com/blog/free-graphic-organizer-templates

Michael C. Friedman, "Notes on Note-Taking: Review of Research and Insights for Students and Instructors," Harvard Initiative for Learning and Teaching, Harvard University. https://cpb-us-w2.wpmucdn.com/u.osu.edu/dist/c/15148/files/2017/03/Notes-on-Note-Taking-qrs2kq.pdf

Step 5

"Exploring College Disability Accommodations and Other Academic Supports," video by the author demonstrating how to explore a DS site. https://www.youtube.com/watch?v=DEP7nRV_cOA&t=493s

Think College, Family Resources, college planning resources and other information for students with intellectual disabilities and their families. https://thinkcollege .net/family-resources

Marybeth Kravets and Imy Wax, *The K&W Guide to Colleges for Students with Learning Disabilities*, 15th ed. (New York: Penguin Random House/Princeton Review, 2021). Provides information about the disability services offices and any specialized programs at several hundred universities.

Campus Disability Resource Database (CeDaR), free database from the National Center for College Students with Disabilities (NCCSD). https://www.cedardata base.org/

College Web LD, database from consultant Judith Bass and her associates. https:// www.collegewebld.com/our-mission

Gap Year Association, offers lists of programs, a planning guide, information about financial aid, and more. https://www.gapyearassociation.org/

Jane Thierfeld Brown, Lorraine Wolf, Lisa King, and G. Ruth Kukiela Bork, *The Parent's Guide to College for Students on the Autism Spectrum* (Shawnee Mission, KS: AAPC, 2012).

Step 6

"What Is a Test Optional College?" FairTest's list of test-optional colleges. http:// fairtest.org/university/optional

Resources for Parents

Books

Peg Dawson, Richard Dawson, and Richard Guare, book series: *Smart but Scattered; Smart but Scattered Teens; Smart but Scattered: The Revolutionary "Executive Skills" Approach to Helping Kids Reach Their Potential* (Guilford), offering tips and advice on helping students work on executive functioning.

Online Resources

ADDitude Magazine, features strategies for improving executive functioning and information on college-related topics. https://www.additudemag.com/

College Parent Central, website and podcast, features helpful points about college, such as how students can transfer, how they can negotiate with roommates, how to talk to students about using their resources. https://www.collegeparentcentral .com/podcast/

Learn Smarter, The Educational Therapy Podcast, educational therapists offer strategies and tips on improving executive functioning. https://learnsmarterpodcast.com/

Seth Perler, a popular executive function coach, offers tips and advice on helping students work on executive functioning on his website and YouTube channel. https:// sethperler.com/; https://www.youtube.com/user/ShineOnEducation

Resources for Professionals

Career Development and Transition for Exceptional Individuals (CDTEI) from Hammill Institute on Disabilities is a peer-reviewed journal featuring studies in the transition field to help educators keep up with current research. https://journals.sagepub.com/home/cde

International Division on Career Development and Transition (DCDT) is a professional organization for educators and administrators working with students on postsecondary transition. https://dcdt.org/

Transition Tennessee, "Supporting Strong Transitions for Youth with Disabilities," features transition-focused resources, including online courses for students and parents, and courses, live events, and webcasts for educators. https://transitiontn.org/

Bibliography

Americans with Disabilities Act Amendments Act (ADAAA) of 2008, P.L. 110-325, 42 U.S.C. § 12101 et seq.

Baggetta, Peter, and Patricia A. Alexander. "Conceptualization and Operationalization of Executive Function." *Mind, Brain, and Education* 10, no. 1 (2016): 10–33. https://doi.org/10.1111/mbe.12100

Banerjee, Manju, Adam R. Lalor, Joseph W. Madaus, and Loring Cole Brinckerhoff. "A Survey of Postsecondary Disability Service Website Information." *Learning Disabilities: A Multidisciplinary Journal* 26, no. 4 (2021): 34–42.

Barshay, Jill. "Evidence Increases for Reading on Paper Instead of Screens." *Hechinger Report*, August 12, 2019. https://hechingerreport.org/evidence-increases-for-reading-on-paper-instead-of-screens/

Bjork, Robert A., John Dunlosky, and Nate Kornell. "Self-Regulated Learning: Beliefs, Techniques, and Illusions." *Annual Review of Psychology* 34 (2013): 417–44.

Brown, Jane Thierfeld, Lorraine Wolf, Lisa King, and G. Ruth Kukiela Bork. *The Parent's Guide to College for Students on the Autism Spectrum.* Shawnee Mission, KS: AAPC, 2012.

Brown, Thomas E. "Executive Functions: Describing Six Aspects of a Complex Syndrome." *Attention* (February 2008): 12–17. https://chadd.org/wp-content/uploads/2018/06/ATTN_02_08_Executive_Functions_by_Thomas_Brown.pdf

Cavendish, Wendy, and David J. Connor. "Toward Authentic IEPs and Transition Plans: Student, Parent, and Teacher Perspectives." *Learning Disability Quarterly* 41, no. 1 (2017): 32–43. https://journals.sagepub.com/doi/10.1177/0731948716684680#

Chiu, Yung-Chen Jen, Hsiao-Ying Vicki Chang, Ann Johnston, Mauricio Nascimento, James T. Herbert, and Xiaoyue Maggie Niu. "Impact of Disability Services on Academic Achievement among College Students with Disabilities." *Journal of Postsecondary Education and Disability* 32, no. 3 (2019): 227–45. https://eric .ed.gov/?id=EJ1236854

Cole, Emma V., and Stephanie W. Cawthon. "Self-Disclosure Decisions of University Students with Learning Disabilities." *Journal of Postsecondary Education and Disability* 28, no. 2 (2015): 163–79. https://eric.ed.gov/?id=EJ1074663

Dukes III, Lyman L., Stan F. Shaw, and Joseph W. Madaus. "How to Complete a Summary of Performance for Students Exiting to Postsecondary Education." *Assessment for Effective Intervention* 32, no. 3 (2007): 143–59. https://doi.org/10.1177 /15345084070320030301

Dunlosky, John, Katherine A. Rawson, Elizabeth J. Marsh, Mitchell J. Nathan, and Daniel T. Willingham. "Improving Students' Learning with Effective Learning Techniques: Promising Directions from Cognitive and Educational Psychology." *Psychological Science in the Public Interest* 14, no. 1 (2013): 4–58. https://doi .org/10.1177/1529100612453266

Francis, Grace L., Jodi Duke, Frederick J. Brigham, and Kelsie Demetro. "Student Perceptions of College-Readiness, College Services and Supports, and Family Involvement in College: An Exploratory Study." *Journal of Autism and Developmental Disorders* 48 (2018): 3573–85. http://dx.doi.org/10.1007/s10803-018-3622-x

Gothberg, June E., Lori Y. Peterson, Maria Peak, and Jennifer M. Sedaghat. "Successful Transition of Students with Disabilities To 21st-Century College and Careers: Using Triangulation and Gap Analysis to Address Nonacademic Skills." *TEACHING Exceptional Children* 47, no. 6 (2015): 344–51. https://doi .org/10.1177/0040059915587890

Individuals with Disabilities Education Improvement Act (IDEA) of 2004, P.L. 108-446, 20 U.S.C. § 1400 et seq.

Kravets, Marybeth, and Imy Wax. *The K&W Guide to Colleges for Students with Learning Differences*, 15th ed. New York: Penguin Random House/Princeton Review, 2021.

Lahey, Jessica. *The Gift of Failure: How the Best Parents Learn to Let Go So Their Children Can Succeed.* New York: HarperCollins, 2015.

Lightner, Kirsten L., Deborah Kipps-Vaughan, Timothy Schulte, and Ashton D. Trice. "Reasons University Students with a Learning Disability Wait to Seek Disability Services." *Journal of Postsecondary Education and Disability* 25, no. 2 (2012): 159–77. https://eric.ed.gov/?id=EJ994283

Lindstrom, Will, Jennifer H. Lindstrom, Trisha T. Barefield, Mary Hall Slaughter, and Erin W. Benson. "Examination of Extended Time Use Among Postsecondary Students with Non-Apparent Disabilities." *Journal of Postsecondary Education and Disability* 34, no. 4 (2021): 297–306. https://www.ahead.org/professional-resources /publications/jped/archived-jped/jped-volume-34

Luebbe, Aaron M., Kathryn J. Mancini, Elizabeth J. Kiel, Brooke R. Spangler, Julie L. Semlak, and Lauren M. Fussner. "Dimensionality of Helicopter Parenting and Relations to Emotional, Decision-Making, and Academic Functioning in Emerging Adults." *Assessment* 25, no. 7 (2016): 841–57. https://journals.sagepub.com /doi/10.1177/1073191116665907

Lyman, Michael, Mark E. Beecher, Derek Griner, Michael Brooks, John Call, and Aaron Jackson. "What Keeps Students with Disabilities from Using Accommodations in Postsecondary Education? A Qualitative Review." *Journal of Postsecondary Education and Disability* 29, no. 2 (2016): 123–40. https://eric.ed.gov/?id=EJ1112978

Madaus, Joseph W. "Let's Be Reasonable: Accommodations at the College Level." In *Preparing Students with Disabilities for College Success: A Practical Guide to Transition Planning*, edited by Stan F. Shaw, Joseph W. Madaus, and Lyman L. Dukes III, 10–35. Baltimore, MD: Brookes, 2009.

Madaus, Joseph W., Nicholas Gelbar, Lyman L. Dukes III, Ashley Taconet, and Michael Faggella-Luby. "Are There Predictors of Success for Students with Disabilities Pursuing Postsecondary Education?" *Career Development and Transition for Exceptional Individuals* 44, no. 4 (2021): 191–202. https://doi.org/10.1177/2165143420976526

Madaus, Joseph W., Nicholas Gelbar, Lyman L. Dukes III, Adam R. Lalor, Allison Lombardi, Jennifer Kowitt, and Michael N. Faggella-Luby. "Literature on Postsecondary Disability Services: A Call for Research Guidelines." *Journal of Diversity in Higher Education* 11, no. 2 (2018): 133–45. https://doi.org/10.1037/dhe0000045

Mamiseishvili, Ketevan, and Lynn C. Koch. "First-to-Second-Year Persistence of Students with Disabilities in Postsecondary Institutions in the United States." *Rehabilitation Counseling Bulletin* 54, no. 2 (2011): 93–105. https://doi.org/10.1177/0034355210382580

Mazzotti, Valerie, Dawn A. Rowe, Kelly R. Kelley, David W. Test, Catherine H. Fowler, Paula D. Kohler, and Larry J. Kortering. "Linking Transition Assessment and Postsecondary Goals: Key Elements in the Secondary Transition Planning Process." *TEACHING Exceptional Children* 42, no. 2 (2009): 44–51. https://doi.org/10.1177/004005990904200205

Monahan, Jessica, Allison Lombardi, and Joseph Madaus. "Promoting College and Career Readiness: Practical Strategies for the Classroom." *TEACHING Exceptional Children* 51, no. 2 (2018): 144–54. https://doi.org/10.1177/0040059918802579

Morningstar, Mary E., Allison Lombardi, Catherine H. Fowler, and David W. Test. "A College and Career Readiness Framework for Secondary Students with Disabilities." *Career Development and Transition for Exceptional Individuals* 40, no. 2 (2017): 79–91. https://doi.org/10.1177/2165143415589926

National Center for Education Statistics. "How Many Students in Postsecondary Education Have a Disability?" https://nces.ed.gov/fastfacts/display.asp?id=60

Nelson, Jason M., Brittany Whipple, Will Lindstrom, and Patricia A. Foels. "How Is ADHD Assessed and Documented? Examination of Psychological Reports Submitted to Determine Eligibility for Postsecondary Disability." *Journal of Attention Disorders* 23, no. 14 (2014): 1780–91. https://doi:10.1177/1087054714561860

Newman, Lynn A., and Joseph W. Madaus. "An Analysis of Factors Related to Receipt of Accommodations and Services by Postsecondary Students with Disabilities." *Remedial and Special Education* 36, no. 4 (2015): 208–19. https://doi.org/10.1177/0741932515572912

———. "Reported Accommodations and Supports Provided to Secondary and Postsecondary Students with Disabilities: National Perspective." *Career Development and Transition for Exceptional Individuals* 38, no. 3 (2015): 173–81. https://doi:10.1177/2165143413518235

Newman, Lynn A., Joseph W. Madaus, and Harold S. Javitz. "Effect of Transition Planning on Postsecondary Support Receipt by Students with Disabilities." *Exceptional Children* 82, no. 4 (2016): 497–514. https://doi.org/10.1177/0014402915615884

Newman, Lynn, Mary Wagner, Anne-Marie Knokey, Camille Marder, Katherine Nagle, Debra Shaver, and Xin Wei, with Renée Cameto, Elidia Contreras, Kate Ferguson, Sarah Greene, and Meredith Schwarting. "The Post–High School Outcomes of Young Adults with Disabilities Up to 8 Years after High School: A Report from the National Longitudinal Transition Study-2 (NLTS2)." National Center for Special Education Research, Institute of Education Sciences (NCSER 2011-3005). Menlo Park, CA: SRI International, 2011. https://ies.ed.gov/ncser/pubs/20113005/

Povenmire-Kirk, Tiana C., Lauren K. Bethune, Charlotte Y. Alverson, and Laurie Gutmann Kahn. "A Journey, Not a Destination: Developing Cultural Competence in Secondary Transition." *TEACHING Exceptional Children* 47, no. 6 (2015): 319–28. https://doi.org/10.1177/0040059915587679

Prevatt, Frances, Laura E. Johnson, Katie Allison, and Briley E. Proctor. "Perceived Usefulness of Recommendations Given to College Students Evaluated for Learning Disability." *Journal of Postsecondary Education and Disability* 18, no. 1 (2005): 71–79.

Rehabilitation Act of 1973, P.L. 93-112, 29 U.S.C. § 701 et seq.

Rojewski, Jay W., In H. Lee, and Noel Gregg. "Causal Effects of Inclusion on Postsecondary Education Outcomes of Individuals with High-Incidence Disabilities." *Journal of Disability Policy Studies* 25, no. 4 (2015): 210–19. https://doi.org/10.1177/1044207313505648

Rowe, Dawn A., and Grace L. Francis. "Reflective Thinking: Considering the Intersection of Microcultures in IEP Planning and Implementation." *TEACHING Exceptional Children* 53, no. 1 (2020): 4–6. https://doi.org/10.1177/0040059920952007

Rowe, Dawn A., Valerie L. Mazzotti, Catherine H. Fowler, David W. Test, Vickie J. Mitchell, Kelly A. Clark, Debra Holzberg et al. "Updating the Secondary Transition Research Base." *Career Development for Exceptional Individuals* 44, no. 1 (2021): 28–46. https://doi.org/10.1177/2165143420958674

Scruggs, Spencer, Shengli Dong, Shelley Ducatt, Jennifer Mitchell, and Whitney Davis. "Impact of High School Transition and Accommodation Experience on Student Involvement in College." *Journal of Postsecondary Education and Disability* 34, no. 2 (2021): 179–90. https://files.eric.ed.gov/fulltext/EJ1319194.pdf

Sparks, Richard L., and Benjamin J. Lovett. "Learning Disability Documentation in Higher Education: What Are Students Submitting?" *Learning Disability Quarterly* 37, no. 1 (2014): 54–62. https://doi.org/10.1177/0731948713486888

Squires, Maureen E., Beverly A. Burnell, Cynthia McCarty, and Heidi Schnackenberg. "Emerging Adults: Perspectives of College Students with Disabilities."

Journal of Postsecondary Education and Disability 31, no. 2 (2018): 121–34. https://eric.ed.gov/?id=EJ1192068

Stixrud, William, and Ned Johnson. *What Do You Say? How to Talk with Kids to Build Motivation, Stress Tolerance, and a Happy Home.* New York: Viking, 2021.

Test, David W., Catherine H. Fowler, Wendy M. Wood, Denise M. Brewer, and Steven Eddy. "A Conceptual Framework of Self-Advocacy for Students with Disabilities." *Remedial and Special Education* 26, no. 1 (2005): 43–54. https://doi.org/10.1177/07419325050260010601

Thompson-Ebanks, Valerie, and Michelle Jarman. "Undergraduate Students with Nonapparent Disabilities: Identity Factors that Contribute to Disclosure Decisions." *International Journal of Disability, Development, and Education* 65, no. 3 (2018): 286–303. https://doi.org/10.1080/1034912X.2017.1380174

Torpey, Elka. "Education Pays, 2020." Career Outlook, U.S. Bureau of Labor Statistics. June 2021.

Torres, Kathryn, Nathanie Lee, and Christine Tran. "Building Relationships, Bridging Cultures: Cultural Brokering in Family Engagement." The Equitable Parent-School Collaboration Research Project. 2015. https://education.uw.edu/sites/default/files/programs/epsc/Cultural%20Brokers%20Brief_Web.pdf

Trainor, Audrey A. "Using Cultural and Social Capital to Improve Postsecondary Outcomes and Expand Transition Models for Youth with Disabilities." *Journal of Special Education* 42, no. 3 (2008): 148–62. https://doi.org/10.1177/0022466907313346

Trainor, Audrey A., Lynn Newman, Elisa Garcia, Heather H. Woodley, Rachel E. Traxler, and D. Nicole Deschene. "Postsecondary Education-Focused Transition Planning Experiences of English Learners with Disabilities." *Career Development and Transition for Exceptional Individuals* 42, no. 1 (2019): 52. https://journals.sagepub.com/doi/full/10.1177/2165143418811830

U.S. Department of Education. "The Family Educational Rights and Privacy Act: Guidance for Eligible Students." April 2020. https://studentprivacy.ed.gov/sites/default/files/resource_document/file/FERPAforeligiblestudents.pdf

———. "Questions and Answers on Report Cards and Transcripts for Students with Disabilities Attending Public Elementary and Secondary Schools." October 2008. https://www2.ed.gov/about/offices/list/ocr/letters/colleague-qa-20081017.html

———. "Transition of Students with Disabilities to Postsecondary Education: A Guide for High School Educators." March 2007, reprinted March 2011. https://www2.ed.gov/about/offices/list/ocr/transitionguide.html

Valenzuela, Rudolph L., and James E. Martin. "Self-Directed IEP: Bridging Values of Diverse Cultures and Secondary Education." *Career Development for Exceptional Individuals* 28, no. 1 (2015): 4–14. https://doi.org/10.1177/08857288050280010301

Verrell, Paul A., and Norah R. McCabe. "In Their Own Words: Using Self-Assessments of College Readiness to Develop Strategies for Self-Regulated Learning." *College Teaching* 63, no. 4 (2015): 162–70. http://dx.doi.org/10.1080/87567555.2015.1053046

Wagner, Mary M., Lynn A. Newman, and Harold S. Javitz. "The Influence of Family Socioeconomic Status on the Post–High School Outcomes of Youth with Disabilities." *Career Development and Transition for Exceptional Individuals* 37, no. 1 (2014): 5–17.

Watson Jr., Michael D., Joan B. Simon, and Lenora Nunnley. "SLD Identification: A Survey of Methods Used by School Psychologists." *Learning Disabilities: A Multidisciplinary Journal* 21, no. 1 (2016): 57–67. https://doi.org/10.18666/LDMJ -2016-V21-I1-6392

Wehmeyer, Michael, and Michelle Schwartz. "Self-Determination and Positive Adult Outcomes: A Follow-Up Study of Youth with Mental Retardation or Learning Disabilities." *Exceptional Children* 63, no. 2 (1997): 245–55. https://doi .org/10.1177/001440299706300207

Zimmerman, Barry J. "Self-Efficacy: An Essential Motive to Learn." *Contemporary Educational Psychology* 25, no. 1 (2000): 82–91. https://doi.org/10.1006 /ceps.1999.1016

Index

Page references for tables are *italicized.*

academic accommodations: Americans with Disabilities Act Amendments Act, 12–13, 14, 15; attendance, flexibility with, 154; auxiliary aids, 17–18; course load, reduced, 153; course substitution, 153–54; legal requirements, 12–18; National Longitudinal Transition Study-2, 183, *183*; registration, priority, 153; requirements, altering, 14–15; Section 504 of the Rehabilitation Act of 1973, 12, 13–18; texts/materials in alternative format, 154; undue burden on college, 13. *See also* tests
academic advisors, 22
academic engagement, 60
academic help at college, 92
academic progress, 51–52
academic responsibilities, 52
academic skills, 75–96; about, 75–76; academic help at college, 92; course selection, 87–90; exams, 77–79; lack of, 75–76; notetaking, 85–86; reading assignments, 82–84; students, all, 76–86; students with disabilities, 86–92; studying, 79–82; technology, 90–92; writing assignments, 84–85. *See also* nonacademic skills
access, as goal, 8
Accessible Information Management (AIM), 32
accommodations: about, 141–42; access to, 9–11; appeals, filing, 38–39, 165; approval rates, 169–70; classroom, 155–56; COVID experiences and, 163; denied, common types, 159–62; disability services office, evaluating, 103; DS decision about, 164–65; DS registration process, 142–45, 168; effectiveness of, 38; exemptions from, 23; gap year, 123; high school team help with, 165–67; housing, 19, 33–34; modifications, 15, *182*, 182; National Longitudinal Transition Study-2, 179–85, *182*,

183; nonacademic, 18–20, 183, *183*; opting out of, 39–40; procedural rights, 36–38; professors and, 32–33, 37, 46–47, 103, 163; rate of receipt, 179, *182*, *183*; rate of receipt, factors influencing, 179–81, 184–85; recommendations for, 148; request processes, 33–34, 46–47; research on, 170–72; retroactive, 39, 143, 172; test, 33–34, 39–40, 44, 156–59, 172; time concerns, 37–38. *See also* academic accommodations; documentation, required for accommodations

achievement tests, 149

ACT, 137–38, 139

action, in executive functioning model, 56

activation, in executive functioning model, 55

ADAAA. *See* Americans with Disabilities Act Amendments Act

add deadlines, 30

ADHD (Attention Deficit Hyperactivity Disorder), 2, 13, 37, 150

administrative burden on college, undue, 13

admission by exception, 139

admissions: about, 127–28; disability disclosure in admissions process, 128–36; disability services queries not tied to, 104, 125n27; flexibility in, 138–39; law and, 136–38; privacy rights, 41; "qualified" students, 9, 136–37; requirements, typical, 62; standards, 136–38

admissions tests, 137–38, 139, 189–90

advisors, academic, 22

aides, 17–18

alertness, regulating, 56

alternatives to four-year college, 120–23, 126n41

Americans with Disabilities Act Amendments Act (ADAAA): academic accommodations, 12–13; academic adjustments, 14, 15; applicability, 4n1, 6, 7; disability, defined, 10–11; mitigating measures, 10–11; privacy rights, 40; purpose, 7–8; undue burden on college, 13

animals, emotional support, 16

anxiety disorders, 15

apparent *versus* invisible disabilities, 179–80, 181

appeals, filing, 38–39, 165

articulation agreements, 121

assignment calculators, 84, 85

assignments, 52, 159–60, 161, 163

assistants, 17–18

assistive technology professionals, 91, 92

athletic teams/clubs, 20

attendance, class, 29, 52, 154

attendants, 17–18

Attention Deficit Hyperactivity Disorder (ADHD), 2, 13, 37, 150

autism, 111, 150

autonomy, 58

auxiliary aids, 17–18

Bass, Judith, 118

batteries, test, 150, 173n5

Beacon College, 108–9

"best" colleges lists, 116–17

Blind/VI students, 2, 147, 154, 158

body doubling, 82

breaks, during tests, 157–58

Brown, Jane Thierfeld, 111

Brown, Thomas, 55–57

calculator use, 16, 159

Campus Disability Resource Database, 118–19

campus visits, 113–15

capital, sharing, 189–90

captioned video recordings of classes, 163

caregivers. *See* parents

case managers: academic skill building and, 88; accommodations, creating list of, 151, 164; nonacademic skill building and, 61–62, 63

Casey, Joan, 139

causation *versus* correlation, 171

Child Find mandate, 20

Clark, Rick, 129, 132, 135

classes: admission requirements, 137; attending, 29, 52, 154; high school, 61–62; learning disabilities support, 129, 140n3; load, reduced, 153; physical education, 20; prerequisite, 10, 37; priority registration for, 88, 153; public speaking, 15; recording, 15–16, 20n11, 86, 155, 163; remedial, 21; remote, 163; required, 14, 24, 88–90, 99; selecting, 61–62, 87–90; size, 163

classroom accommodations, 155–56

clinical interviews, 148

clinical summary, 148

clubs and activities, 53

coaches, 119

cognitive ability/aptitude tests, 149

cognitive flexibility, 55

collectivist cultures, 187–88

college and career readiness skills framework, 59–60

college capable students, 66

college completion rates, 185, *185*

college enrollment statistics, 178–79, 188–89

college paperwork/tasks, 46

college ready students, 66

college search, 97–126; alternatives to four-year college, 120–23; campus visits, 113–15; disability services office, evaluating, 100–104; fit, finding good, 97–100; nonacademic skills, building, 64; parents, help from, 115–16; postsecondary choices, generally, 123–24; resources, 116–19; support, choosing right level of, 104–13; supports, off-campus, 119–20

college transcripts, 42

CollegeWebLD.com, 118–19

communication, 57, 64–65

community colleges, 89–90, 120–21, 126n41

complaint process, 38

conditional admission, 21

control group, 171

Cooper, Elizabeth, 66

coordinators, 3–4, 63

core requirements, 14, 24, 88–89, 99

correlation *versus* causation, 171

counseling and placement services, 19–20

course substitutions, 14, 24–25, 103, 153–54. *See also* classes

COVID experiences, accommodation requests arising from, 163

critical thinking, 60

cultural awareness, 187–88

cultural capital, 189

culturally and linguistically diverse students: capital, sharing, 189–90; college enrollment rates, 188–89; college planning considerations, 190–91; self-awareness and cultural awareness, 187–88

deadlines, 29–30, 33–34, 161

Deaf/HOH students, 2, 13, 29, 163

degree audit/progress report/evaluation, 95n26

deliverables, 55–56

developmental classes, 21

DiAndreth-Elkins, Leann, 107

Dickinson College, 133

dictation software, 85

DiGalbo, Laura, 109–10, 115

disabilities: ADAAA definition, 10–11; apparent *versus* invisible, 179–80, 181; colleges just for students with, 108–9; high schools just for students with, 130–31; intellectual, 111–13; legal coverage, 10–11; mental health, 109–10; physical/medical, 110; reading, 8, 154, 158; rule out of, 148; students with, statistics, 5; as term, 3. *See also* learning disabilities
"disability cap," 138
disability disclosure in admissions process, 128–36; admissions data, lack of, 133; admissions decision, no effect on, 132–33; admissions directors, advice from, 133–34; disability inquiries by colleges not allowed, 128; documentation not included with admissions application, 131; high school documents and, 128–31; Level 3 services not determined by admissions staff, 131–32; as optional, 131; test score/grade anomalies explained by, 134; tips, 134–36
disability evaluations, 21
disability inquiries, preadmission, 128
disability-related information, protecting, 41–42
disability services office (DS): accommodation requests, 46; college paperwork and tasks, 46; complaint process, 38; contacting, 104; coordinators, 3–4, 63; decision from, 164–65; dedicated, 101; dual-enrollment programs, 94; e-book accommodations, 34; evaluating, 100–104; location, 113–14, 125nn28–29; names of, 100–101; office setup and staffing, 102; parents, communication with, 48; processes, 102–3; registering with, 31–32, 35–36, 47–48, 168;

registration process, 142–45, 168; registration requests from parents, 47; releases from students, signed, 47, 48; staff size, 101; staff training, 101–2; student workers and privacy rights, 41; as term, 3; test accommodations, 33, 34, 39–40; tours, on-campus, 113–14, 125nn28–29
discrimination, 15–16
documentation, required for accommodations: about, 145–46; achievement tests, 149; ADHD or autism, requirements for students with, 150; age of documentation, 146–47; clinical interview, 148; clinical summary, 148; cognitive ability/aptitude tests, 149; conclusion/diagnosis (or rule out of disability), 148; evaluator qualifications, 147; history, 148; information processing tests, 149–50; insufficient documentation, 168–69; learning disabilities, requirements for students with, 145–46, 149–50; recommendations for accommodation, 148; requirements, general, 146–49; testing scores and narrative, 148; transition packets, 150–51
dogs, service, 16
dorm rooms, private, 162
drop deadlines, 30
DS. *See* disability services office
dual-enrollment programs, 93–94

e-books, 34, 154
economic capital, 189–90
educational effectiveness, 22
educational standards, 22
effectiveness, educational, 22
effort, 56
electronic text (e-text), 34, 154

emotion, in executive functioning model, 57
emotional support animals, 16
employment assistance, 19
empowerment, psychological, 58, 59
Endlich, Eric, 66, 135
engagement, 53, 60
English language learners (ELLs), 191
ethnicity and college enrollment rates, 188
exams. *See* tests
executive assistants, 54–55
executive functioning, 54–57
extended test batteries, 173n5
extended time for tests, 157, 172
eyeglasses, 17

fail, letting students, 66–68
Family Educational Rights and Privacy Act (FERPA), 40, 45, 48
fellowships, 19
financial and employment assistance, 19
financial burden on college, undue, 13
504 plans, 7, 93–94, 129, 167
focus, 55, 90
formats, alternative, 34, 154

gap year, 122–23
general education requirements, 14, 24, 88–89, 99
general education settings, 190
Georgia Tech, 129, 132, 135
Gift of Failure (Lahey), 67
goals, setting, 21–22, 61
GPA, maintaining, 29
graduate school applications, 42
graduation requirements, 99
graphic organizers, 85
Grigal, Meg, 112–13

hard of hearing students, 2, 13, 29, 163
hearing loss, 2, 13, 29, 163
helicopter parenting, 68–69

help, using available, 54
high school course selection, 61–62
high school plans, 6–7
high school preparation for academic skills: course selection in college, 88; exams, 78; notetaking, 86; reading assignments, 83; studying, 79–81; technology, 91–92; writing assignments, 84–85
high school profiles, 130–31
high school services not mentioned in laws, 20–22
high schools just for students with disabilities, 130–31
high school transcripts, 128, 129–30
holistic admissions process, 134
homeschooled students, 3, 64
housing accommodations, 19, 33–34, 162

IDEA (Individuals with Disabilities Education Act), 6, 7, 20, 21, 60
identification-based tests, 77
Indiana University Bloomington, 135
individualistic cultures, 187
Individualized Education Plans (IEPs): applicability, 6–7; dual-enrollment programs, 93–94; high school courses, selecting, 61; postsecondary goals, identifying, 61; student involvement in development of, 167; student participation in, 62–64; transcript concerns, 129; transition planning, 60–61
Individuals with Disabilities Education Act (IDEA), 6, 7, 20, 21, 60
information processing tests, 149–50
inhibitory control, 56
instruction, specialized, 21
intake meetings, 142, 143, 144, 145, 168
intellectual disabilities, 111–13
internal locus of control, 59

invisible *versus* apparent disabilities, 179–80, 181

Johnson, Ned, 67

Kravets, Marybeth, 117–18
The K&W Guide to Colleges for Students with Learning Differences, 117–18

Lahey, Jessica, 67–68, 70
Landmark College, 108–9
Langford, Mike, 130
language-based disorders, 15
laptop use, 156, 159
laws: about, 5–6; accommodations, academic, 12–18; accommodations, access to, 9–11; accommodations, exemptions from, 23; accommodations, nonacademic, 18–20; admissions policies, 136–38; course substitutions, 14, 24–25; coverage, 6–11; disability, defined, 10–11; discrimination forbidden by, 15–16; high school plans and, 6–7; high school services not mentioned in, 20–22; purposes, 7–9; "qualified" students, 9–10; requirements of, 11–22. *See also specific laws*
lawsuits, 39
leadership, 58
Learning and Study Strategies Inventory (LASSI), 95n12
learning differences, as term, 74n22, 166
learning disabilities (LD): achievement tests, 149; cognitive ability/aptitude tests, 149; college enrollment statistics, 178; documentation requirements for, 145–46, 147, 149–50; information processing tests, 149–50; support classes, 129, 140n3; as term, 2
learning processes, 60

lectures, recording, 15–16, 20n11, 86, 155, 163
Level 1 services, 105
Level 2 services, 105–6
Level 3 services, 106–8, 131–32
leveling the playing field, 8–9, 44–45, 162, 172
life skills, 71–72
locus of control, internal, 59

Madaus, Joseph W., 169, 170, 178, 180–81, 182–83, 185
majors, 9–10, 14, 24, 99
materials, purchasing, 29
medical disabilities, 110
medical professionals, 119–20
medication for ADHD, 13
memorandum of understanding, 94
memory, working, 56
memory aids for tests, 160
mental health disabilities, 109–10
Miller, Gabrielle, 107–8
mindsets, 60
mitigating measures, 10–11
modifications, 15, 159–60, 182, *182*
modified tests, 78, 93, 160
monitoring, 56
Moyer, Gregory, 133
Muskingum University, 107

National Center for College Students with Disabilities, 118–19
National Center for Education Statistics, 5, 169
National Longitudinal Transition Study-2 (NLTS2), 177–85; about, 177–78; accommodations, 179–85, *182, 183*; accommodations, academic, 183, *183*; accommodations, nonacademic, 183, *183*; college completion rates, 185, *185*; college enrollment, 89, 178–79;

disabilities, apparent *versus* invisible, 179–80, 181; modifications, 182, *182*

National Secondary Transition Technical Assistance Center, 60

neurotypical, as term, 2

Newman, Lynn A., 178, 180–81, 182–83, 185

NLTS2. *See* National Longitudinal Transition Study-2

nonacademic accommodations, 18–20, 183, *183*

nonacademic skills, 51–74; assessing, 60; building, 61–64; college search process, 64; communication, 64–65; executive functioning, 54–57; goals, identifying postsecondary, 61; high school courses, selecting, 61–62; IEP and meetings, participating in, 62–64; life skills, 71–72; parent help with, 66–72; self-advocacy, 57–58; self-determination, 58–60; self-management, 51–52; success tips from DS directors, 52–54; transition planning, 60–61. *See also* academic skills

notes and notetaking: challenges, 85–86; laptop for, 156; peer notes, 34, 86, 95n24, 156; privacy rights, 41, 42, 156; from professor, 161–62; technology for, 91

Office for Civil Rights (OCR), 4, 13, 38–39

office hours, 52, 78, 82, 85, 87, 163

on-campus tours, 113–15, 116

online assistance, 119

online professor rating sites, 89

online resources, 118–19

open book tests, 77–78, 95n5, 160

organization, 55

overnight campus visits, 115

ownership, taking, 53

parents: college search, 115–16; disability services, communication with, 48; disability services, registering with, 47–48, 168; encouragement for, 175–76; helicopter, 68–69; intake meetings, 168; as term, 3; transition help, 66–72

peer notes, 34, 86, 95n24, 156

persistence, 53

perspective taking, 188

pets, 16

physical education classes, 20

physical/medical disabilities, 110

placement services, 19–20

plagiarism, 84–85

Pomodoro Technique, 80–81

positive, accentuating, 135

PowerPoint slides, 162

prerequisite courses, 10, 37

printing allowance, 83

prioritization, 55

priority registration for classes, 88, 153

privacy rights, 40–42, 45, 156

probation, 29, 72n1

procedural rights, 36–40

processing speed, 56

procrastination, 161

professional/advocate involvement in DS registration process, 168

professors: academic progress of students and, 51–52; accommodations and, 32–33, 37, 46–47, 103, 163; classes, recording, 155; extra time with, 163; notes of, 161–62; office hours, 52, 78, 82, 85, 87, 163; privacy rights of students and, 42; rating sites, online, 89; talking with, 87

profiles, high school, 130–31

program costs, Level 3 services, 107

progress reports, 95n26, 164

prospective students, 143

psychological empowerment, 58, 59
public speaking classes, 15

"qualified" students, 9–10, 136
Quinlan, Jeremiah, 132, 133

race/ethnicity and college enrollment
    rates, 188
reading assignments, 82–84
reading disabilities, 8, 154, 158
recommendation, letters of, 135–36
recording classes, 15–16, 20n11, 86,
    155, 163
reduced-distraction sites, 158
registration, priority, 88, 153
registration form, disability services,
    142, 143–44
releases from students, signed, 47, 48
remedial classes, 21
remote classes, 163
resilience, 53
responsibility, taking, 53
retroactive accommodations, 39, 143,
    172
rights: knowledge of, 57; privacy,
    40–42, 45, 156; procedural, 36–40;
    student, 36–42
role-playing, 63
rolling admissions, 138, 140n15
rules, following, 28

Sarouhan, Jane, 122, 123
Sarouhan, Jason, 122, 123
SAT, 137–38, 139, 189–90
Scales, Keyana, 130–31
schedule adjustment period, 30n1
scholarships, 19
Schwartz, Michelle, 58, 59
screen readers, 84
Section 504 of the Rehabilitation
    Act of 1973: accommodations,
    academic, 12, 13–18;
    accommodations, effectiveness of,
    38; accommodations, nonacademic,
    18–20; admissions tests, 137–38;
    applicability, 6, 7; classes, recording,
    155; course substitutions, 14, 24;
    disability cap in admissions, 138;
    disability inquiries, preadmission,
    128; privacy rights, 40; purpose,
    7–8; "qualified" students, 9, 136;
    transcripts, 129
sections, class, 89
self-advocacy, 57–58
self-awareness, 187–88
self-determination, 58–60, 94, 181
self-efficacy, 59
self-knowledge, 57, 63
self-management, 51–52
self-realization, 58, 59
self-regulation, 56, 58, 59
service dogs, 16
sign language interpreting, 13
Singleton, Korey, 91–92
skills: life, 71–72; social, 60, 111. See
    also academic skills; nonacademic
    skills
smart pens, 155
social capital, 189, 190
social organizations, 20
social skills, 60, 111
socioeconomic status, 188–89
SOP (Summary of Performance), 4
special education, 21, 26n22
specialists, 70–71
spellcheckers, 159
standards, educational, 22
STEM schools, 129
Stixrud, William, 67
student responsibilities: academic
    responsibilities, 52; class attendance,
    29; college paperwork and tasks,
    46; deadlines, meeting, 29–30;
    everyday responsibilities, 28–30;
    GPA, maintaining, 29; materials,
    purchasing, 29; rules, following,

28; specialized responsibilities for students with disabilities, 31–36, 46–48. *See also* student rights

student rights: accommodations, appealing denial of, 38–39; accommodations, opting out of, 39–40; accommodations, requesting, 36–38; disability, choosing whether to identify as person with, 41; disability-related information, protecting, 41–42; DS registration, opting out of/delaying, 39, 40; privacy rights, 40–42, 45, 156; procedural rights, 36–40. *See also* student responsibilities

students: Blind/VI, 2, 147, 154, 158; college capable, 66; college ready, 66; Deaf/HOH, 2, 13, 29, 163; homeschooled, 3, 64; prospective, 143; "qualified," 9–10, 136; transfer, 32, 121. *See also* culturally and linguistically diverse students

student workers, 41

study buddies, 82

study groups, 78–79, 82

study guides, 164

studying, 79–82

study space, quiet, 163

study strategies for tests, 78

subvocalization, 158

success tips from DS directors, 52–54

Summary of Performance (SOP), 4

summer sessions, 89

support: Level 1 services, 105; Level 2 services, 105–6; Level 3 services, 106–8, 131–32; off-campus, 119–20; scaling back, by parents, 69–70; services, general, 99; types of, 104–13. *See also* accommodations

tasks, completing, 28–29

teaching assistants (TAs), 78, 82, 87, 109, 164

teams, as term, 3

Tech Act Project, 91

technology, 90–92

terminology, 2–4

Test, David, 57

test anxiety, 170

testing centers, 158

test-optional policies, 139

tests: accommodations, 33–34, 39–40, 44, 156–59, 172; achievement, 149; admissions, 137–38, 139, 189–90; batteries, 150, 173n5; challenges, 77–78; cognitive ability/aptitude, 149; format information, 164; high school preparation for, 78; identification-based, 77; information processing, 149–50; legal requirements, 16; memory aids for, 160; modified, 78, 93, 160; open book, 77–78, 95n5, 160; questions, someone to explain, 160–61; strategies for taking, 78; study strategies, 78

texts/materials in alternative format, 34, 154

text-to-speech software, 17, 90–91, 92, 158

therapists, 119

Thieme, Sacha, 135

Think College, 112, 113

thinking, critical, 60

time management, 79–81, 84, 85, 161

Title II, 129

tours, campus, 113–15, 116

Trainor, Audrey A., 189–90

transcripts, 42, 128, 129–30

transfer students, 32, 121

transition knowledge, 60

transition night with DS representative, 45

transition packets, 43, 150–51

transition planning, 42–45, 60–61, 181

Tulkin, Annie, 110

tutors: evaluating, 70–71, 99; off-campus, 119; SAT, 189–90; specialized, 18; using, 92

undue burden on college, 13
Universal Design for Learning, 26n21
University of Arizona, 107–8
University of California system, 139
U.S. Department of Education, 23, 129, 168–69
U.S. Office for Civil Rights, 4, 13, 38–39

video recordings of classes, 163
violation, addressing, 57
virtual tours, 113
visually impaired students, 2, 147, 154, 158

waivers, course, 26n24, 62
Walker, Jennifer, 124

Wax, Imy, 117–18
Wechsler Intelligence Scale for Children–5 (WISC–5), 150, 173n6
Wehmeyer, Michael, 58, 59
Western Carolina University, 130
What Do You Say? (Stixrud & Johnson), 67
Wilkerson, Belinda, 135
winter sessions, 89
withdrawals, class, 30
Wolf, Lorraine, 111
working memory, 56
writing assignments, 84–85
writing centers, 85, 96n31

Xavier University of Louisiana, 130–31

Yale University, 132

Zimmerman, Barry, 59

About the Author

Elizabeth C. Hamblet splits her time between working with students as a college learning disabilities specialist and educating parents and professionals about how to prepare students with disabilities for successful college transition. She is author of two previous book editions, two brief guides, and numerous articles on this topic, and she gives presentations on transition around the country. Hamblet has been a columnist for *Disability Compliance for Higher Education* since 2009.